STRATEGIC SALES PRESENTATIONS

JACK MALCOLM

Booktrope Editions
Seattle, WA 2010

Cover Design by Greg Simanson

Cover Image by Heather Holt

Edited by Jane Radke Slade

Layout by Victoria Wolffe

ISBN 978-1-935961-52-9

For further information regarding permissions, please contact

info@booktrope.com.

Library of Congress Control Number: 2012943080

DEDICATION

For George S. Malcolm

Contents

INTRODUCTION: YOUR LEADERSHIP MOMENT

When your leadership moment comes, will you be ready?

If you've been in sales for any length of time, you can probably look back on several moments in your sales career where you have had an extraordinary opportunity to close a large sale. As a result of your hard work and positioning you have managed to get the customer's high-level decision makers together to listen to your sales pitch.

Such moments are precious because they are rare and valuable, and they are *leadership* moments for two reasons. First, because they are occasions that have an outsized impact on your success — they may determine whether you make quota that year or even the arc of your career. Second, regardless of the rank or position of the people in the room, when you are standing in front of them delivering your presentation, *you are the leader in the room*.

One such leadership moment happened to me in 2003, when I flew from Fort Lauderdale, Florida, to Auckland, New Zealand, to deliver a sales presentation. My audience was a committee of sales, marketing and operations executives for a New Zealand company that has sales offices around the globe, and they were there to evaluate four companies that had made the short list for their potential sales training contract.

Each company that made the short list was given an hour and a half time slot, with specific instructions that we should present for forty-five minutes and answer questions for another forty-five, and that is precisely what each of my competitors did.[1] They gave very detailed and professional descriptions of their company, their sales processes, and their capabilities, and then gave (mostly) effective answers during the Q&A period.

---

[1] This is what I found out later. We were not permitted to see each other's presentations.

My turn came last on the agenda. That was not an accident, by the way; why and how I arranged this will be covered in Chapter 4. When my turn came, I gave a brief introduction, and then rather than launching into a talking brochure, I gave a high-level overview of what I saw as their major challenges and asked for their feedback. What followed was a dialogue with the audience members in which they mostly confirmed my understanding of their needs, and also brought out some additional needs that had not been in their original request for proposal. By a remarkable coincidence, these needs happened to coincide with my company's strengths, and in fact constituted the bulk of the presentation that I did deliver.

My slide presentation took about ten minutes instead of forty-five, and said very little about my company and its capabilities. (They already had that information in their packets.) Instead, it focused on the problems they faced and what a solution would mean to them. At the end of it, they were interested enough to spend an hour and a half asking me questions.

When it was over, one of their executives approached and complimented me: "Superb presentation. Thanks, Jack."

I ended up winning the business as a result of that presentation, and that one leadership moment resulted in a long and profitable customer relationship. In retrospect, the presentation was successful because I unknowingly followed four critical precepts which will be recurrent themes throughout this book: customer focus, clear thinking, intensive preparation, and being genuine.

WHY ARE EXECUTIVE SALES PRESENTATIONS SO IMPORTANT?

You need to excel at executive sales presentations for the same reason that Willie Sutton supposedly gave when asked why he robbed banks: "Because that's where the money is."

Generally, decisions that require a high-level presentation are the important ones, so the stakes are high for your company and for you personally. They are also relatively rare events for most presenters, so you don't have too many chances to try again if you don't achieve your objectives the first time.

Exceptional salespeople know the fastest way to close complex deals is to win over senior-level decision makers with compelling business value propositions. When the sale is large enough or strategic enough, senior executives usually have to make the decisions. The good news for salespeople is that those executives are used to making important decisions, so if they see the advantages of acting, they're not going to involve you in long months of analysis paralysis or picayune wrangling over every last dime. To quote Mack Hanan in *Consultative Selling*, "Buyers can wait for a lower price, while operating managers cannot wait for added value."

People at the top will have to get involved if you're truly selling consultatively because by definition you will bring solutions to problems your customers don't even know they have. If that's the case, they will not have funds budgeted for your solution. Lower-level people are given budgets that they have to follow; only higher-level people have the authority to change budgets if they see the need. In fact, the lack of budgeted funds can be a good thing for your sales situation: because they haven't addressed the issue, it also means that they haven't gone out and talked to a bunch of competitors.

Although most complex sales require months — if not years — worth of meetings with people at all levels in the buyer's organization, they usually culminate in a crucial presentation to a committee of high-level decision makers. According to research cited in Shell and Moussa's *The Art of Woo*, important corporate decisions (and this surely includes those involving complex sales), involve an average of eight people in the decision, and that number has grown during this recent period of economic austerity. That means that you are almost guaranteed to have to make a presentation to an audience in order to win the sale, and that at least one senior-level person will be in the room.

It does not have to be a closing presentation at the end of the sales cycle. If you get to high-level decision makers early in the process, you can shape what the final request for proposal will look like, and you can also instill an urgency among lower-level recommenders and influencers.

Even if you are not required to sell directly to the top-level decision makers, you should want to. At some point, *someone* has to sell them on the idea. You can leave it up to your allies and champions, but do you want to put your destiny into someone else's hands when the decision is crucial to your success?

When you analyze it objectively, your performance during an executive sales presentation should have almost no influence on an important purchasing decision. It should pale in comparison to the quality of your solution, the reputation and performance of your company, value for the money, technical performance, etc.

Yet your performance can have a huge, even decisive, impact. According to research conducted by the HR Chally Group, which analyzed a database of over 300,000 purchasing decisions, salesperson effectiveness accounts for 39% of customer buying decisions. By contrast, the total solution came in at 22%, quality of offering 21%, and price 18%.

This is both a challenge and a unique opportunity for you as a sales professional to crystallize your value proposition, stand out from a crowded competitive field, and make that all-important personal connection. In short, the ability to excel in this situation is crucial to your sales success.

WHAT'S SPECIAL ABOUT STRATEGIC SALES PRESENTATIONS?

Although much of what we will cover in this book applies to any presentation for the average audience — how to choose a clear message, organize your ideas for maximum persuasive effect, and deliver credibly and confidently — strategic sales presentations pose special challenges.

The two key differences are that your audiences are generally higher-level executives, and that your presentations fit within a defined sales strategy — they are not free-standing events.

Of course, there will be many times in your career when you will present to lower-level audiences, but the good news is that the principles that apply to executive presentations will make you even better at those. The C-suite is like New York — if you can make it there, you'll make it anywhere.

Additionally, this book focuses squarely on business-to-business (B2B) complex sales. That means that every step of the process of crafting and delivering your presentation is explained within that context. I presume you're reading this book not only to become a better speaker, but to make a measurable improvement in your sales effectiveness.

DON'T FORGET: IT'S STILL A SALES CALL

Although there are differences, never forget that every presentation to a customer is a sales call. Your listeners are there to give and receive information that will help them make a decision about whether or not to purchase your solution, or to continue doing business with your company.

Because it's a sales call, it will be more interactive than a regular presentation. Your listeners will feel free to ask questions or challenge you, and will probably not wait quietly for the end of the formal presentation. That's not a problem for you — in fact, you want to encourage their participation as much as possible.

Here's how a professional sales presentation compares to a normal sales call or a speech:

Sales call: The least formal of the three. More free flowing, with the most interaction. Properly done, the customer does most of the talking. It will typically involve up to five or six people on the customer's side.

Speech: Most formal and structured. All the communication is one way, from speaker to audience, and there are usually more than twenty people in a much larger venue.

Sales presentation: Much more talking done by the presenter, but allows for a significant amount of interaction between presenter and audience. In fact, good presenters encourage early and active audience participation. The number of participants is somewhere between six and twenty. Above about six people, there is a different dynamic than there is with an individual conversation.

WHAT QUALIFIES ME TO WRITE THIS BOOK?

This book is about you, not me, but perhaps I should take a few moments to tell you what I bring to the table and why I'm confident I have something to say that will make a significant difference in your sales career. (If you've already bought the book, I don't want to talk past the close, so you can skip this part.)

I have trained thousands of salespeople over the past twenty years in business-to-business (B2B) complex sales, which is ironic because I did not begin my career intending or wanting to go into sales. I began my career as a commercial banker with an MBA in Finance. Banking interested me because at the time it was a heavily regulated industry that did not require too much in the way of sales. We used to joke that we would never go wrong if we followed the "3-6-2" rule: pay 3% on deposits, lend it out at 6%, and hit the golf course every day at 2 p.m. I saw myself as a numbers person and not a people person, and sales did not interest me at all.

Fortunately for me, soon after I entered the industry the US Congress passed sweeping legislation that began the process of deregulating banking, and it opened us up to far more competition. We hot-shot know-it-all young MBAs had to learn how to sell, and quickly. While I wasn't happy about it at the time, it began my own personal transformation.

At about the same time, a friend finally convinced me to attend a meeting of his Toastmasters club, beginning the practice that converted me from terrified introvert into a confident speaker. I soon acquired a reputation for speaking, and that got me some high-profile opportunities to speak in front of the top leaders of the bank.

I noticed something unfair: it seemed that fifteen minutes in front of the right people made more of a difference in my ascent up the career ladder than months of plugging away at my real job. Those who did great work but lacked the skills or the motivation to seek out speaking opportunities continued to plug away as my career took off. Of course, I wasn't complaining.

In 1991, I made the switch to sales training, and since 1996 I have had my own firm specializing in consultative selling in complex sales for B2B companies. That has given me a solid background in sales processes, sales techniques, and the elements of personal influence, as well as affording me multiple opportunities to put my skills to the test. In order to win contracts to train salespeople at some of this country's top companies, I have to successfully execute precisely the ideas and techniques that I teach in this book.

In addition to my own considerable experience, I've had the privilege of working with thousands of successful sales professionals, and I've seen what works and what does not work for different people. My ideas have been tested and refined through years of training others; most of my students are not shy, and are quick to point out where they disagree with my ideas. That's how I learn from every class I teach, and that's one of the reasons I can't wait for the next twenty years. (Future editions of this book will be even better, but please don't wait — we'll both be much older then.)

On the other hand, while experience is the best teacher, it can also mislead. If I try something and end up closing the sale, the only valid conclusion that I can draw from that is that it did not *lose* me the sale. Maybe I closed the sale in spite of what I did, or it made no difference, or it made a difference to that specific audience but it does not carry over to others, etc.

I work hard to keep up on research related to my work, so you will also see a lot in this book about what other experts have to say — not just about sales presentations, but about presentations in general, and about the psychology of how people think, perceive, and decide. This book strives to combine the best of academic rigor and practical, hard-nosed selling.[2]

WHAT WILL YOU LEARN?

This book is organized into three parts: planning and positioning, preparing, and delivering.

Part 1: Plan and Position. So much of your success in strategic sales presentations depends on what you do before you show up. In complex systems sales, strategy matters as much as your personal selling and communication skills. This section shows you how to prepare and what to think about before building the presentation.

Chapter 1 introduces four ideas that should help you get your head in the game, right at the outset. Chapter 2 takes us into the fascinating and quirky world of the human mind that you are trying to persuade: it covers the psychology of how people react to persuasive communication efforts. Chapter 3 focuses further on the particular thought patterns and expectations of executive audiences; and how to analyze your audience within the context of your sales cycle and strategy. In Chapter 4 you will get ideas on how to shape the conditions for success, so that you can stack the odds in your favor to achieve the purpose of your sales presentation.

Part 2: Craft Your Presentation. This is the meatiest part of the book, in keeping with the philosophy that solid content, backed by sound evidence and made compelling for the audience, is the most important ingredient in any successful presentation.

Chapter 5 shows you how to choose the right message for the right audience, and how to focus and shorten it so that it is absolutely

---

[2] You can be sure that if you ever come across the phrase "studies show" in this book, you will be able to see the citation (in the back of the book) so you can see for yourself if you want.

crystal clear to you first. As Cato[3] said, "Find the message and the words will follow."

Chapter 6 outlines the importance of a clear structure and introduces a comprehensive range of choices for structuring your arguments to provide clarity and impact regardless of the situation. Chapter 7 focuses on choosing the best building materials for your presentation: how to select the right type and amount of evidence to support your claims. Chapter 8 is all about taking the raw materials of structure and evidence and polishing your material so that it is clear, concise, and compelling.

You might be surprised to learn that one of the *last* things you'll do is to figure out what you're going to say *first*. In Chapter 9 you learn how to take advantage of the most important moments in any presentation by writing an introduction that grabs the attention and interest of your audience and closing decisively on a high note. Chapter 10 talks about how to prepare and deliver visual aids that aid, rather than hinder, the persuasiveness and impact of your presentation.

Part 3: Stand and Deliver. Of course, even with great content you still have to execute. In this section you will see how to ensure a great presentation through confident and dynamic delivery.

In Chapter 11 you will learn how to project an executive presence: to speak and carry yourself in such a manner that you project authority and create trust. Chapter 12 will tell you everything you need to know about projecting confidence even when you don't feel it, by channeling your nervous energy into superior performance. Chapter 13 will provide practical advice on what to do between crafting the presentation and getting up to speak, to ensure top performance and productive audience engagement. In Chapter 14 you will learn how to use your voice, stance, and gestures to engage and influence your audience.

Chapter 15 is about how to plan, prepare and present an effective team presentation. Chapter 16 is about how to use the Q&A session

---

[3] The Roman fellow, not Inspector Clouseau's sidekick.

as reinforcement and competitive differentiator rather than a period to be dreaded and survived.

Finally, the shortest and final chapter in the book, Chapter 17, sends you on your way with a message about personal excellence and growth.

To aid understanding and provide examples, we will follow a hypothetical scenario in which an account manager works through the process of planning and crafting a Strategic Sales Presentation. The scenario is introduced in Chapter 3, with additional details emerging throughout the book, at the end of each relevant chapter, set off by the shaded background. Chapters 8 and 16 each have their own separate case studies.

PART 1: PLAN AND POSITION

The aim of strategy is to win before you show up, whether it is for battle, a game, or a presentation.

In complex systems sales, strategy matters as much as your personal selling and communication skills, and the work you do before you even begin to craft your presentation can make a huge difference in your success. While you're probably eager to learn how to craft a compelling message and deliver it dynamically, proper planning and positioning acts as a multiplier for your effectiveness.

This section shows you how to prepare and what to think about *before* building the presentation. You'll learn about the peculiar quirks of the minds you are trying to persuade, with particular emphasis on how executive-level decision makers view their world and what they expect from you. Next, you will see how your presentation must fit within the context of your sales cycle and strategy, and then use those insights to shape the conditions for success and stack the odds in your favor.

1
FOUR RECURRING THEMES IN STRATEGIC SALES PRESENTATIONS

Although you may work for a huge company that has thousands of employees, numerous locations and billions worth of assets standing behind you, the audience hears and sees only you and your team. During the presentation, you *are* your company.

Customers attend these presentations to hear what you have to say and to see who you are, so you must pay careful attention to your content *and* the message you send about yourself.

At least subconsciously, and sometimes explicitly, decision makers will make a multi-million-dollar decision based on their perceptions of you, personally. Besides forming an opinion about your verbal content, they will form a general impression of you, which will in turn affect their comfort level in doing business with your company.

Are you competent and honest, and do you have their best interests at heart? They will find the answers to these critical questions in your presentation — in its content and in its delivery.

I hope to make this book well worth your time by covering a lot of useful material in great detail, but I want to make four key themes very explicit right up front:

- Outside-in thinking: It's not about you. It's about your listeners.

- Clear thinking: Persuasive ideas begin with sound logic and strong support. Content is king.

- Preparation: You can't guarantee success, but you must *deserve* it.

- Being genuine: Be yourself — at your best — when presenting.

OUTSIDE-IN THINKING

It's not about you — it's about your audience or your listener. Audience-focused communicators know that the quality of the reception is more important than the elegance of the transmission. They make the listeners the heroes of their stories, not themselves. They use *outside-in thinking*, which looks at the persuasion process from the point of view of the other person first. What do they know and not know? What are their needs? Why would they say yes or no to your idea? How do they like to receive information?

We've all heard the *Alice in Wonderland* quote to the effect that if you don't know where you're going, any road will get you there. Yet knowing where you want to go is not always enough, and that's where sales presentations tend to go wrong. After all, even a man lost in the woods knows where he wants to go. Any presentation, sale, or other persuasive effort aims to take the other person from Point A, where they are now, to Point B, where you want that person to end up. You can't go anywhere without knowing both the start and end points.

It goes even further than that: You may want to get to Point B, but the customer wants to get to Point C. As a sales professional, you already know very well that ultimately the road to your own goals must go through your customer's intended destination. People do things for their reasons, not yours.

Persuasion is not about getting people to see things your way; it's about getting them to see your point in their way.

I learned about customer focus quite by accident. When I was a banker, I managed to get an appointment to see the CEO of a reasonably large local company to try to pitch him our banking services. I'm sure the only reason he gave me his time was because I worked for one of the larger banks, not because of any special skill that I had in C-level selling.

I walked into his imposing mahogany-lined office and introduced myself. We chatted for a short time, and then he got down to business. "So, tell me why I should bank with you."

I'd dealt with this question many times before, but this time, I looked at him for a couple of seconds, and all that came out of my mouth was, "I don't know."

I'm not sure which one of us was more surprised by my answer. There was an uncomfortable silence for a few moments, and then in a tone that implied he was trying to figure out whether to get angry or laugh at me he asked, "You want me to bank with you but you can't tell me why?"

Thinking fast, I said, "Well sir, I have a lot of customers who are very satisfied with the services we can provide. We help some of them grow their businesses with loans and credit lines; we help some with cash management services or investment advice. But until I know more about your business, I don't know if you *should* bank with me. Do you mind if I ask you a few questions?"

He said, "Interesting approach. Go ahead, ask me a few questions."

I don't remember exactly what I asked, but as the conversation went on his answers grew longer and soon he was telling me about how he founded the company and the pride he felt in what he had achieved. By the end of the meeting, he agreed to give us a small piece of his business, and he later became one of my largest and most important clients.

That's the day that I learned the essence of selling. I realized for the first time that selling is not about who you are, or the products you sell, or the price you charge. These are all important, but selling is first of all about customers. It's about understanding them and their needs first. It's about asking before telling. It's about having the humility to admit what you don't know, and the ego to find out. It's about realizing that while your customers may see you and your competitors as all alike, they always see themselves as unique.

There's an old bit of sales wisdom that says: "Leave the product in the car." That is excellent advice for presentations. For many salespeople, their favorite topic is their product — or their company. How many sales presentations begin with slides that tell your corporate "story," for example?

I call this approach outside-in thinking. We naturally look at the world from the inside out. We have our own thoughts, desires, needs, and aspirations, and we look at the world — and at others — and try to figure out how we can get what we want through them. What may feel unnatural, but is far more effective in the long run, is to begin by seeing the world through their eyes first, and then work backward to figure out *how they can get what they want through us.*

Of course, there's nothing new about this idea. On a business level, the most eloquent exponent of the idea is Peter Drucker, who said:

> *It is the customer who determines what a business is. For it is the customer, and he alone, who through being willing to pay for a good or a service, converts economic resources into wealth, things into goods. What the business thinks it produces is not of first importance — especially not to the future of the business and its success. What a customer thinks he is buying, what he considers "value," is decisive — it determines what a business is, what it produces and whether it will prosper.*

It's also embodied in the works of these sales-minded authors: Tony Alessandra, who made a slight alteration of the Golden Rule to state his Platinum Rule: "Do unto others as *they* want done to them"; Stephen Covey, who tells us: "Seek first to understand and then to be understood"; and Fisher and Ury, who encapsulate the idea in their "win-win" approach to negotiating.

Inside-out thinking, by contrast, is characterized by outputs instead of outcomes — pushing things out the door to unwilling and unreceptive audiences. In the old Soviet Union, the economy was run by five-year plans handed down by a central planning office, which led to some strange decisions at the local level as factories did what they could to meet their targets. There's a story told of a shoe factory that constantly exceeded its production targets — by producing only left shoes of one size! You have probably attended enough presentations that seem to have been produced under the same principle, where efficiency of production is more important than whether the message fits the audience.

Show the audience you care about them, and they will reciprocate that regard. Do you want people to listen to you and be interested in what you have to say? Then begin by listening to them and being interested in what they have to say. Do you want to influence them? Be open to being influenced yourself. Abraham Lincoln once said that when preparing a speech he would devote two-thirds of his time to thinking about what the audience wanted to hear and one-third to what he wanted to say.

In her book *Resonate*, Nancy Duarte quotes Ken Haemer, who says, "Designing a presentation without an audience in mind is like addressing a love letter 'To whom it may concern.'" To ensure a strong customer focus, filter your presentation through the simple two-word question that is uppermost in your listeners' minds when you speak:

So what?

I refer to this important customer focus filter as the *so-what test*.

CLEAR THINKING

You can easily find plenty of presentation books that focus on style, on making an emotional connection with your audience, and on telling stories that will appeal to their right brains. A lot of them are well worth reading — after you're sure you have the fundamentals down pat.

Just as a master chef begins with quality ingredients before deciding on the flavorings and arrangement on the plate, effective communication begins with clear thinking. Presenters spend far too much time worrying about their fonts and decorations, or their delivery skills, when most of the battle is won in terms of clear thinking. In the end, content is still king.

Being dynamic and charismatic can take you far, but only for so long. As Lincoln said, you can't fool all of the people all of the time. Here's what another president said about it:

> *And in all of that time I won a nickname, "The Great Communicator." But I never thought it was my style or the words I used that made a difference: it was the content. I wasn't a great communicator, but I communicated great things...*

Complex sales follow a clear path and a process, and even if your compelling presentation makes an impact on your audience, the good feeling may have worn off when they actually make the decision a week later. There is nothing wrong with emotional appeals, but they are much more effective when wrapped around a hard core of logic and fact. Emotions wear off, but, as John Adams says, facts are stubborn things.

In our era of information overload, clear thinking is more critical than ever. Your listeners will appreciate the value you bring by cutting through the clutter and distilling masses of data and information into nuggets of knowledge that make sense and affect them personally.

Clarity of thought also says something about you personally. Besides improving the content of your message, the clarity of your thinking sends a strong underlying message to your listeners about how competent you are and, by extension, how much they can entrust their business to you.

This discussion so far begs the question: what kind of content is important to your customers? Whatever passes the so-what test. We've already seen that they're not that interested in your company history or even in your products that much. Instead, the content that resonates with them at high levels is useful, validated and quantified information about how to improve their business.

Here's a quote from Minelli and Barlow's *Partnering with the CIO*:

> *...CIOs want suppliers to partner with them by understanding the specific business needs of their organizations and by providing technology engineered to address those specific needs. Furthermore, the CIOs we interviewed want IT sales reps to talk less about technology and talk more about business value.*

Content that relates to business value includes solving known problems, taking advantage of opportunities, growing their top and bottom lines, lowering risks, streamlining processes, and economic value add. In addition, it helps to be able to translate all of these into financial metrics such as return on investment, payback, economic value add, and so forth.

PREPARATION

Audience focus and clear thinking don't come easily; they take work and preparation. With so much at stake, you owe it to yourself and to your audience to give it your best.

Giving your best requires three related but distinct areas of focus that are each critical in their own right: preparation, rehearsal, and ongoing practice.

Preparation refers to the time and effort spent crafting your message and your presentation. It is where you can make the biggest difference between mediocrity and excellence.

Bill Lane, Jack Welch's speechwriter at GE, emphasizes the importance of preparation with a story about Welch being asked to deliver an eight-minute presentation at a panel sponsored by Bechtel. Welch's so-called competitors on the panel included Charles Schwab and George Schultz. He recounts that they spent about eight hours together putting down ideas, followed by another eight to twelve hours each refining the presentation — all adding up to about four or five days of work for eight minutes in front of an audience.

Although that's a lot of work for a short presentation, here's what Welch said before flying to San Francisco for the event: "I can't wait to get out there and do this. I can't wait. It's so good." When you can take that mindset into any presentation, you will be unbeatable, and your confidence and enthusiasm can't help but be contagious.

Some people think they can be more creative if they "wing it." (Now *those* are the competitors you want to go up against.) It's actually preparation that improves creativity: if you prepare with plenty of time, you can have a day or two to let things marinate in your mind and spark new ideas.

After preparing you need to rehearse. There's a big difference between putting ideas on paper and hearing them aloud, and rehearsal gives you a chance to try the sound of your ideas under the most realistic conditions. Solo rehearsal is definitely worthwhile, but it's even better to try your ideas on someone else — and ask them to be completely honest. It's better to have your feelings hurt than to lose a deal. You might find something that is clear to you is confusing to your listeners, usually because they lack a key piece of knowledge that you take for granted.

Steve Jobs made his performances look naturally flawless, but only because he would spend two full days rehearsing with his team (who by that time had spent weeks putting things together) before his presentations.

Finally, long-term practice — constantly working on your skills for purposes of continuous improvement — is the only way to become great. You can't become a great speaker without speaking a lot. Martin Luther King is celebrated for his "Dream Speech," but he could not have done it without having spoken thousands of times before, without having given some version of that very speech dozens of times in churches, protest meetings, and civic functions. Winston Churchill saved a nation, and maybe western civilization, with his magnificent speeches, but of course he had been speaking in one of the finest speech schools in the world — the British Parliament — for forty years.

In the press of daily selling, you won't be able to put in the same hours that they did, but you simply *can't* get better without practicing, trying new things, getting feedback, and learning, then repeating this cycle again and again.

BEING GENUINE

Regardless of all the audience focus, clear thinking, and preparation you do, you still have to execute effectively when you talk to your audience, whether it is a large group or a single person. Too many presenters and salespeople blow it by forgetting that within the presentation, there is a conversation in which one human being connects with another. It has to be a genuine conversation and a dialogue.

Ideally, there should be no difference between a presentation, a sales call, and a conversation. The president of the bank where I used to work was a charismatic, confident speaker in small groups, but sounded like an incompetent fool when the group size reached double digits. You can see a similar phenomenon in sales calls where salespeople either sound like they're mechanically reading from a script or they fire numerous questions at their prospects but don't take the time to truly listen to the answers. There are some differences between interpersonal dialogue and a presentation, but most people exaggerate them.

Here's a blinding flash of the obvious in case you haven't figured it out: you never speak to an audience. An audience does not react to you. An audience does not buy anything. There is no such thing as an audience; it's an abstraction and abstractions don't make decisions. *People* in the audience do those things. Speak to the people as individuals, pay attention to their reactions, connect with them, and you will not have a problem with being genuine or even with pre-speech jitters.

It's easy for your audience to be passive during presentations — like watching television. Make it a conversation with each individual in the room, and they won't have a choice; they have to get involved, because it's a dialogue, and it's personal.

That passive audience effect is one of the reasons I'm leery of canned presentations that have been prepared for salespeople by the marketing department. While there's often some good material in there, it usually sounds like it was written by someone in an office far removed from the actual flesh-and-blood customer.

As part of my research for this book, I interviewed dozens of senior executives to find out what they like and dislike about sales presentations. Here were some of the comments I heard:

"Don't pitch me. Teach me."

"Don't use $75 words. It makes me think you're full of it."

"I don't like salespeople who come across as too hard, too coiffed, too canned."

SUMMARY AND KEY TAKEAWAYS

Whether or not you make a sale is dependent on so many variables that it would be ludicrous to try to reduce success in strategic sales presentations to simple formulas. Yet if you can skillfully, clearly, and sincerely show your customers how you can improve their lives, you will have an outstanding and lucrative sales career.

That goal translates into those four guiding principles, which should serve as your guide in the pages to come:

- Outside-in thinking is critical. You must make the customer the main topic and the hero of your stories.

- Clear thinking is the foundation of any successful sales presentation. You may wow them with your charisma, but when they meet again a week later to make the decision, the charisma will have worn off and the logic must stand on its own.

- Preparation is absolutely essential. Regardless of how good you are at thinking on your feet, you will always be better with preparation.

- Prospects and customers can spot a phony from a mile away. Be your best professional self, but always be yourself.

2
CAPTURING THE LISTENER'S MIND: HOW INDIVIDUALS DECIDE

What we call a mind is nothing but a heap or collection of different perceptions, united together by certain relations and supposed, though falsely, to be endowed with a perfect simplicity and identity.

—David Hume

The ultimate goal of any sales presentation is to capture enough of your listeners' minds to gain the decision you seek, so it makes sense to begin with a practical understanding of how their minds work: how they receive and process your message and what goes on in their heads during the process of making a decision.

A major corporate purchase or investment seems like it is fundamentally an economic decision, so common sense would tell us that your audience members will listen carefully to the relevant information, rank alternatives against carefully selected and weighted criteria, and select the option that scores the highest.

That's the view of the world that classical economists have, and if it were true the accountants and systems analysts would earn all the commission dollars. If it were true, better mousetraps would sell themselves. Fortunately for us salespeople, the real world does not work that way, or our persuasive skills would not make a bit of difference.

The real world is much messier and more complex than the rational choice model admits. People are not as much in control of their own perceptions and decisions as they think they are. The members of your audience miss some information, they bring their own personal experiences and prejudices to the meeting, they react to how you come across as a person, they may be distracted, they're influenced by far more information than your words contain, and their decisions might even be affected by how hungry they are or whether they had an argument with their spouse that morning.

Besides, most of the information you say is not 100% "true" in the sense that you can guarantee what will happen in the future if they buy your solution. On top of that, they have to try to remember everything you said when it comes time to make a decision. (And this only scratches the surface of all the possible deviations from the rational choice model.)

So, before we begin with the practical nuts and bolts of putting together winning presentations, we must have a good working knowledge of how your listeners' minds work. We'll consider the interplay of logic and emotion, and examine some biases and glitches in reasoning processes that may affect how your message is received.

Armed with this understanding, then, you will be able to tap into the psychology of persuasion and of cognition to add persuasive power to your executive sales presentations.

This chapter deals with individual minds in general, and in Chapter 3 we consider the specific ways in which those minds work within the context of corporate buying decisions.

WE HAVE TWO DIFFERENT MODES: SYSTEM 1 VS. SYSTEM 2 PROCESSING

We process information on two levels. By definition, we are only aware of our conscious thoughts, which comprise the chatter running through our head at any particular moment and involve that to which we have currently directed our attention. But beneath that surface current runs a vast torrent of submerged thought processes that are always going on beneath our conscious awareness and which can have an enormous influence on what we decide and how we behave.

Both systems are involved in making decisions, so if you want to influence someone you can emphasize either or both of the two systems. In the psychological literature there are several overlapping and basically similar terminologies, but for our purposes, we'll use the simpler terms popularized by Daniel Kahneman in his book *Thinking, Fast and Slow*: System 1 and System 2.

In some ways our brains are like the control system of an airliner on a long flight. System 1 thinking is like being on autopilot; it's good enough to get us through most of the journey with little effort on the part of the pilots. It's fast and effortless and mainly runs below the level of our consciousness. But there are times when the pilots need to take over and become fully engaged in flying the aircraft; that's System 2 — slower, more logical, and requiring conscious effort to use.

System 1 processing is also known as intuition, or gut feel. Intuition is more than just emotion, although emotions certainly play a dominant part. Intuition is basically very fast pattern recognition, by which we unconsciously and quickly react to cues in the situation. Maybe we like someone, and therefore will be more likely to agree to their request. Conversely, we may not have a favorable first impression, and that will color our reaction to any information we receive after the initial rocky start. System 1 is blindingly fast: *thin-slice* studies, so-called because researchers show progressively thinner slices of a speaker's behavior, have found that we can make reasonably accurate judgments about speakers (at least certain qualities) in seconds.

System 2 processing takes place in the logical processing centers of the brain. Using it, we pay careful attention to the information presented to us, weigh the evidence, analyze the logic, and make an objective decision. System 2 is slow and deliberate, and in the long term can be much more accurate, but it is difficult to master.

We all function in the world using both types of processing, in greater or lesser proportions depending on who we are or the situation in which we find ourselves. One would think that senior-level executives are very good at overcoming or filtering out their unconscious biases and reactions and being "hard-headed" in their decision making. If you think that's true, let's digress for a brief story told by John Kotter in his book *The Heart of Change*:

> *A procurement manager of a major corporation tried to convince division executives to centralize purchasing in order to cut purchasing costs. Although his analysis showed savings of close to a billion dollars over five years, no one got excited about it or took the lead in trying to implement the change. Then the executive asked an intern to find out how many different types of gloves the company purchased in its far-flung operations, and to order one pair of each type. He piled the gloves on a boardroom room table, arranged by division and tagged with individual prices, and invited executives to come in and take a look.*

> *What they saw astounded them: a huge pile containing 424 pairs of gloves! Executives quickly called others and insisted they had to come right over and see it. Word spread like wildfire, and the decision to centralize followed soon afterwards.*

As Kotter summarized the lesson, if you're trying for real change, you have to change the way people feel before you work on changing their thinking. Even decisions that make perfect economic and logical sense sometimes require some sort of emotional impact to drive action.

But don't get carried away by Kotter's story, because System 2 is also very important to get the action you want. For one thing, if you change someone's opinion through changing their thinking, that change will be longer lasting and more resistant to counterargument. You could, for example, deliver a knockout presentation that strongly influences your listeners to lean towards buying your solution. Maybe they're going to reconvene the following week to discuss their options and make a decision. By that time, the psychological impression you made has worn off, and logical considerations are back on the front burner. If your logic and evidence don't hold up a week later, you're going to be in trouble.

Besides, there is still a polite fiction within most of the corporate world that decisions are based on hard data and reason, so you had better give your audience something they can use to defend their decision.

WE TAKE MENTAL SHORTCUTS

Because System 2 processing is such hard work, we take mental shortcuts to reduce our workload. One of the most common ways we do this is by substituting an easy question for the hard one in front of us.

What psychologists observe in experiments is replicated thousands of times a day in sales presentations. For example, the question: "Will this multi-million dollar investment achieve the ROI we expect?" is extremely difficult to answer. An easier question to answer is: "Do I trust this person who is telling me it will?"

In *Partnering with the CIO*, Michael Minelli tells us that the process going on in a CIO's head is very simple: "When a CIO sizes up a salesperson, there are only two questions on his mind: *Can you help me?* and *Can I trust you?*"

Those questions tend to get answered by System 1, in spite of our best efforts to rely on data and logic as much as possible. For example, Olivia Cabane tells us in *The Charisma Myth* that CEOs and HR professionals often admit they'll decide whether to hire someone within the first few seconds. "The rest of the interview is just window dressing." A sales presentation in front of a larger audience will not be so extreme, but it underscores the necessity to pay attention to even the smallest detail.

This tendency is difficult, if not impossible, to shut off. Your listeners want to make their decisions based on data as much as possible, but System 1 thinking is always working in the background and nudging their decisions in one direction or the other, often in response to cues it picks up from the environment.

SOCIAL CUES AFFECT OUR THINKING

One of the best-known books in the persuasion literature is *Influence: the Psychology of Persuasion*, by Robert Cialdini of Arizona State University. Cialdini shares compelling research that demonstrates the powerful effect that unconscious cues can have on our decisions. The six powerful persuasive cues are:

Reciprocation: You scratch my back and I'll scratch yours. We are hardwired to respond to gifts by giving something in return. Gifts do not have to be tangible material objects: one of the easiest gifts to give a customer is the gift of listening, which will encourage them to return the favor when you speak.

Commitment and consistency: It's important to us to be consistent. We don't like to say one thing and do another, or apply one principle in one situation and a different one in another similar situation. In presentations, this may come into play when you connect your approach to values they espouse and hold dear.

Social proof: We often take cues about how to behave in an unfamiliar situation from what others are doing. Salespeople have long known how to use testimonials to reassure their prospects that it would not be a foolish risk to try something new — because it's not new to others.

Liking: No surprise here, we're more willing to agree to requests from people we like than those we don't. One of the key themes as we saw in Chapter 1 is to be genuine, which is one of the best ways to get your listeners to identify with you and like you personally.

Authority: We defer to people in authority. The authority does not have to come from a title; we grant it to others who have expertise in some area that we don't. Even subtle cues such as the way you dress and carry yourself will convey authority or the lack of it. There is in fact some indefinable aura of authority that seems to apply when one person stands in front of a group to speak.

Scarcity: Things always seem more valuable when there aren't many of them, or they are hard to obtain. As you will see in Chapter 4, you can sometimes make your presentation more special in the eyes of your customers by making them work a bit to get you there.

Persuasive cues such as these are no substitute for good sound business reasoning, but they can definitely add or detract from the effectiveness of your message, so it's important to be aware of them as you prepare your presentation and sales campaign.

There are times when persuasive cues may work in your favor, and you want to accentuate them. At other times, you may want to mitigate or counteract them. When people are not engaged in System 2 thinking, for example, they tend to stick with the default option. So if you're doing an account review for an existing account, maybe you don't want them thinking too hard! Emphasize the positive cues and avoid too much information. On the other hand, if you want to get them to switch to your product or service, you have to engage their analytical processes much more heavily.

The key point is not that one approach is better than the other. The people you are trying to influence during your presentation are just that: people. No matter how exalted their titles, they still make decisions with the same brain that regular folks use, and that brain is affected by cues that may or may not be within its conscious control.

WE RESIST CHANGE

One reason that intuition and emotion can't be taken out of executives' decision processes is that decisions about spending money always entail some risk. After all, any purchase is fundamentally a prediction about the future, and the future never holds guarantees. If the investment turns out wrong, there may be personal consequences.

Consultant and business coach Mark Goulston says: "Something I know about seemingly confident people, and especially people who work in large companies, is that often they're more afraid of making a mistake than they are of wanting to do something right. (That's especially true for managers or CEOs in their mid-forties, and even truer if they're men.)"

People are more afraid of errors of commission than of omission, meaning that it often appears safer not to make a decision. Potential regret can be a powerful motivator. Kahneman tells us: "People expect to have stronger emotional reactions (including regret) to an outcome that is produced by action than to the *same outcome*[4] when it is produced by inaction."

Here's a little thought experiment to illustrate: You're given a choice between two options:

A: 90% chance to win $1 million

B: $150,000 for sure

Which would you choose? (If you chose A and lost, would you tell your spouse about it?)

All things being equal, people will stick with the most secure option, often the status quo. It's easier and more comfortable to stick with what you have than to make a change, even if you're not completely satisfied with the current situation. That's one reason why so many members of Congress get reelected every two years even though no one is happy with the institution in general.

Under conditions of uncertainty, we cling even more tightly to the status quo. So, for example, if your listeners get confused, either because they don't understand some aspect of your presentation or because you give them too many choices, they will be very reluctant to change.

If you're the industry leader or the incumbent, status quo bias works in your favor, but if you're trying to break in, it's potentially a serious obstacle. Computer systems salespeople knew this all too well when their buyers had the attitude that "nobody ever got fired for buying IBM."

We will look at ways to mitigate risk and reduce fear. But even more powerfully, we will see in Chapter 6 how our choice of presentation structure can make risk work in our favor, by making it riskier *not* to buy.

---

[4] Emphasis added.

Sales presentations are basically about getting people to change, and change is one of the hardest things for people to do. The prospect of change actually produces a reaction in those regions of the brain that are primed to respond to danger and stress. To improve the personal connection, you may even want to acknowledge the stress and pain of change in your presentation.

It also means that getting agreement to change is only a first step. Beyond agreement, you have to get *commitment* and *action*. In Chapter 9 you will learn how to plan for this in your close, by getting clear agreement and eliciting what are called *implementation intentions*.

On the other hand, people find it easier to change when it's their idea. This is especially true of senior-level people, who are used to telling others what to do. Usually the most credible ideas are those people come up with themselves, so we'll examine how to structure your message and your approach so that your listeners feel as if they are participating in designing the solution to their problem.[5]

WE MISS OR FORGET A LOT OF WHAT IS SAID

Many presenters seem to think that just because they told someone something, that person will remember it when it comes time to use the information. They seem to think that knowledge transfer is like filling a glass with water. The problem with that analogy is that the glass is half empty at best. According to one study, immediately after a ten-minute presentation the average listener has either missed or already forgotten 50% of what you just said; by the next day the amount remembered has dropped to 25%, and that number drops to 10% a week later.

What does this mean to you? Two things:

If they will only remember 10%, you must be absolutely sure which 10% they will remember, especially if they then have to sell your

---

[5] It's like the joke: How many psychologists does it take to change a lightbulb? One, but the lightbulb has to *want* to change.

solution internally. You'll see this concept again when you choose the focus for your presentation.

Second, there are many ways to increase that 10% to a much higher number, including your choice of evidence and support, your introduction and close, your visual aids, and your delivery.

If listeners have forgotten that much of your message, it's either because some of it did not sink in at the time they received it, or it did not stick in their long-term memory. There are potential problems and inefficiencies in three mental processes that may derail your intended effect: attention, working memory, and long-term memory.

Partial attention

In today's frenzied society it is hard enough to capture and maintain anyone's attention for more than a few moments, and this is compounded when your listeners think they have seen it all, anyway.

When you have the floor, it can be very disconcerting to notice that most of the members of your audience seem to have their attention directed anywhere but at you.

We are probably the most attention-deficit generation in history, and our constant connection means that often your audience members are disconnected from what you are saying, beguiled by their latest email message or thinking about something else.

In effect, your listeners may be in a state of continuous partial attention, which means that while paying attention to you some portion of their minds is scanning their environment for higher-priority information.

What makes it worse is that they overestimate their ability to fully capture what you're saying while doing something else at the same time. For example, many people say they have a bad memory for names, but it's usually an attention not a memory issue. Have you ever been introduced to someone only to have no clue seconds later what their name is? It's because you were not focusing on their name when they spoke it.

As a speaker, your listeners' distractions pose two challenges: you have to seize their attention from the beginning and you have to sustain it during the time of your complete presentation. And you have to do both things tactfully.

In Chapter 9 we will look at ways to seize their attention right from the beginning, and throughout the book we'll discuss how to keep them fully engaged with your message and with you personally.

Working memory limitations

Even when we are fully paying attention, we rely on our working memory to make sense of the huge amount of stimuli that can occupy our attention. Although we can perceive millions of bits of information at a time, we can only consciously process a limited number of them.

You can passively take in huge amounts of information, but if you want to actively think about the information, and mentally process it, those thoughts must pass through the bottleneck of your working memory. Working memory is like a mental scratch pad on which you temporarily record and manipulate bits of information in order to make sense of them.

Working memory can be easily overloaded. In 1956, George Miller, a researcher at Bell Labs, published a paper titled "The Magical Number Seven, Plus or Minus Two." His point was that we can only process approximately seven pieces of information at one time. Some can do more, and some can do less, but that's about it.

More recent research has found that seven may actually be very optimistic. It's one thing to try to memorize numbers as they are read to you, but the difficulty level shoots up when you try to manipulate those numbers in your mental scratch pad. For example, if I asked you to add 24 + 17 in your head, you might not have too much trouble, but if I asked you to add 247 + 175, you might begin overloading your working memory as you try to remember the digits and add them together at the same time. Finally, when the pieces of information you are trying to process are complex or abstract ideas, they become even harder to manipulate in the mental scratch pad.

When working memory limits are reached, it's like pouring too much water too quickly into a funnel — some will overflow and not make it into the container. You've probably seen this yourself when a presenter puts up a slide that looks like a blueprint for the space station.

Or maybe, as presenter, you bring out new and surprising information that causes listeners to compare it to what they know. As they are doing that, they are bringing their own internal bits of information into working memory, so there is less capacity left for taking in more detail as you continue speaking.

In short, there is a real risk that your listeners may get left behind as you speak. When this happens, the best case is that they may interrupt you and ask questions, but usually they just tune out.

We'll go into detail throughout the book on ways to deal with working memory limits, including being very selective about the information you provide, having a clear structure, and designing visual aids and leave-behinds so they don't have to remember every detail.

Long-term memory

Even if you have managed to sustain their full attention and have not exceeded their working memory limits, there are still several reasons your listeners may not remember important points or details when it comes time to make a decision.

Sometimes the material simply won't stick. One major reason is that your presentation may be a competitive one, which means that at least one other vendor is trying to achieve the same thing you are. You can imagine the conversation on the following day:

> I really liked what they said about the scalability of the system; by the way, which vendor was the one who said they could do it?

> Vendor A really brought out some important points. One was that…, but I can't remember the other two.

The key is to make your message and your content so memorable that they *can't* forget what you said. Chip and Dan Heath wrote a book, *Made to Stick*, which examines the qualities of messages that tend to stick in peoples' minds. They list six qualities:

Simplicity: One of the most common mistakes that presenters make when they're facing C-level audiences is to make things much more complicated than they have to be. Making something simple is not the same thing as dumbing it down; in fact, if you can't simplify it you may not understand it well enough. If you don't simplify, they will simplify it in a way that makes sense to them, but it might not be the message you had intended.

Unexpectedness: The human brain reacts to anything that breaks a pattern; it's what enabled our ancestors to survive long enough to produce us. For example, you may drive down a crowded freeway at seventy miles per hour and be totally at ease, not even consciously paying attention to what's going on around you. But if the car next to you begins to drift even just a few inches into your lane, you become instantly alert and react. You will learn ways to break out of your listeners' ordinary patterns and engage their full attention.

Concreteness: We remember things that we can see, hear, touch, and feel much better than abstract concepts. For example, you can say your solution increases productivity, which is a very abstract term. Or, you can say it enables Chris behind the counter to serve four customers in an hour instead of three.

Credibility: When people are disposed to believe you they will pay more attention to your message and its details. You can enhance the credibility of your presentation by your planning, preparation, your use of evidence, the confidence of your delivery, and your presence. In fact, we devote all of Chapter 11 to the development of a credible presence.

Emotions: Events and information that strike our emotions get engraved more deeply into our minds. In a business presentation, there's a fine line between adding impact with emotions and turning off your audience, but, if properly used, appealing to emotions can take you beyond a simple "yes" to heartfelt commitment.

Stories: As humans, we passed on information and meaning in the form of stories for millenia before we developed a written language. Our minds are built for remembering and responding to stories. We'll look at ways to select the right stories and tell them properly.[6]

BAD IS STRONGER THAN GOOD

A popular song tells us we should accentuate the positive and eliminate the negative. Intuitively, it just feels right, and many writers on persuasive communication share this view.

But if you examine the evidence instead of your preferences, you will see that the negative can be a much more powerful persuasive tool than the positive — at least for parts of your persuasive task.

In 2001, Roy Baumeister and colleagues wrote a paper titled "Bad Is Stronger than Good," in which they surveyed the landscape and literature of psychology and noted a clear and substantial difference between the impact of negative information and events and positive information and events. From child-rearing to learning to memory to first impressions, we seem to place inordinate weight on the bad. It makes evolutionary sense for our minds to work this way. Finding something tasty might feed you for a day, but missing a sign of danger could kill you for a long time.

What does this mean in terms of sales presentations? First, people tend to process and remember negative material better than positive material. As politicians know all too well, one small glitch or wrong note can command far more attention than an entire well-crafted speech. Second, it means that losses loom larger in our minds that the equivalent gains. Daniel Kahneman is most famous for being the only non-economist to be awarded the Nobel Prize for Economics, partly for work he called _prospect theory_, which examines the different ways in which people respond to negative and positive frames.

---

6 By the way, acronyms can also help you remember; you may have noticed that these six qualities spell out "SUCCES."

To illustrate some of his research, let's create an example. Your plant, which employs 600 people, is losing money, and you have to recommend a course of action to the board. Consider the following choices:

> A)   You can scale back production in the most unprofitable lines and keep the plant open. This choice means that 400 jobs will be lost.

> B)   You can invest in new equipment to try to salvage the unprofitable lines. This choice means there is a 1/3 chance that no jobs will be lost, and a 2/3 chance that all 600 will be lost.

Which course would you choose? [Please answer before proceeding.]

If you chose B, you were in the clear majority. Now consider these options with a different frame:

> C)   You can scale back production in the most unprofitable lines and keep the plant open. This choice means that 200 jobs will be saved.

> D)   You can invest in new equipment to try to salvage the unprofitable lines. This choice means there is a 1/3 chance that all jobs will be saved, and a 2/3 chance that none of 600 will be saved.

In this case, a large majority chose C. In effect, three out of four people made one choice when presented one way, yet only one out of four made the same choice when it was worded differently! The only difference between the two situations was in how the choices were framed.

These results show up in properly designed studies, where each group only sees the information presented one way. Yet what is especially fascinating is that when I run this experiment in my presentation classes, the same results apply. In other words, people change their choice *even when they know there is no difference!*

If you're still not convinced, consider the following life-or-death choice. A person with lung cancer can choose between radiation or surgery. Surgery has a better record for long-term survival, but it is riskier in the short term. In a study, participants were given one of the following two descriptions of the surgical outcomes:

- The one-month survival rate is 90%.

- There is 10% mortality in the first month.

Which would you choose? 84% *of physicians* chose surgery when the survival rate was posed. Only 50% favored it in the second frame. Apparently, training and education are not enough to counteract the effect: surprisingly (and disturbingly) the framing effect applied equally to doctors as to the general population.

These examples demonstrate that *people are much more willing to take risks or action to avoid loss than to achieve gains.* So, a choice that is framed as the avoidance of loss is more likely to spur action than one that is portrayed positively. If a key goal of your persuasive efforts is to get listeners to take action, consider stressing the negative consequences of inaction. It also demonstrates that words matter. Mortality is a scary word that invokes specific emotional reactions.

Does this mean that your entire presentation should be negative? Of course it doesn't. If all you've done is scared the audience or made them uncomfortable, you've just ruined their day without accomplishing anything for yourself. Negative gets them moving, but you must have a positive direction or destination for them to follow.

You can actually harness your own bad news to good effect. It doesn't hurt to bring up some of the shortcomings of your solution. Doing so can boost your credibility and allow you to control the perception of the information. If there is bad news to deliver, make absolute sure you are the one delivering it so that you can counteract it.[7]

If you plan for it, you can turn a negative into a positive. When you eat a cherry pie, an unexpected pit can ruin the entire experience. But if the label says, "Real cherries — watch out for pits," you might be more likely to buy it.

---

[7] Another tidbit from reading Baumeister's paper: when it's a good news/bad news scenario, 77% to 88% of people prefer to hear the bad news first.

SOCIAL STYLES

Every single person in your audience is a unique individual, different from everyone else just as no two snowflakes are alike. No one responds in exactly the same way to your message or the information you provide.

People like to receive information in different ways. Some want to go through the thought process step by step, while others want you to get to the point immediately. Some people want to see passion in your presentation; others get suspicious if they think your passion is a substitute for analysis. Some care mostly about the bottom line, while others say the real bottom line is people and how the proposal will affect them. Strategic persuaders consider the listener's preferred mode of receiving information when they craft their message.

There's a rich body of literature in sales and communication that addresses the issue. One of the better-known approaches segments the population into four quadrants. This approach appears under many different labels, but the terminology I'm most familiar with is that of global consulting firm Wilson Learning's social style selling strategies, which uses the terms *analytic, driver, amiable* and *expressive*.

Let's use an example using Wilson Learning's categories to see how this applies to a presentation scenario. Suppose you're presenting a proposal that solves a business problem. This type of presentation usually comprises a description of the problem, a consideration of alternatives, and a recommendation. Ideally, you would know who the most important decision makers are in the room and would tailor your presentation so that the evidence you bring to support your points fits their styles best. If you want to appeal to the analytics in the room, you will spend extra time on the problem definition, particularly the process by which you analyzed the problem and determined the root causes. For the amiables, you can stress how you have talked to the relevant stakeholders and received their blessing for the solution. For the drivers, keep it short and present two options and let them choose. For the expressives, paint a vision of what the future will be like with the solution in place.

If you don't have the luxury of knowing who the key deciders are, or their preferred styles, it's best to default to the driver mode, especially with a more senior-level audience. Give them your solution up front and then be prepared to back it up with additional support as necessary. Try to keep it conversational and friendly and gauge their reactions to know how much to loosen up.

There is yet another dynamic to consider as you plan. You have your own preferred style, which may not always be the most effective for your particular audience. Approaches and evidence that seem most compelling to you may not work for your listeners.

There are two major challenges in adapting your presentation to others' social styles: one is finding out in advance which styles are favored by key audience members, and the other is figuring out how to tailor your approach for a mixed audience. We'll look at ways to do the former in Chapter 4 and the latter in Chapter 6.

OTHER BIASES

At the beginning of this chapter, we saw that the workings of our minds are messy. Returning to the substitution principle, thinking deeply and critically about something is hard work. Most people will do everything they can to avoid it. Psychologists call it being a *cognitive miser*, which is a euphemism for being mentally lazy. That sounds harsh, but it complies with what Kahneman calls the "law of least effort": when there are several ways to do something, we'll choose the least demanding option. Anyone who has ever raised a teenager knows this all too well.

Neurologically, our brains default to decisions that require the least amount of energy. [8] This means that we take mental shortcuts (technically called *heuristics*). Some of the shortcuts that are relevant to our discussion include *anchoring, contrast, primacy/recency, availability,* and the *halo effect*.

---

[8] It's a bit humbling to realize that the brain runs on about twelve watts of power, which is less than a refrigerator lightbulb.

Because of your attention and memory limitations, we're not going to cover those just yet. You will see more of them in the chapters where they have the most relevance and application.

SUMMARY AND KEY TAKEAWAYS

As you can see from this chapter, the human mind is not the neat, rational, and linear machine that we sometimes pretend it is. Changing minds is not rocket science — it's much more complicated than that. Rocket scientists can calculate the exact amount, timing and direction of forces to take a payload from the Earth to the moon and land within inches of their target.

For a speaker, the sheer unpredictability of your listeners' thought processes, coupled with the fact that others are trying to convince them of their point of view at the same time, mean that the few inches between your listeners' ears can be harder to navigate than the quarter of a million miles between the Earth and the moon. That thought may be daunting to some, but to me it's what makes selling, persuading, and presenting so much fun. Besides, if it were easy, anyone could do it, and you wouldn't be paid the big bucks!

- Our brains are hybrid engines, with two systems running concurrently: sensing intuition and logical analysis. Your presentation needs to appeal to both systems.

- We prefer easy questions, and, when choosing answers, respond to cultural and emotional cues without even knowing it.

- Bad is stronger than good. Take advantage of this when framing choices, and take special care to avoid even minor errors in presentation.

- We resist change. Make your solution the least-risky path, and let the specifics be the customer's idea.

- We have attention and memory limits. Be clear and concise.

- Be sensitive to your listeners' preferred modes of receiving information.

3
DECISION MAKING IN ORGANIZATIONS

In this chapter, we'll narrow our focus from decisions in general and take a more specific look at how individuals make buying decisions within organizations.

Chapter 2 showed us that individual perceptions and decisions are messier and more complicated than they seem on the surface. Companies have long known about these deviations from the standard utility-maximizing model for a long time, so they have put in place formal processes to guard against them. Yet because it's still individual people within the organization who do the thinking, these intelligently designed formal rules and structures quickly evolve into informal processes.

All of this adds up to yet another level of complexity, so we need a clear template to help us organize the myriad details into a coherent picture that will allow us to proceed.

A STRATEGIC TEMPLATE FOR PRESENTATIONS

What makes a sales presentation strategic? It's one that delivers the right content, to the right people, at the right time, to advance or close your sale.

For a successful sale to take place, the following conditions must be in place:

> The **right people** are **committed** to satisfy a **need**, and perceive your solution to be the **right choice**.

These seemingly simple eighteen words provide a crystal-clear outline of what you need to do to *understand* and *shape* the conditions for success in your strategic sales presentation. They should serve as the context and measuring stick you use as you analyze your audience, gather information, and craft your sales presentation.

In this chapter and the next, we will consider what you need to know and what you need to do to ensure that you are in the best position possible to have a successful *strategic* sales presentation.

We'll begin with a look at how decisions are made in organizations. Next, we'll also examine how senior-level executives are different from ordinary mortals, and what that means to you in terms of how you prepare and deliver your information.

For every person in your audience, it is important to know their:

- Role and function in the decision process
- Stake in the decision outcome
- Knowledge level and technical sophistication
- Attitude toward your solution
- Thinking and deciding style
- Personal history

WHO IS INVOLVED IN THE DECISION?

The standard term "B2B sales" glosses over that fact that businesses don't make buying decisions, people in those businesses do. Also, as anyone who has sold complex solutions knows, it's extremely rare that only one person talks to all the vendors, evaluates their offerings, and makes the final decision. Most of these decisions are made by teams of people, and just like a sports team they tend to have their own specialized functions. (Although, unlike most sports teams, individuals can play more than one function at once.)

If you've had any training in strategic selling methodologies, you've no doubt seen or created a decision process chart, which depicts the various roles in the decision process and the lines of influence between them. The decision-making process in a sales opportunity may look like an organizational chart, but it is not. An org chart may depict the formal levels of authority within an organization, but it cannot begin to portray the true paths through which influence flows in the typical buying decision, or any other corporate decision, for that matter.

Everyone in the process has informal levels of influence sustained by their perceived expertise, experience, or interest. Pat in accounting may be a low-level worker but is seen as the only person who truly understands the entire accounts receivable process; Ted in IS may be the only person who has worked with cloud technology. Joan may be a user who takes an active interest in ensuring that everyone is comfortable with whatever solution is implemented.

Unlike an organizational chart, the decision process will change with every opportunity. Unlike an organizational chart, you may be in a position to influence the decision process. By contacting the problem owner, for example, you may be able to convince them to get involved to ensure that their interests are met.

Always remember that everybody in the decision process sees the problem to be solved in a different way, depending on their position in the organization. They all have different levels of knowledge about your technology, and they have different personal styles of processing information and making decisions.

Let's start by defining the respective roles and functions in the decision-making process, listed roughly in order of their importance to you, as a sales professional. In overview, they are:

- Problem owner
- Decision maker
- Approver
- Recommender
- Influencer
- User

Problem owner: the person with ultimate responsibility for the business or operational results that are occurring or will occur once the solution is implemented.

If you think of your presentation as a problem-solving exercise, every business problem impacts someone in the organization; the people most impacted are the problem owners. This is an important definition. The person charged with solving the problem is not necessarily the problem owner — it's the one who suffers if the problem is not solved. For example, the VP of Sales may be concerned about decreasing margins, so she asks the Director of Training to find a course that will teach salespeople to better sell value. The Training Director may be asked to solve the problem by recommending or choosing a course, but in the end the VP of Sales feels the pain of decreasing margins and owns the business results to be generated from the purchasing decision.

There may be multiple problem owners, depending on the impact that your solution will have on the enterprise. Unlike the rest of the roles below, "problem owner" is not a separate formal role. Most problem owners will also play one of the roles below.

Decision maker: the person who will make the final decision on what is purchased. This person is the keystone of your sales strategy and is at the center of all the discussions and inputs during the sales process.

Approver: the person(s) who has the power to commit funds to the decision. Don't automatically assume this is the decision maker's boss; it may be someone in finance, for example, who controls the budget.

Recommenders: any individual involved in the decision who makes formal recommendations or otherwise influences the decision maker and others. Two of the most common recommender roles are technical and procurement. But recommenders may also be chosen because their department might be affected by the chosen solution, because their judgment is valued, or simply for political reasons. Sometimes recommenders are outside consultants who are retained to advise in the procurement decision.

Influencers: people who might have influence on the decision even though they are not "officially" recommenders. One of the best examples might be an executive assistant who can play a gatekeeper role and have a huge influence on whom you can talk to before your presentation.

Users: the person(s) who will actually use the product or service during the normal course of business.

For all of these participants, there are some key pieces of information which you must know. We'll discuss those next.

WHAT DOES EACH CARE ABOUT?

There is an old saying: "Where you stand on an issue depends on where you sit." It simply means that everyone in the decision-making process looks at a purchasing decision through the lens of their own self-interest within the organization. Everyone has a slightly different view of the need and therefore will have different buying criteria. The astute salesperson takes the time to see the opportunity through the eyes of each of the players in the decision process, and adjusts the sales approach to best meet the needs of each.

No one in the decision process has a complete view of the problem; they're like the blind men in the poem who encounter an elephant. One feels a leg and says the elephant is like a tree; one feels the tusks and thinks an elephant is like a spear, and so on. If you talk to just one problem owner, you're missing a lot, but it's even worse than that. Often, salespeople don't even talk to any problem owners; they only talk to problem solvers, or in the common sales terminology, recommenders.

Recommenders are one step removed from the elephant so they don't directly feel the pain like the problem owners do. As a result, they have different and often conflicting decision criteria. To the problem owner, speed is paramount because the situation has a cost — the meter is ticking. A reasonable solution which works now is better than a perfect solution much later. Recommenders don't have the same urgency; their incentive is to collect as much information as possible to make an accurate and justifiable decision. Wrong recommendations can be career-limiting, so they analyze every possible aspect of the choice in order to make the safest and most defensible choice. They love putting together elaborate tables of price comparisons and weighted decision matrices to show how thorough they have been.

Often the recommender is someone in the purchasing function, and you can be certain that their buying criteria will center on lowering the price and making it easy on themselves in the buying process. As a result, they step over dollars to pick up dimes. Or, they spend an inordinate amount of time in a continuing round of negotiations to squeeze the last price concession, while the problem owners are bleeding.

The following is a general overview of what people in the different roles care about.

The approver is usually interested in financial and operational criteria. They may not know or care about technical or performance characteristics. They may be willing to listen to a salesperson who can make a compelling business case for their solution, but often they prefer to delegate decisions to people at lower levels. To gain their attention, you must convince them that their guidance is necessary to ensure the best possible fit between the solution and the company's business issues.

The decision maker is caught in the middle between the demands for financial impact driven from upper levels, and technical, political, and user issues at lower levels. This makes it difficult to determine in advance what their primary criteria are; knowing their personal background may help.

Problem owners are concerned with resolving business and personal needs as expeditiously as possible.

Recommenders' needs and buying criteria will depend on their position in the company and their reason for involvement in this decision. For example, recommenders involved for technical reasons might be very concerned with performance features, and with compatibility with existing systems. Recommenders want to ensure that they make a defensible recommendation, in case things don't turn out as well as expected. They will want a lot of supporting data, especially social proof.

Influencers usually have a personal stake in the ultimate outcome; that's why they get involved. Sometimes the personal stake may be at odds with the needs of the organization or end users. For example, someone concerned with security may oppose connecting nonstandard devices to the network, even though everyone wants the latest type of phone.

Users are interested in criteria that will make their jobs easier and more productive, but without too much disruption. They will look for factors such as ease of use and similarity to existing systems.

One last thing: for all these people involved in the decision process, it can be enormously useful to know how they are personally measured. What are the key performance indicators that they pay attention to?

HOW MUCH DO THEY KNOW ABOUT THE SITUATION AND YOUR SOLUTION?

Almost any complex solution sold today involves some sort of high technology, so you will always have the challenge of figuring out how technical you need to get. In addition, your audiences will usually be mixed, which makes finding the right balance even tougher.

You have to find the sweet spot between boring them (or worse, insulting their intelligence) by giving too much information, or confusing them by not giving them enough. How do you strike just the right balance? One way is to know how much the audience members want to know. This is dependent to a certain extent on their role in the organization and their personal styles, as we will see a little later in this chapter.

But it also depends on where you are in the sales cycle and what decision has to be made. Every complex purchasing decision essentially requires *two* major decisions:

Do we make this investment?

If so,

Which do we buy?

Earlier in the sales cycle, your sales task is to get a "yes" to the first question. Although this seems obvious when you're looking at it in black and white, in my experience it is one of the most overlooked points in complex selling efforts. So many salespeople focus their efforts on showing why their solution is the best choice when the prospect has not even committed to solving the problem. That's one of the major reasons forecasts are so far off and why senior-level executives don't like spending time with salespeople.

Until you get that first yes, keep in mind that usually the decision makers and approvers care more about *what* your solution does than *how* it does it. Your material should be heavy on the business case and light on the technical details. Make sure you have the business case covered, and you can always dive deeper into the how during the Q&A or offline with those who need to know.

If the customer has decided that they do want to move ahead with their project, then it might be important to dive into the esoteric technical issue because at this stage the decision has moved to a choice between systems, and that choice may hinge on small details.

Yet even at this stage, any discussion of technical details has to be conducted under the discipline of "need to know." Give them everything they need to know in order to make the right decision, and drop the "nice to knows." This is where outside-in thinking comes in. Put yourself into the place of the audience members and apply the so-what test, while keeping in mind that the answer may be different for each person in the room.

There may be so many technical differentiators between your solution and the competitor's that talking about all of them will overwhelm all but the geekiest members of your audience. Focus on the meaningful few — the top two or three differentiators — tie those differences to operational and business improvements, and leave the others for the written proposal.

WHAT ARE THEIR ATTITUDES COMING IN?

Although I stress repeatedly in this book that clear thinking is paramount, even the most carefully reasoned and well-supported message can fail to change someone's mind if their mind is not prepared to hear it.

In fact, your listeners will hear your message differently depending on what their initial attitude is to your position on the issue. They may have their own opinion about whether your solution is the best fit for their need, or even about whether the need is worth addressing.

According to *social judgment theory*, there is a range of possible attitudes a person can take on an issue. Roughly, they can reject, accept, or be neutral about the issue.

FIGURE 3-1: BROAD RANGE OF POSSIBLE ATTITUDES

But these three terms don't really describe positions; they are more like zones because there are differences *within* the zones, as you can see in the more detailed diagram below.[9]

FIGURE 3-2: DETAILED RANGE OF POSSIBLE ATTITUDES

---

[9] These labels are *not* the labels that psychologists use. They are labels used in sales-strategy thinking.

The baseline is *neutrality*. Members of your audience may be neutral for one of three reasons: apathy, ignorance, or indecision.

Ignorance: They are not aware of the issue. In fact, if you're truly engaged in consultative selling, there is an excellent chance that they will be ignorant of the issue. That is because consultative selling, by my definition, means that you are bringing fresh ideas — in effect, solutions to problems they don't know they have.

Apathy: They know about the issue but don't care about the outcome or decision. Maybe it does not affect their profit center, or they are not yet aware of the impact it might have on them, or it's not yet a priority.

Indecision: They know and care about the issue but don't know which course of action is the best.

If you want to move someone from neutrality, you must know the reason they are neutral. You must either inform them, demonstrate why they should care, or make the case for your solution to the issue.

The negative attitudes as they relate to your proposal — the ones that social judgment theory says put someone in the mode of *rejection* — are:

Skepticism: They don't support your idea but are not necessarily resisting. Maybe they don't trust you or haven't heard enough to make them feel comfortable with the idea.

Opposition: In this case they are actively resisting your idea, perhaps seeing disadvantages for themselves or favoring a different approach.

Blocker: Besides resisting your idea, they are taking an active role in fighting against the idea. Maybe they favor the competitor's approach, or possibly they view your proposal as too risky or causing too much work.

The positive attitudes related to *acceptance* are:

Ally: They go along with your idea. They may say yes, or agree not to block your efforts.

Coach: They personally commit to seeing that the idea gets implemented. They take an emotional and personal interest in the idea and become enthusiastically committed to it. This is the difference between following the letter of your request and promoting the spirit as well.

Champion: Others make the idea their own and take an active leadership role in promoting and extending it. They may have a vested interest in seeing your solution implemented, probably because it will help them solve a problem or take advantage of an opportunity.

When you closely examine the range of positions that someone in the decision-making process can take, several critical considerations emerge.

First, there is a *latitude of acceptance* that each person is comfortable with. It's reasonable and possible that someone who is opposed, for example, can be moved to skeptical or even, possibly, neutral. In most cases, people can be moved slightly from their current positions.

But it is very difficult to move people outside their latitude of acceptance in one shot. No matter how charismatic or persuasive you are, it's unlikely that you will get someone to do something they are strongly opposed to just because of one presentation. With people like that, the phrase "You can't get there from here" applies.

In fact, if what you're selling is too far outside their latitude of acceptance, you run the very real risk of a boomerang effect, meaning that your message will have the effect of strengthening their opposition. In some cases, that means that it's better not to even try — or at least dial down your target and expectations.

Think of it like trying to pull a heavy weight with a string. If you pull too hard or too suddenly, the string will snap. But if you apply a bit of pressure and then patiently add to it, you have a chance.

Second, the listener's initial position will determine how they perceive your message. If what you say falls within their latitude of acceptance, they will see your message as more similar to their position than it actually is. If it does not, they will perceive it as more different from their position than it actually is.

Third, it takes time to move people to the right. That's why every sales presentation should be seen in the context of a complete sales campaign and not an end in itself. In Chapter 4 you will learn how to use your time wisely and shape the conditions for success.

WHAT ARE THEIR PERSONAL HISTORIES?

Finally, if at all possible you should also try to learn as much as possible about individuals' involvement in similar decisions in the past. If it's an existing customer, you may be able to find the information in customer files or your CRM records. Or you might be able to ask colleagues who had prior experience with the company. You may also be able to find out about them through their LinkedIn profile.

It's especially helpful to know if anyone in the audience was the person who implemented the existing system that you hope to replace with your solution. No matter what the situation, nobody likes to be told their baby is ugly, so you have to be extremely tactful.

THE ABSENT AUDIENCE

As if it's not enough to learn about your prospective audience members, there is one more "attendee" you need to take into account: your absent audience. The absent audience is the person or persons who are not there but will also be part of the decision process. You don't always have the luxury of having the ultimate decision maker or approver present during your presentation, but you can bet his or her shadow looms large in the minds of the people attending.

They are weighing everything you say with regard to how they will explain it or sell it to the absent audience, so you should too.

KEEPING TRACK

The appendix at the back of this book contains a blank template you can use to keep track of all your audience analysis data. It's especially helpful for team presentation briefings because it gets all presenters on the same page.

THE EXECUTIVE MIND

Everything we have covered so far in this chapter applies across the board to anyone in the decision making process who might be an audience member at one of your sales presentations. It's time now to turn our attention to the thinking and special concerns of top-level people. How are they different, and what do they want to hear, see, and feel when they listen to you?

EXECUTIVE AUDIENCES ARE NOT AVERAGE

When it comes to executive sales presentations, you are not presenting to an average audience. Certain characteristics are present in extreme amounts, and your presentation must take these into account:

Sophisticated audience: Most of your listeners have "heard and seen it all," or at least they like to think they have. They are smarter and more knowledgeable, on average, than a general audience, so they will get your point more quickly and need less repetition and detail. Their ears are extremely sensitive to fluff, unclear thinking, and baloney.

Pressed for time: They are very much in demand and guard their time jealously, and don't suffer time-wasters gladly. They even think differently about time: research has shown that people who feel entitled experience wasted time more painfully. Fortunately, this means that they are more decisive, so make sure you know what you want from them.

Broader vision: They don't know the details as well as you do, but they have a clearer view of the big picture, and know how to get to the heart of the matter to see how your proposal fits into their larger picture.

WHAT DO EXECUTIVES WANT TO HEAR FROM YOU?

For high-level executives to carve out time in their agendas to see a salesperson, it had better be worth their time.

There's an old saying in sales that "you get sent to who you sound like." If your presentation is mostly about your product and your pricing structure, executives will tune you out (or just walk out) because they have purchasers and technical experts to concern themselves with such things.

They also don't have the time or inclination to listen to a talking brochure in which your focus is on your own company and your capabilities. I'm sure you've sat through a few talking brochures yourself: the first few dozen slides look like a blown-up version of your company's annual report — with pictures of your HQ, message from your CEO, etc.

They don't want or need to hear your story. Executives interviewed about their perceptions of sales presentations consistently complained about the number of slides devoted to telling company history. As one CEO put it, "Even the presenters seem bored with it." A story in which you are the hero is not as fascinating to them as it is to you; they want to hear stories in which *they* are the heroes.

What they want to hear is what *they* think about constantly: their business processes and how you can improve them, their problems and how you can solve them, and your ideas to improve their profits. They want insights that they can't get anywhere else.

These insights can generally be found in the three "PROs" of professional selling: problem, process, and profit. How can you solve my problems, improve my processes, or increase my profits?

FIGURE 3-4: THE 3 PROS OF PROFESSIONAL SELLING

You will notice that this diagram does not contain product or pricing information. They pay people to listen to those kinds of presentations.

WHAT DO EXECUTIVES WANT TO SEE IN A SALES PRESENTATION?

The ideal presentation is like a fine watch. Your audience usually just wants to know what time it is, but they expect it to be accurate and they appreciate the craftsmanship behind it. They are looking for these qualities in your presentation:

Relevant: It addresses issues that are important and timely, and may have a personal impact on them as well.

Concise: It is as short and efficient as possible; packs a lot ideas into few words and provides just enough detail. If they want more, they will ask for it.

Simple and clear: Executive-level people are judging your thinking. If you can't explain your proposal clearly and in simple terms, they may suspect you don't understand it yourself. It's tempting to try to impress people with your brains by making things seem more complicated than they are or using puffed-up language, but this will actually make them perceive you as less intelligent.

Strategically focused: Demonstrate your own leadership credentials by not taking too narrow or parochial a view of your subject. Show how it fits in with their corporate goals; follow the three PROs.

Interactive: Any audience likes to be included and engaged, and even more so when they consist of high-ranking individuals who are used to being in charge. Even if you don't plan to make it interactive, they will.

Friendly and relaxed: The best way to make a good impression is to not try too hard. Presenters who are just themselves come across as personable and confident. Inject some of your own personality and conviction into the talk. As we noted in Chapter 1, be yourself — your best self.

WHAT DO EXECUTIVES WANT TO FEEL?

As we saw in Chapter 2, feelings and emotions creep into even high-level business decisions, and you want your audience to feel good about entrusting their business to you. In his excellent book, *Achieve Sales Excellence*, Howard Stevens lists the results of 80,000 interviews with senior-level executives in which they explain what they expect from salespeople. The top three items on their combined wish list are listed here because they are directly relevant to the approach we take in this book:

Will you take responsibility for my results?

Are you simply going to stand up and give us a talking brochure that focuses only on your company's capabilities and strengths, or are you going to show us how those capabilities will deliver results to our business? Can we count on you to personally take responsibility?

Do you know my business?

The last thing I want is a canned presentation that could have been delivered to anyone. I want to know that you have invested the time to understand my business. You don't have to be an expert; we'll be happy to help you get educated, but only if you earn the right by doing your homework first.

Will you be on our side?

Can we count on you to get things done for us inside your own company? We're not asking you to cross any lines, but we expect you to orchestrate your company's resources as though we are one of your most important customers.[10]

SUMMARY AND KEY TAKEAWAYS

When you consider everything covered in this chapter, there is a lot to think about and keep track of with respect to the people who will comprise your audience. It's a lot of work, and you may not be able to get all the information you would like. But there is one guarantee: the process of thinking about it and of trying to collect the information will make you one of the most customer-focused and best-prepared presenters they have ever seen.

The time pressure of selling is going to tempt you to cut corners, but keep in mind the stakes involved and the potential payoff — and do the right thing.

- Organizations don't make decisions; people do. Make sure you know who makes which decisions and why.

- Analyze their current attitudes to the situation and to your solution, and craft your message to move them to a favorable zone.

- Be sure to focus on the needs and criteria of the important stakeholders.

- Tailor your message to the traits and concerns of top-level executives.

---

[10] Stevens' complete list can be found in the notes section.

CASE STUDY: INNOVATIVE MANUFACTURING SOLUTIONS (IMS) STRATEGIC SALES PRESENTATION

Brian Carpenter is an Account Manager for Innovative Manufacturing Solutions (IMS), which does contract manufacturing for the electronics industry. One of the prospects in his territory is the Mobile Products Division of Visionary Industries, a rapidly growing manufacturer of mobile phone handsets.

Brian has been trying for a long time to get a foothold into Visionary Industries, but because of their vertical integration strategy, they have not been receptive. They prefer to control every aspect of the manufacturing process, which they feel has given them a competitive advantage in their market because of their reputation for innovative, high quality products.

Brian finally sees an opportunity, however. Through the industry press and information gathered through his network contacts, he has learned that VI has been experiencing an unusually high number of product returns and complaints from its major customers, specifically for the latest version of its SmartCall phone. They have traced the problem back to their power modules, which are failing too often. Although they have identified a solution which involves upgrading their production equipment to improve manufacturing tolerances for a specific component in the module, Brian is recommending that they consider outsourcing production of the entire modules to IMS.

Based on his knowledge of the decision process at Visionary Industries, Brian takes a first cut at the audience analysis (Figure 3-5) and realizes he has more work to do. He needs to find out more about the issues and concerns of the approver, and, although it will be uncomfortable, he decides to reach out directly to the Plant Operations Manager, who seems to be the principal opponent of the idea.

AUDIENCE ANALYSIS

GENERAL DESCRIPTION

The mobile products division is the largest division of Visionary Industries, and the fastest growing. They currently are fifth in global market share for mobile phone handsets, with the publicly stated goal of achieving #1 status by 2020.

They are known for their innovative and high quality products, and rapid new product introductions. Recently, their reputation has suffered due to quality problems which have been traced to excessive heating caused by misalignment of the HBT fingers on the power module semiconductor substrate. We are proposing to take over the design and manufacture of the entire power module, which is something they have resisted because they've preferred to control every aspect of the manufacturing process.

However, due to current conditions they are now open to the idea.

Key audience member: Pat Jones
Title: CFO
Role in decition: Decision maker
Attitude: Neutral
Issues and concerns: Financial stability of supplier, contract terms, costs

Key audience member:
Title: Plant Operations Manager

Role in decision: Recommender
Attitude: Opponent

Key audience member: Feng Li
Title: Director of Product Planning
Role in decision: Recommender
Attitude: Champion
Issues and concerns: Concerned that a repetition of this problem can seriously jeopardize potential customer relationships and slow down new product development. Wants to increase the average selling price by concentrating on higher-end units.

Key audience member:
Title: AD, Power systems
Role in decision:
Attitude: Opposed
Issues and concerns: We think he is concerned that outsourcing power modules for SmartCall will reflect on his design and potentially limit growth, although he has not publicly said this.

"Hidden audience": Chris Tilberg
Title: President of Mobile Products Division
Role in decision: Approver
Attitude: Unknown

FIGURE 3-5: BRIAN'S PARTIALLY COMPLETED AUDIENCE ANALYSIS

4
SHAPE THE CONDITIONS FOR SUCCESS

Don't be a hero. We all admire the heroic view of persuasion, where the hero deploys his impeccable reasoning, formidable presence and eloquent words to sway an audience. Think *12 Angry Men*, or "Win One for the Gipper," or, for the more literary-minded, Mark Antony's eulogy for Caesar, where he artfully turned the anger of the mob away from Caesar and against his murderers. It's easy to be fascinated because that's where the drama is.

If drama is what you want, put down this book and rent a movie. The most effective salespeople in the long run usually do it without the dramatics. They understand that, as Sun Tzu teaches in *The Art of War*, the best general is not the one who wins the most battles, but the one who wins without having to fight battles.

Don't get me wrong, all those things mentioned in the first paragraph — reasoning, presence, words — can mean the difference between success and failure, and we will spend a lot of time in this book looking at ways to make those as powerful and effective as possible. But sales presentations are a means to an end, and what counts in the end is an increase in sales. This chapter is about doing all the things *before* your presentation that will ensure that you come through it successfully. It's about applying a little positive paranoia and doing what you can to stack the odds in your favor.

I learned this well in my banking days, when I used to bring loan proposals to a committee for approval. After a few rough presentations, I gradually figured out how to work the system. I would bring the rough version to one of the more influential members and ask his help in structuring the deal so that it would make sense. Besides giving me the benefit of his experience to improve the proposal, it would also get him committed to the deal, and I would then have an influential champion. I could then go to another member and say, "Chuck and I think this deal would work this way. What do you think?"

This approach would also make it easy to quickly figure out if there was going to be a deal-breaker, in which case it made sense to "lose early." This approach can improve your overall success rate at the same time as it improves your reputation for only bringing in sound proposals. Credibility must be painstakingly built, brick by brick, over time; but once it's built, assuming you don't get complacent or arrogant and do something stupid, it's a gift that keeps on giving.

In large organizations the complexity of persuasion mushrooms because of the number of people involved. Strategic sales professionals learn to figure out the informal paths of influence within the customer's organization; they find out who has the most influence in each type of decision, how they perceive their interests, how they like to receive information, and dozens of other bits of information that go into completing the presentation mosaic.

Because of their complexity, some sales opportunities can take on the character of a military campaign, where countless details need to be considered, resources marshaled on your behalf, allies to be lined up, and opponents' moves and countermoves to be considered. Today's military planners are taught to "shape the battlefield"; the last thing they want is a fair fight.

Just as seasoned negotiators know that their personal performance at the negotiating table can only influence the final agreement within a narrow range that has been dictated already by the respective power and positioning of the participants, expert presenters know fairly precisely what is likely to happen because of their presentation — in good part because they will make it happen.

Of course, because people are unpredictable and circumstances change, you have to strike the right balance between planning and flexibility. Football coaches game-plan very meticulously, but quarterbacks and defensive captains still need to be able make changes based on what they see the opponent doing. While no sales presentation has ever gone exactly as planned, the *process* of planning has personally saved me on numerous occasions. As Eisenhower said, "Plans are nothing; planning is everything."

FIGURE OUT NEXT STEPS

Let's go back to the description of the conditions that must be in place to win your sales opportunity:

> The **right people** are **committed** to satisfy a **need**, and perceive your solution to be the **right choice**.

Your audience analysis provides a detailed and accurate picture of where you stand in relation to these conditions before you present. If you've filled it out, you've probably uncovered several areas where you fall short. You may have some skeptics, the approver may not see an urgent need, you may have some unknowns, and so on.

You can take a chance and go ahead with the presentation, or you can apply a little healthy paranoia and do what you can to improve your position. Better to sweat the details beforehand than to sweat during the actual presentation!

GET A CHAMPION

Easily the most important step in shaping the conditions for success is to recruit someone to be your champion: someone in the customer organization who actively works to see that you succeed. They are on the far right side of the attitude range.

Why would someone be your champion? There may be a number of reasons, but the most likely and the most powerful is that buying your solution will make their life better in some way. It might solve a problem, make them look good, improve their political standing within the organization, or make their life easier.

For this reason, a champion will sell for you when you're not there. Regardless of how industrious you are, the simple fact is that you spend very little of your time actually talking to someone from the prospect's organization. (And in some cases, your ability to talk to them may be constrained — by conditions of the RFP, for example.) Champions are always there. Besides, they usually carry a lot of credibility and know far more about the inner workings of their company than you do.

Champions are usually found at middle levels in the organization. They are the "box two" operational and functional managers who own the processes that produce corporate performance and are best placed to see what needs improvement and why.

How do you use your champion?

- Collect intelligence. It's very difficult to collect all the information we discussed in Chapter 3 without having someone on the inside to help.

- Ask them to do something for you. The chief difference between a coach and a champion is that they will do something for you besides furnish information. For example, a champion could arrange for your presentation to go last on the agenda, as we saw in Chapter 1.

- Run your presentation by them for honest feedback. You may not want to share your entire presentation, but at the very least it's helpful to confirm your understanding of the customer's business situation and issues, fine-tune how you would position certain messages with specific individuals, and learn what to avoid.

- There's nothing wrong with educating your champion on the weaknesses of your competitors, and maybe even suggesting questions they should ask them during their presentations.

- Do not presume upon their willingness to help to ask them to put themselves into an awkward situation or cross any ethical lines. For example, in a competitive situation, I would never ask my champion about what my competitors are proposing.

By the way, if you can't find a champion for your idea before you go into the presentation, maybe you'd better reconsider the whole idea. It might mean that no one in the customer's company recognizes the importance of the problem or sees enough value in your solution.

Finally, if one champion is good to have, more than one is that much better. Knowing as much as you can about all the different ways that your solution can help your customer's business will help you target different problem owners who may champion your solution when they see how it can help them.

WORK WITH YOUR SPONSOR

If you can't recruit a champion, the next best thing is to work with the person who sponsored the meeting. Your sponsor may or may not be your champion, but they usually care about your success because a poor showing by you is bound to reflect on them. So, help them to help you. Let them know who should come, how the room should be set up, when the meeting should be, etc.

The sponsor can also give you information about the key members who will be attending. In effect, just going through the process of gathering the information will help you to shape the conditions for success.

Since the sponsor is probably the one who will introduce you, give him or her a brief description of how you would like to be introduced.

FIGURE OUT WHO SHOULD BE INVITED

"The truth is that in most complex selling situations, anyone who agrees to see your sales representative for any amount of time, without additional preparatory conversation, has more time to waste than most senior-level executives."

—Dan McDade, *The Truth About Leads*

You don't have to passively wait to see who is going to show up for your presentation, especially if it's a concept presentation early in the sales cycle. Try to get the major problem owners to attend, and anyone else whose influence might be important during the sales cycle. If they are not willing to bring in some of the participants that you feel should be there, that may be a bad sign.

You will boost your chances for success, and possibly trim the sales cycle significantly, if you have high-level people in your audience during the initial presentation where you interest the customer in the concept. Executive sponsorship early in the sales cycle will do several things for you:

- Properly define the problem and help keep the focus on true needs

- Increase the sense of urgency for the information gatherers, which may ward off "analysis paralysis"

- Qualify that a real opportunity exists

- Open doors for you in other parts of the decision process

You may note that the first three benefits help the customer as much as they do you, which is useful in case a gatekeeper asks why the boss needs to be there.

One of the first mistakes that salespeople make in any complex sales cycle is to be so happy about getting their foot in the door that they don't set certain conditions as the price for showing up. If it's too easy to get that first meeting, you should remember Groucho Marx's quip that he would not join any club that would take him as a member!

If you don't set some parameters, you run the risk of spending a lot of time and your company's money doing a dog-and-pony show for a bunch of tire-kickers who are just using you to educate themselves on new technologies and products. Even if they have any intention to buy, they won't have the budget or ability to make the decision.

You have to get the prospect to put skin in the game. If none of their more important or influential people have enough interest to attend the first presentation, the likelihood of a successful sale plummets. On the plus side, if you ask your contact to get a higher-level problem owner involved, they have to do some selling for you in order to make that happen.

Another very practical reason to get your prospect to put skin in the game is to make sure they honor their commitment and actually show up. If you've ever flown to a meeting only to find that the VP of Sales who had agreed to meet with you had left for the day, you won't forget this lesson!

One way to do this is to get a commitment for additional people to attend; it's highly unlikely they will blow you off if the meeting includes other key personnel. Building a strong meeting roster is also a very effective way to cultivate relationships, gather information, and develop allies before the presentation.[11] Just be sure you have a value proposition worked out that explains what value *the customer receives* by inviting others to attend and by allowing you to speak to them.

It's very important to guard against the tendency to over-focus on problem owners and decision makers. Regardless of their importance in the decision, they are still going to rely on others to gather information, give necessary input to the decision, and make sure the final decision is implemented properly. In fact, recent sales research by the Corporate Executive Board has found that widespread support for the supplier is the number one thing senior decision makers look for in making their decision.

Make sure they're brought in early, and make sure you attend to their needs also. Others who are helpful to have attending:

- Technical buyers. They're the ones who can easily veto your solution, so you need their stamp of approval.

- Purchasing function. Although they are not usually the problem owners, they can make your life very difficult if you try to exclude them.

- Implementers and users.

If it's a closing presentation, it should go without saying (but I'll say it anyway) that you had better have the decision maker present. Once I made a sales presentation to an office equipment company

---

[11] It also helps if you're prone to presentation jitters — when you know someone it's generally easier to talk to them.

that went so well that the decision maker decided to skip the next presentation being made by my competitor. About a year later I met my competitor at a conference. He told me that when he walked in and found out that the decision maker had not showed up, he knew it was over before he began.

Besides the decision maker, the following people should be at the closing presentation:

- CFO, Controller, or Financial Director, depending on what level of authority is needed to write the check.

- Anyone whose cooperation will be instrumental in implementing the solution.

MAKE SURE YOUR OPPONENTS ARE THERE

It's natural to hope for an easy presentation with no tough questions, so it can be very tempting to try to arrange that your opponents not be there during your presentation. I think that's a mistake. You can't deal with objections if you're not there to hear them. You have to smoke them out — let them make their objections public and make sure you're well prepared for them. Otherwise, they can come back later and begin a whispering campaign behind your back. If they don't bring up objections during the presentation, they'll be hard-pressed to bring them up later.

As I was working on my sales opportunity for the New Zealand prospect, I found out that the highest-ranking person who would be in the audience was opposed to hiring my company. I found out some of his reasons from my champion, but I also picked up the phone and called him directly.

I probed for his concerns, and as he explained them all they sounded serious enough that I said, "If you were in my position, would you even come to New Zealand?"

His reply? "I don't know that I would."

Considering that it's a very long and expensive trip, the prudent decision might have been not to go. (Did I mention he was the highest-ranking person who would be in the audience?) But I thought I had a strong offering and could come up with answers for his concerns, so I went anyway.

What did that phone call get me? At the very least, it got me advance information on what his objections were going to be. I also believe it got me some respect.

It's human nature to want to avoid blockers and opponents in the sales cycle, but you're going to face them during the presentation so what do you have to lose by reaching out to them beforehand?

If you do, it's extremely important to avoid turning this call into a sales call. The most you can try for is to nudge them slightly in the direction you want, maybe from opponent to skeptic. Don't try to win them over or change their minds, because you run into the danger of the inoculation effect.

Trying to persuade another before you're ready increases the risk not only of failure but of hardening their position. If your arguments are easy for the other person to counter, they act as an inoculation, in which fighting off a weaker version of the disease strengthens the immune system against the stronger version. By causing them to bring arguments against your position, they strengthen their mental immune system against your position.

Also, if they oppose you publicly, they are much less likely to shift from their original position. We all admire those who are persistent in the face of disagreement, but it's usually better to put in the time *before* the first persuasion attempt rather than after.

If you can handle the call to your opponents, it should be a breeze reaching out to the other participants.

Reaching out does not have to be in the form of a personal conversation. You can also send an email to the expected attendees a few days before your presentation. Keep it brief, but introduce yourself and the reason for the presentation; confirm the time and place of the meeting, and invite them to let you know if they have any specific issues they would like to see addressed during the meeting.

WHEN NOT TO INVOLVE THE C-SUITE

You don't always need a senior executive present in the room during your presentation. The general rule is to only go as high as you add value. Most executives like to push decisions as far down the organization as they can, both to develop their people and to manage their time more efficiently.

Executives should *not* be there when you find yourself in either of these situations:

- Your solution does not have a strategic or broad impact on their company. You will be wasting their personal time and their company's resources asking for that person to be there.

- You have not done the right groundwork with lower-level members of the decision process. There may be some cases where you're being blocked at lower levels and feel that an end-run can save your position, but you'd better be absolutely certain that doing so is in the best interests of your customer, not just in yours.

RESEARCH THE COMPANY AND THE INDUSTRY

You will probably have done a lot of this in the normal course of working on your sales opportunity, but here's a reminder of the steps to take in your research.

Read their annual report. You may not have to read the whole thing, but you should definitely read the Chairman's Letter to Shareholders, which will bring you up to date on their recent performance, key events, corporate strategies, etc. You may also find some key phrases, concepts, and corporate buzzwords that are important to them. You can get a lot of the same information from their 10-K report if they're a public company, and casually mentioning that you read their 10-K makes you sound even more sophisticated and professional.

Whether or not you go so far as to read their financial statements depends on how much of a financial sale you're working on.

Regardless, it's a good idea to be familiar with their general numbers, including revenues, profits, general growth rate, etc. If you want to be extra-prepared, read the Management's Discussion section.

Scan a copy of their latest quarterly reports. By the time the annual report is published, it's almost a quarter out of date, and things can change fast.

Check the news releases and the press on the day that you're going to make the presentation. You may find information you can use in your presentation to make it sound very timely and personalized, or you might even avoid stepping into a major pile of embarrassment.[12]

Check the LinkedIn profiles of the attendees. You never know when you might find a useful tidbit or a connection you might have in common.

If you're not a specialist in the customer's particular industry, you should also research the industry. The following is a bare minimum:

- Who are the key players, and how does your prospect compare to them?

- What are the critical success factors and key competitive differentiators?

- What specific operational metrics do they track?

- What are the key issues and trends in the industry?

ANTICIPATE QUESTIONS AND OBJECTIONS

When I think about the depth of knowledge that you should strive for, I'm reminded of a story that involved the great physicist, Max Planck. Planck traveled around Germany delivering lectures, and

---

[12] A client told me the story of the presentation he attended at Frito-Lay just a couple of days after their purchase by PepsiCo had been announced. When they were asked if they would like a drink before the meeting started, his sales engineer asked for a Coke. It was not an auspicious start.

one day his chauffeur said, "Professor, I've heard your lecture so many times that I am sure I could deliver it word for word. Why don't I pretend to be you at the next lecture and see how I do?"

The chauffeur delivered a perfect rendition of the lecture, but he had not reckoned on having to answer questions. When one of the members of the audience asked for an explanation of a particular point in the lecture, the Chauffeur replied: "Professor, I am surprised that a man of your standing should ask such a question. It is so easy that I will let my chauffeur answer it."

The point of the story is that although it's more work, you should strive for a deep cushion of knowledge rather than the bare veneer that you think you will need for your presentation. As we will see in Chapter 16, often the presentation itself is less important to your success than the dialogue with the audience members. When executives recognize that they don't have the subject matter expertise to choose between complicated options, they like to use questions to dig a little deeper and test your depth of knowledge and confidence.

The most important thing you can do to excel during the question-and-answer period is to prepare thoroughly by trying to anticipate — and answer — every conceivable question your listeners might throw at you.

Preparation brings three benefits. The most obvious is that you will have a good answer prepared. Second, preparation will give you genuine confidence, which will make you feel better and help you come across to the audience more credibly. Finally, anticipating your audience's reactions and questions will force you into their frame of mind, which might even cause you to go back and refine your presentation.

Depending on how confident you want to be that you have anticipated every possible question or objection, there are five progressively stronger steps you can take:

Wing it. Probably the most common method practiced by salespeople, it has the advantage of taking no time and letting you be totally natural in your responses. Unfortunately, it can turn out to be the most expensive approach, for obvious reasons.

Anticipate general objections. This is the most obvious approach, which is nevertheless overlooked by even some of the most experienced salespeople. What are the principal objections you get all the time from your customers and prospects when you are selling this particular solution? Most salespeople think about these, but I'm constantly amazed at how many never actually take the time to write out their responses.

The reason for writing out your response is not to have a script that you will recite when the question comes up. You will sound like a politician — or a well-coached defendant. The real reason is to find the gaps and solidify the thinking in your head. As we've already discussed, writing or saying things out loud is a great way to clarify your ideas and make sure they sound right to others.

For particularly important presentations, you might want to check your own internal corporate network to find out what questions others have been getting and what approaches have worked for them.

Think through specific objections. The next step is to go through your own presentation and try to figure out which parts will get which types of questions from which participants. They may question your facts: be sure you have solid references to back them up if asked. They may question your interpretation of the facts: try to think of alternative interpretations and be prepared to refute those or explain why your conclusion is more likely.

As if going through your own presentation trying to find objections isn't stressful enough, keep in mind that anything is fair game for the Q&A. They may ask you about something totally unrelated to the subject of your presentation — maybe something your organization did or did not do in the past offended one of the attendees. Or, while you are focusing on the merits of your solution, the CFO may ask you questions about your own company's financial strength.

Although you can't anticipate all of these questions, your best protection is thorough audience analysis. In general, what are their needs and motivations for being at your talk? Specifically, if you know certain individuals will be there, try to find out about their personal hot buttons, history, and anything else you might want to be prepared for.

Anticipating general and specific objections and questions will probably put you far ahead of the game compared to most salespeople. But since strategic sales presentations carry such high stakes, and because a bit of healthy paranoia is one of the qualities of top sales professionals, here are two additional steps you can take to pressure-test your ideas.

Take the chess master approach. Think at least two steps ahead. If you have written down expected questions in one column and outlined your answers in a second, add two more columns to the right of your worksheet. In the third column, imagine that you've just given the answer in column two, and some skeptical audience member asks a follow-up question to your answer. Then write your answer to that.

Red-team it. Remember that there is usually at least a third participant in the decision making process besides yourself and your customer — the competitor. Smart competitors will know that you are presenting and may have champions of their own. They may even have planted questions designed to trip you up. (I know because I've done it myself and I know for a fact it has been done to me.) Try to put yourself in your competitor's place and figure out how you would attack you. Better yet, get some of your peers to do it.

PREPARE PRESPONSES

One of the benefits of anticipating challenges is that it can help you defuse them before they even come up. *Presponse* is a word I made up that means anticipating objections or questions and answering them even before they come up by building them into your presentation. This does several things for you:

- It demonstrates your outside-in thinking. Even skeptics and opponents will appreciate the fact that you understand their concerns.

- It steals their thunder. When you bring an objection up during your presentation and answer it, it loses a lot of its power.

- It allows you to define the terms of the discussion.

- It makes you look really smart and well prepared.

SUMMARY AND KEY TAKEAWAYS

In the movie *Glengarry Glen Ross*, Alec Baldwin plays the hard-nosed sales manager who tells his salespeople: "A-B-C. Always Be Closing." When you see sales as an event instead of a process, ABC is about your only choice. But in high-level B2B sales, that approach is unprofessional and ineffective. In the long run, it's better to remember that the way to succeed is to use the three Ps: Process, Positioning, and Preparation.

- Sales presentations become strategic when they are an integral part of your sales strategy rather than disconnected events. Get a champion and line up your support before the presentation.

- Don't leave the attendance to chance. Make sure the relevant stakeholders are invited, including your opponents.

- You don't always have to present to the C-level. Know when and when not to get them involved.

- Research the company and the industry — right up until the last minute, if you want to avoid surprises.

- Anticipate likely — and unlikely — questions, and have answers prepared.

CASE STUDY, CONTINUED: IMS STRATEGIC SALES PRESENTATION

Following the ideas in this chapter, Brian begins working the decision process, talking to key players and gathering useful information. You will note from his updated audience analysis form that he has found some new and potentially useful information about the company, identified specific concerns that his principal opponent will have, and invited a potentially useful ally to attend. The amount of information that goes into the audience analysis may depend on whether it's intended to be a briefing document for a solo or a team presentation — a team's audience analysis form gathers several different perspectives together in one place, and may be quite a full document. (Look for a separate case study about team presentations in Chapter 16.)

AUDIENCE ANALYSIS

GENERAL DESCRIPTION

The mobile products division is the largest division of Visionary Industries, and the fastest growing. They currently are fifth in global market share for mobile phone handsets, with the publicly stated goal of achieving #1 status by 2020.

They are known for their innovative and high quality products, and rapid new product introductions. Recently, their reputation has suffered due to quality problems which have been traced to excessive heating caused by misalignment of the HBT fingers on the power module semiconductor substrate. We are proposing to take over the design and manufacture of the entire power module, which is something they have resisted because they've preferred to control every aspect of the manufacturing process.

However, due to current conditions they are now open to the idea.

Based on latest Annual Report, we have seen updates to the company's Vision and Strategies. VI intends to realize its "2020 Vision" through:
- Fast responses to market changes
- Strengthening market leadership through differentiation
- Focus on core competencies

According to analysts, the substantial growth in market share has been a mixed blessing, as the companing is running into capacity constraints in its manufacturing, leading to cash flow constraints and increased borrowing costs. We believe this may resonate with the CFO.

Key audience member: Pat Jones
Title: CFO
Role in decition: Decision maker
Attitude: Neutral
Issues and concerns: Financial stability of supplier, contract terms, costs, capacity constraints?

Key audience member: Jim Coppedge
Title: Plant Operations Manager
Role in decision: Recommender

Attitude: Opponent

Issues and concerns: Resistance to change, history with supplier of current equipment, worried about setting a precedent, very much measured by throughput and capacity utilization

Key audience member: Feng Li
Title: Director of Product Planning
Role in decision: Recommender
Attitude: Champion
Issues and concerns: Concerned that a repetition of this problem can seriously jeopardize potential customer relationships and slow down new product development. Wants to increase the average selling price by concentrating on higher-end units.

Key audience member: Nancy Alaoui
Title: SVP of Sales and Marketing
Role in decision: Influencer
Attitude: Neutral
Issues and concerns: Primary concern is keeping major customers happy and preserving reputation for quality.

"Hidden audience": Chris Tilberg
Title: President of Mobile Products Division
Role in decision: Approver
Attitude: Unknown
Issues and concerns: He will not be at presentation (traveling

in China) but will rely heavily on input from subordinates, wants to ensure consensus. One of his major personal wins is to crack the double-digit barrier in handset market share.

FIGURE 4-1: BRIAN'S UPDATED AUDIENCE ANALYSIS

In addition, Brian lists some of the top objections and questions he expects to get from members of the audience. This list is far from complete for a presentation of this strategic importance, but he expects to add to it after he circulates his initial audience analysis to his team members.

EXPECTED QUESTIONS/OBJECTIONS	RESPONSES
What makes you think you can do this better than we can?	• We are specialists. • Maybe you can do it better; is that the best area to devote your resources, especially as capacity gets tighter?
We like to keep control of the entire manufacturing process, because it's the	• Distributed manufacturing lowers supply chain risk • Economies of scale

best way for us to ensure top quality.	• Show our quality certifications; performance contracts; demonstrate prototypes; references and testimonials
This could lead to labor problems	This is actually the best way to continue operating at capacity and growing, thus keeping full employment. Can you redeploy existing staff to other functions?
We may need to do this in the future, but right now we can handle our immediate capacity issues.	This is the best time to start, so that we can take the time to do it right and ensure a seamless transition. When we are called in too late, costs and risks go up substantially.
Do you have the financial strength to grow with us?	Show latest financial statements.

FIGURE 4-2: SOME ANTICIPATED OBJECTIONS AND QUESTIONS

PART 2: CRAFT YOUR PRESENTATION

With all your planning and positioning complete, you're probably pretty eager to get on with it, to get in front of your executive audience and deliver your message.

Yet there's still some hard work to do. All of your planning and positioning will go to waste if you can't deliver solid, well-supported content that engages, convinces, and inspires action.

In this second section, we will look at how to choose the right message for your audience, back it up with solid support, and express it in a memorable and compelling way.

As you can see in the diagram on the next page, the process is basically linear, but you will probably spend a lot of time going back and forth between the steps as you polish your presentation.

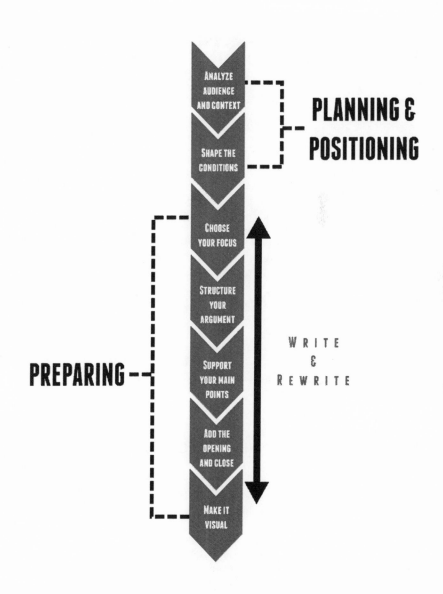

FIGURE 5-1: CRAFTING THE STRATEGIC SALES PRESENTATION

5
CHOOSE YOUR MESSAGE

Find the message and the words will follow.

—Cato

This chapter is the shortest and most important in the whole book. In fact, you could boil its message down to just one line:

> **You should write a clear theme because it is the most important step in creating an exceptional presentation.**

As obvious as it may sound, you have to be absolutely crystal clear in your own mind about what you want your listeners to take away from your presentation. That becomes your overriding theme.

Your theme provides focus, which infuses your presentation with purpose, clarity, and power. It also saves time in the preparation and in the delivery of the talk.

The bottom line is this: you want your listeners to be perfectly clear about what you want them to do and why they should want to do it. If you aren't clear, why should they be?

THE CRITICAL IMPORTANCE OF A FOCUSED THEME

Every time you address an audience, you face three constraints: time, attention, and memory. Focus is the antidote to those constraints because it provides brevity, clarity, and impact.

Brevity

Time is the physical limitation you face. You probably won't have as much time as you think you need to fully explain the issues and the thinking that led you to your conclusions. Your listeners are busy and their agendas are crowded, so you will need to work within those tight constraints.

The paradox you face is that, while the executives want to know you've thought of everything, they don't want to hear all of it. In fact, if you try to cover everything, there is a good chance they will remember nothing.

For most of your presentations, the least of your problems is having enough to say. It's much more likely that you will have the opposite problem. How many presentations have you attended that seemed to ramble on and on with no apparent direction or point? How much of those did you remember? (Probably far less than the 10% we talked about in Chapter 3.) If you tell your audience everything, and they don't remember any of it, what did you accomplish?

You have no doubt gathered a ton of information about your customer during the sales cycle and the preparation phase, including their business goals and challenges, their operations and processes, and their options. Plus, you have a lot of knowledge about your own solutions and products. Your main task as a sales professional and as a presenter is to turn all that data and information into one meaningful message.

That means your first job is to decide what the customer needs to hear, and then to use that as a framework to ruthlessly weed out everything else. Your theme guides you in deciding what to leave out. It serves as a litmus test for what your audience needs to know to make a favorable decision.

Incidentally, did you ever hear anyone complain that a presentation was too short?

Clarity

Focus provides clarity. Participants in my presentation classes go through the exercise of identifying and writing presentation themes. On the first pass, they think it's a very simple exercise. Inevitably, when they read the themes out loud to the class, their ideas fail to make the anticipated impression on everyone else. Remember, you have much more background on your topic than your listeners do, so you must decide what's important and make it lucid to the non-expert.

Focus is to a presentation what a magnifying glass is to the sun's rays: it improves your concentration and theirs. It magnifies the impact of your presentation in that when you are sure what you want to say and why, you are much more likely to be direct, confident, and decisive in your presentation.

Impact

In martial arts such as tae kwon do, small people can produce tremendous power, as when they break impossibly high stacks of bricks. They can only do this by focusing all the power and energy in their bodies at the decisive point at the right time. Without this, even the strongest striker with the strongest determination will fail.

It's the same thing with presentations. Your theme channels your main points, evidence, and words to one decisive point.

HOW TO CHOOSE YOUR THEME

Think a few weeks out from your presentation. If you asked a member of your audience to describe what they remembered about your speech, what would you want them to say, in thirty seconds or less? If you can't think that far out, imagine that you have to sell your speech to the organizer of the event, just to get in the door.

Your theme is like an elevator pitch, but for a very short building. It's the headline you want the audience to take away from your presentation, and to be uppermost in their minds when they discuss it internally, guiding their final decision.

The purpose of any persuasive presentation is to get someone to take action that they would not otherwise take. That's the difference between persuasive presentations — sales presentations — and education or entertainment. In order for them to act, they must be given a good reason (or they would have done it already). So the first thing you should do with all the information you have gathered during the sales cycle is figure out *what* you want your customer to do and *why* they should want to do it.

Boil all that down into about twenty-five words or less, as in the example at the beginning of this chapter (repeated here, in case you've forgotten).

> **You should** write a clear theme **because** it is the most important step in creating an exceptional presentation.

Your theme builds a bridge from your goal to your audience's need. Think of your theme as the completion of this sentence:

> **You should** _____ **because** _____.

While this looks simple, it's not as easy as it looks.

If you've ever done any formal sales call planning, you know that the first two things to figure out are your call purpose and your value proposition. The call purpose tells you why you are investing that time out of your life to go on the call, and the value proposition answers that question from the customer's point of view. Without a purpose and a value proposition, somebody's time is being wasted, and that's never a good thing.

The same holds true for a sales presentation, which, after all is said and done, is still a sales call. You will go through the discipline of specifying your purpose and then expressing the value the customer receives. As a final step, you will distill that down to just a few words, to make it crystal clear.

STEP 1: WHAT IS YOUR GOAL? (CALL PURPOSE)

Why are you giving this talk or making this presentation?

Presentations, in general, can persuade, inform, instruct, or entertain. However, strategic sales presentations have only one purpose: to advance the sales process to the next logical step.

Ultimately, your goal is to obtain a purchase decision. But not all presentations are "closing" presentations, so the next best reason to present is to gain agreement for some action that advances your sale.

You still may need to teach or inform — to share information, explain a process or a product, describe a situation or project — but even in merely informative presentations, your goal is to improve your position relative to an eventual sale, perhaps by changing attitudes.

You must know exactly what you want the outcome to be — before you can even begin to prepare your speech. The more specific and focused you can make your goal, the more likely you are to create a compelling presentation that will impress your audience and get them to take the actions you want them to take. Executives are confident and decisive, and will respect anyone who comes across to them as such.

Your goal will depend on where you are in the sales cycle and what advance you want. For a closing call, the goal might appear to be obvious: get agreement to buy your solution. Yet even closing calls have their nuances or additional actions. While you might get agreement in principle, you still have to negotiate the actual price and terms, and you can accomplish things in your closing presentation that will better position you for the negotiation.

I experienced a significant demonstration of the power that little details during the presentation can have on subsequent negotiations. During my closing presentation to the prospect's Americas Management Team, they asked to see my sales call plan for that meeting. (As someone who sells sales call planning, I get that a lot.) Fortunately, I had anticipated this, and I switched to the template that showed my plan. One of the parts of the plan was expected questions and my responses, containing the following: Q: "Will you lower your price?" R: "No."

A week later, I sat with the GM to nail down the contract, and he said, "I was going to ask you to lower your price, but I already know the answer."

During the earlier stages of the sales cycle, your purpose might not be so clear. Do you want them to approve a pilot project? Assign resources? Agree to put together an RFP? Agree *not* to put together an RFP?

Your purpose has to be based on more than hope — it should assess what is realistically possible, based on your analysis of the audience and their attitudes toward your solution. As we saw in Chapter 3, there is a latitude of acceptance that most people have with regard to their attitude on a particular issue. If you try to stretch them too far, you run the risk, not only of failure, but of hardening their resistance.

It's important to write your goal as output, and not as input. For example, your goal is not to present the benefits of your solution, but to gain agreement on the benefits.

Your goal should also be measurable in some way. You can have a vague goal of getting them interested in your concept, but how will you know? One of the most common examples of this is when a company brings in its technology experts to present a "technology roadmap" outlining where they see the technology evolving. At the end of about sixty or seventy slides, the customer thanks them for their time and nothing much happens.

You need to specify some action that will confirm the customer's interest — and move the sale down your funnel.

STEP 2: WHY SHOULD THEY LISTEN OR DO WHAT YOU WANT? (VALUE PROPOSITION)

Every presentation should bring value to your audience. At the beginning of the presentation, everyone in the room will be thinking the same thing: "Why should I listen to this presentation?"

During the presentation, they're thinking: "Why should I do what you want me to do?"

By the end of the presentation, you want them thinking: "We need to act now!"

As you consider what will interest the audience as a group, remember the 3 PROs of selling from Chapter 3. Your theme has to match the level and interests of your audience. At lower levels you can address product performance issues, but a higher-level audience will be attuned to profit and process improvement, and will consider excessive discussion of price and product to be a waste of time.

At executive and operational levels, the *why* is generally expressed in terms of solving problems, improving processes, and growing profits and cash flow. While these are important enough in a business sense, you can make them even more meaningful to the individuals in the room by expressing the value in the language of the goals that they each care about. You can show how investing in your solution may help them achieve corporate goals, such as key initiatives or strategy attainment. For example, an account manager for an organic food company might put together a presentation for Walmart in which his theme centers on Walmart's green initiative and the related mandate to its suppliers. He could also tie it to related key performance indicators he collected during the audience analysis phase.

You must consider individual audience members in choosing the theme of your presentation. As Al Monserrat, SVP of Sales and Services for Citrix Systems, told me, "Ultimately, all decisions are personal." That includes even corporate investment decisions, although you have to be very tactful in deciding how overtly you want to express how the proposal benefits any one person in the room. Let's say you know one of the decision maker's personal goals is to give herself the inside track in the race for the COO position. You can't come right out and say that in your presentation, but you can make sure your theme focuses on those areas that will make her unit stand out.

During your sales cycle and audience analysis, you have probably uncovered a range of potential benefits you can offer, but don't let that diffuse your focus. The compelling reason for them to take action should be one overriding reason, not a laundry list of benefits. There's nothing wrong with benefits, but you can encapsulate them into a headline, and that's what you're looking for when you craft the *why* portion of your theme.

Here are some examples of value propositions for various sales presentation situations.

For an initial meeting:

> Good: *It will enable you to get an advantage over the competition.*

Better: *If you don't do it, your competition will get an advantage over you in responding to changing market dynamics.*

Good: *It will make you money.*

Better: *It offers the highest and fastest return of any investment this year.*

For a competitive sales situation:

Good: *No one ever got fired for buying IBM.*

Better: *If you don't buy us, there's a good chance your project will fail.*

For an account review with an existing account:

Good: *You're in good hands with us.*

Better: *The best is yet to come!*

For a technology presentation:

Good: *We have some great new technology on the horizon.*

Better: *Our new technology can ensure you extend your industry lead.*

As you consider these examples, keep in mind that they are purposely short on detail. The detail will come during your presentation.

STEP 3: DISTILL ALL OF THIS INTO A CLEAR AND CONCISE THEME

Hopefully, these first two steps have clarified your thinking tremendously. Now it's time to take it one step further. You must combine your purpose and value proposition into one short statement of your theme.

Buy our solution because if you don't buy from us, there's a good chance your project will fail.

Write, in twenty-five words or less, what the audience should do and why. There is no magic to the number twenty-five — it's just that brevity forces clarity, and clarity serves both you and your listeners. At this point, the theme is for your own use only; it serves as the organizing principle around which to build your presentation, so don't worry if the theme is not "pretty" or expressed the way you would say it. In the example above, while what you will actually say will probably be more subtle and indirect, that is definitely the idea that you want to impress on their minds.

In effect, the theme is the headline that summarizes your entire presentation. With so much else potentially distracting the minds and memories of your listeners, when it comes time for them to make their decision, a headline might be about all they will remember, and you want to be certain that they'll remember your headline, not the one they think they heard. That is what will happen if you message is not tight and focused. *You must control the headline.*

The theme is not just for your audience, however. Just like a newspaper headline summarizes the story that is written below it, your theme prepares you to choose the structure of your story that supports the main message.

SUMMARY AND KEY TAKEAWAYS

Choosing a clear theme is the most important step in any presentation because it provides focus, clarity, and impact.

- The theme is even shorter than an elevator pitch. It builds a bridge between your purpose and their need.

- Your purpose depends on the next realistic advance you can target in the sales cycle.

- The value proposition should be targeted to this unique customer in this unique situation.

CASE STUDY, CONTINUED: IMS STRATEGIC SALES PRESENTATION

Brian narrows down his theme. Because he knows the decision maker will be in the audience, his purpose is very clear. His value proposition was more difficult to crystallize, because there is so much he wants to say about his company. Finally, he distills it all down to the theme shown here.

PRESENTATION GOAL (CALL PURPOSE)
Gain the committee's agreement to outsource production of power modules.
VALUE PROPOSITION: WHAT'S IN IT FOR THEM?
We can help with the challenges you will face as you continue to grow at a rapid pace, by offloading some of your capacity needs and freeing up resources so you can concentrate on your critical competitive differentiators. It will provide the quality, capacity, and flexibility you need to continue your aggressive growth.
PRESENTATION THEME
You need to team with IMS as soon as possible in order to put yourself in the best position to achieve your 2020 Vision.

FIGURE 5-2: CRAFTING THE THEME

6
STRUCTURE YOUR ARGUMENT

Up to this point, you have worked to pull together a lot of information and analysis about your customer's situation, your solution, and their needs, in order to concentrate everything into a single theme. With that theme providing focus, it is now time to expand from that point in order to develop the presentation. The first step is to provide a clear structure that will comprise your argument.

Remember in school how you were told to outline what you were going to write before starting an essay or a report? There was a good reason for that. A builder would not just start putting up walls and windows without a plan, and neither should you.

WHY IS STRUCTURE SO IMPORTANT?

Let's start with what structure does for you as the presenter, and then see what it does for your audience.

Structure improves your thinking, boosts the quality of your communication, and can actually make you more flexible during your presentation.

Structure improves your thinking

Without structure, it is easy to write down a lot of information and unconnected thoughts and feel like you have accomplished something. Suppose you're packing for a camping trip. You can throw a bunch of stuff you think you will need into the back of your car, and when it's full you will probably feel like you have everything you will possibly need. But you will never know until you get there — and by then it will be too late. In my own experience with these situations, you never forget the big things; you just forget the little things (like a lighter or a bottle opener), and they become big things when you don't have them.

It's the same with a presentation. You can be very confident that you know the customer's situation and how your solution addresses it, and feel secure that, as a seasoned sales professional, you can think on your feet and put it all together when you need it.

This may be the case most of the time, but you're not a superhero. The reality is that until you force yourself to put your ideas into some logical order, you can't be sure how well prepared you are. In my own experience, the discipline of prodding my ideas into a logical structure always exposes opportunities for improvement, and it's much better to find these *before* you get in front of the customer.

Think of structure as your quality control filter. It gauges how well prepared you are. When you select a clear structure and then begin filling in the detail, you will begin to spot weaknesses in your thinking, gaps in your knowledge, potential objections, etc. For example, in the problem/solution structure covered later in this chapter, you may find that you have not dug deep enough into some aspect of the problem, such as the cause or its consequences, and this may leave you unprepared for objections or questions from audience members who are closer to the situation than you are.

Structure boosts the quality of your communication

The discipline of structure is also going to help you to be concise. It gives you the right openings in which you can insert just the right evidence and detail that supports your points. One key principle of brevity is to separate the "nice to knows" from the "need to knows," and structure can help with this.

Structure allows you to control the narrative. The human mind likes stories and patterns; if it does not get them, it will make up its own. Don't leave it to chance; guide your audience's thought patterns into your chosen structure.

Structure makes you look smart and boosts your credibility. You come across as organized and prepared. Don't forget that, to your customer, you are the company. You may have billions of dollars of assets and thousands of people behind you, but the customer only sees you. If they are going to entrust some key aspect of their operations with you, they are at least unconsciously gauging your company's competence by how you come across in your presentation. Whether you're organized or sloppy, they will expect the same from your company and your product.

Structure can actually make you flexible

Finally, for those who pride themselves on being able to "wing it," structure actually increases your flexibility. Have you ever prepared for a one-hour presentation only to find out that someone is running late and now you only have fifteen minutes? People respond to this situation either by talking real fast, or by going ahead with their prepared remarks and cutting their presentation short, neither of which is very effective.

The alternative way is to know clearly what your main points are, and make sure that you cover those, while leaving out some of the supporting evidence or minor points. You can always refer to your leave-behind material for the detail you omit.

In other words, structure can make your presentation scalable — you unfold as much or as little detail as the occasion calls for.

HOW DOES A CLEAR STRUCTURE HELP YOUR CUSTOMERS?

Structure does your audience a favor by making it easy for them to follow your logic. As we saw in Chapter 2, even high-level executives prefer not to have to think too hard, and it can be hard work to follow an unclear or meandering presentation.

Remember two things: first, they don't know as much about the topic as you do. What seems perfectly obvious to you now was probably not as clear to you at one time. In essence, you have forgotten what it was like not to know what you know now.

Second, presentations are oral. At 130 words per minute, a ten-minute presentation will contain 1300 words, which is a lot of information, even on paper. But unlike paper, your listeners don't have the luxury of being able to re-read something that was on a previous page to connect the dots with what you are saying at the moment; they have to keep up.

By providing structure, you are adding value — making it easier for them to keep up. If they have to dig the meaning out of a mass of unrelated words, they may not make the effort. In effect, you're doing their thinking for them. They're free to disagree, of course, but if you've prepared well that is much less likely.

A clear structure helps you pinpoint exactly where you are at any time in your message, like the hybrid view on Google Maps, with markers overlaid on a satellite photo.

Finally, because it's easier for your listeners to follow your logic, they will be much more likely to remember your points.

RULES OF STRUCTURE

We'll begin with two general rules of structure that are useful in all presentations, apply them to the simplest and oldest structure of all, and then add a few more rules that apply specifically to persuasive presentations.

The power of three

This well-known rule is not strongly supported by scientific evidence, but it has been so well woven into the fabric of literature, communication, and rhetoric that it's a good idea to pay attention to it. It's the curious fact that our minds like ideas in threes. Stories tend to have a situation-conflict-resolution structure. Even with jokes, it's usually three guys that walk into a bar — not two, and not four or five.

Max Atkinson says, "One of the attractions of three-part lists is that they create an impression of completeness." In fact, his analysis of political speeches showed that three-part lists regularly trigger applause.

You may have five reasons why someone should buy your product. Should you tell them all five? Although research shows that it depends on the situation, the short answer for you is no. When the audience is not that intellectually involved with the situation, then more reasons tend to be better. However, when the audience members are involved and are engaging their central processing, you run the risk that the weaker reasons will dilute the stronger. If they are going to forget some of what you told them, there's a chance that they will remember the weaker and forget one of the stronger reasons. You want to give your audience only your strongest arguments to consider.

Sometimes people overstuff their presentations because of a lack of confidence. They worry that they might leave out a reason that is important to *someone* in the audience. I have two answers to that. First, you should know your audience well enough to make sure that does not happen. Second, you can always have those reasons in your backup material in case they come up during the conversation, or in case the top three you chose need reinforcement.

The order of your points matters

Suppose you are going with a simple topical structure, in which you list three reasons to choose your solution. Does it matter whether you talk about the strongest reason first, second, or third?

The answer, according to the research on persuasive communications, is "not much." The studies that have been done do not find clear differences between positioning the strongest first or last, although they suggest you should not bury your strongest reason in the middle.

When presenting to senior executives, you should definitely lead with your strongest arguments. There are two reasons for this:

The first reason is short attention span. If your listeners' attention can be hijacked at any time, it makes sense to lead with your strength to make sure you get in your best shot before they check out.

Secondly, executives tend to be impatient and decisive. If they have heard enough to make a decision, they may cut you off and decide right there. Years ago, when I was first beginning to use PowerPoint in my presentations, I slaved for hours over a sales presentation in St. Louis. I was on the second slide when the President cut me off and said, "Let's go with it." You can bet I did not insist on finishing all the slides I had prepared!

TOPICAL STRUCTURE: MODIFIED "THREE TS"

We begin with what is possibly the oldest presentation structure in the books, the *topical structure*, which is sometimes called the *Three Ts*. This traditional, time-tested process for presentations is to:

- Tell them what you are going to tell them. (Introduction)
- Tell them. (Main points plus supporting detail)
- Tell them what you told them. (Conclusion)

It has been around forever for one simple reason: it works. It's simple and clear and takes advantage of repetition to drive your points home. So you may be surprised that I am going to recommend *against* using it during an executive presentation.

You'll do it a little differently for an executive audience:

- Tell them what you are going to tell them. (Introduction)
- Tell them. (Main points plus supporting detail)
- Test them. (Call to action)

Put the bottom line at the top. Give them the executive summary up front. In other words, tell them your theme; it will eliminate guesswork and provide focus and structure for the rest of the message.

Bill Lane, who wrote Jack Welch's speeches for 20 years at GE, advises:

> *State clearly what you want right away. Give very little background. Offer very little methodology. Be clear about what it is you want them to know.*

Imagine how difficult it would be to complete a jigsaw puzzle without looking at the picture on the box. That's why it helps to give your listeners the big picture before you begin — so they can orient themselves and see how the parts fit into the whole. Think of it as a verbal map.

Even at the risk of oversimplifying at first, it helps to begin with just the broad outlines of the big picture. You can always add qualifiers and exceptions later.

In a sales presentation, the decision makers know you're going to ask for a decision, so you might as well let them know right up front what you're going to ask. This can sometimes significantly shorten your presentation in three possible ways:

- They may agree as soon as they have heard enough to support their decision.

- They may tell you what they need to hear before they will buy your solution.

- They may shut you down right away, but sometimes it's better to lose early.[13]

Because you wrote your theme for yourself, you might have to re-word it slightly so that it sounds good to your audience. For example, in Chapter 5 we saw this theme:

> *Buy our solution because if you don't buy from us, there's a good chance your project will fail.*

Dressed up for your audience, that theme may look like this:

> *You're facing a critical decision that will significantly impact your performance over the coming year. We're here today to show you why our solution ensures the fastest and surest path to...*

Tell them. Your main points can be organized along several lines, but they generally resemble a straightforward list of points or topics. The two most effective approaches are as follows.

List the top 3 reasons that support your recommendation.

- Reason 1 + supporting detail

- Reason 2 + supporting detail

- Reason 3 + supporting detail

---

[13] Your audience analysis and groundwork before the presentation should alert you to this possibility before going in. You may decide to postpone the presentation in that case. If you decide to go ahead anyway, see suggestions at the end of this chapter for dealing with a hostile or skeptical audience.

or

- Advantage/Benefit 1 + supporting detail
- Advantage/Benefit 2 + supporting detail
- Advantage/Benefit 3 + supporting detail

Regardless of the pattern you choose, be very selective in your choice of main points and supporting detail. Avoid the temptation to show off how much you know about your topic. Quality trumps quantity every time. It's not a good idea to stray very far from the rule of three. Make sure that if you're going to exceed three points, you have an excellent reason.

Test them. The traditional Three T's presentation calls for a summary at the end, but *don't* do it for an executive presentation. Your listeners are astute enough not to require one and may find it condescending or, at best, superfluous. Bill Lane again: "I would never use one, and neither would Welch."

Instead, end with a call to action to test the effectiveness of your presentation. Ask for the decision you targeted as your call purpose, whether it's to close the sale or to move the opportunity to the next important step in the buying process.

PERSUASIVE STRUCTURE: CREATING AND RESOLVING TENSION

A topical structure works very well for straight information transfer, and often that's enough for some simple sales situations, such as when your audience is reasonably positive or not too emotionally involved in the topic. It works well because it is clear and easy to follow.

But in most sales situations, your listeners may not be so eager to follow you. When there's some risk, skepticism, or resistance to change (which is the majority of the time in complex sales situations), the audience is not going to passively sit and absorb each of your main points. In this case, you need a persuasive structure that draws them in and carries them along from beginning to end.

Persuasive structures achieve this by applying the power of loss avoidance, narrative, and forward flow.

Loss avoidance

As we saw in Chapter 2, people are much more willing to take risks or action to avoid loss than to achieve gains. So, a choice that is framed as the avoidance of loss is more likely to spur action than one that is portrayed positively. Since a key goal of your persuasive efforts is to get listeners to take action, it doesn't hurt to remind them of the negative consequences of inaction. A little negativity up front will grab their attention and make them uncomfortable enough to look for relief.

Loss avoidance is such a natural a part of the way we think, that it is a fundamental reason stories work so well; they represent the struggle to avoid loss and achieve a happy ending.

Narrative flow: conflict and resolution

For millennia, stories have been the vehicles through which human beings have passed on meaningful lessons — long before we had a written language.

As a result, our brains are hardwired to respond to narrative. Stories help people make sense of information. If it does not make sense, they will either tune out, forget what you said, or make up their own story.

Although a story is a powerful format for a presentation, do not confuse this with a strict chronological approach. The key attribute of story is not chronology, but conflict followed by resolution. In other words, the story creates some tension in our minds — a mismatch between what is happening and what we want to happen; that mismatch is what grabs our interest, and the promise of having that tension resolved is what sustains our interest.

That's why sales presentations are so well suited for some sort of narrative structure: they are about solving problems for customers. From his classic book, *Moving Mountains*, Henry Boettinger's description is worth quoting at length:

Present your idea in this structure and sequence: statement of the problem, development of its relevant aspects, and resolution of the problem and its development. Use this structure and you send your idea rolling down the well-worn grooves of the human mind.

Call it conflict, tension, challenge, or a problem; it is an indispensable part of any story. You set up the conflict by first describing the situation, and then you offer a resolution. So the standard story structure is situation-conflict-resolution, or SCR for short.

Anyone who has been in sales for even a short time will recognize another fundamental reason for incorporating conflict and resolution. Have you ever had a sales conversation that seemed to be flowing well, only to watch the prospect's eyes cloud over when you launched into your pitch? That happened because the prospect was not yet ready to hear about a solution — he or she was not prepared to listen to the resolution because the tension was not high enough.

They have to need the information before you give it to them. Just as a cold drink tastes so much better when you're thirsty, if you create the need, they will *want* the information you provide. That's going to keep their attention and make them much more accepting of your points.

Tension and resolution both exist in time. They juxtapose the present, which contains some element of tension, with a better future. The comparison of *what is*, with *what could be* gets the audience to look forward to the future, and that is what propels the presentation and moves it forward.

A good presentation structure should have a sense of forward movement; it should flow naturally from one point to the next.

Stories are a natural vehicle for forward flow. When you hear the beginning of a story you almost feel compelled to hear the end, and that's how you keep listeners engaged. It also adds credibility to your argument because it implies a natural order in your thought process.

There are two main ways to use SCR structure to make your presentation flow. One way is to make the entire presentation fit the SCR structure. The other way is to make it a series of linked mini-stories, so that each contains SCR and then links to the next.

But that forward movement should not be a relentless rush from start to finish. You have to have momentary pauses to allow your main points to sink in and take hold in their minds. The best way to do this and keep their attention is to provide examples or analogies after you have made a point.

In the next section, we'll look at several different ways to create tension and capture the forward flow of a good story.

VARIATIONS OF PERSUASIVE STRUCTURES

PROBLEM/SOLUTION

Solution selling is a hugely popular concept, and for good reason, but too many salespeople forget that you can't really sell solutions unless the customer has a real problem. This is not a trivial observation, in my experience. The word "solution" has become a cliché in sales, often serving as a synonym for product — as though the fact that a solution exists is enough evidence of a problem.

That's why you see so many sales presentations leave out the problem part and begin by launching right into the solution, becoming just another talking brochure. The problem/solution structure is an antidote to this tendency. It has five sections, and you cover each in greater or lesser depth depending on the customer's current understanding of the situation.

Define the problem

There is an old saying that if you can define the problem on your own terms, you can define the solution. In this phase, you describe the business or operational problem the customer faces, including the cause(s) of the problem and the consequences.

By addressing the causes, you are setting up your solution as a mechanism for eliminating or changing the causes, and demonstrating your credibility and knowledge of the customer's situation.

It's important to address the costs of the problem during this phase. There has to be a compelling reason for your prospect to make a change. What is the problem costing them, in terms of revenues, actual costs, risks, personal hassle, etc? They have to be willing to move *from* the current situation before you introduce the solution. Even if you are selling an opportunity to improve, you can frame it as the solution to a larger problem, such as how to grow market share.

Notice that the problem section has its own three-part structure: showing a problem actually exists, showing why they should care, and analyzing the causes. This ties in to the point made in Chapter 3 that there are three reasons for an audience to be neutral about a situation: ignorance, apathy, or indecision. You will put greater or lesser emphasis on each part depending on your analysis of where the audience is.

List the criteria for a solution

Next, list the principal criteria for the solution. Naturally, as a salesperson you want to get agreement from the customer on the criteria that align with your advantages. One way to do this is simply to list the criteria you want them to use to evaluate solutions. But if you do this, you run the risk that someone will object to your criteria or to the priorities you assigned.

There is a way that you can make your ideal criteria their idea, and that is through the use of an interactive presentation. In *Secrets of Question Based Selling*, Thomas Freese suggests having a flip chart at the front of the room, and using it to ask the audience, "To what extent is ____ important?" If you've done your prep work properly you're going to get the audience agreeing that it's very important. If you do this two or three times you will have a list of criteria that dovetail very nicely with your advantages — and the best thing is that they were suggested by the audience![14]

List alternative solutions

This one sounds wrong. If you're selling, why would you even bring up alternatives the customer has? Isn't that giving the competitor an advantage and courtesy they won't extend to you?

Remember that intelligent, involved audiences find two-sided messages to be more credible. By acknowledging that they have other feasible alternatives you can bolster your credibility and maybe even seem a bit different and, quite frankly, more professional. You can also steal the thunder of the opposing arguments because people in the room are well aware of the competing alternatives. And there always are competing alternatives; even if you don't have another company as a competitor, you are always competing against status quo.

Select the best

This is the section where your sales pitch actually begins — after you've positioned it for maximum effect. You give the reasons why your approach is the best solution to the customer's problem. It's a mini-version of the topical structure.

Describe how it will be implemented

One of the key considerations in getting people to take action is to make it easy and risk-free for them. Telling them how your solution will be implemented can smooth the path and also make the solution "real" in their minds by getting them to envision the steps they will take.

If you use some interactive questions to get their agreement on implementation steps, you can get them to take mental ownership of the solution. But don't push too hard. They may not be ready to make a decision or might resist telling you anything even if they have decided, so be tactful. Ask once, and then back off.

---

[14] If you do this during the shaping phase of the sales cycle, you won't need to do it during the presentation.

YESTERDAY, TODAY, TOMORROW (YTT)

YTT is an excellent structure to use in many situations because it has a strong narrative flow. It is especially useful in account reviews, or when you are trying to change a decision that was made by people currently in your audience.

Yesterday — where we began

The current solution was put in place to address the problem of... At that time, the decision was made to adopt this approach because it offered the following advantages...

Today — what we face today

Today the market and the economy are significantly different in several ways... At the same time, technology has evolved and the current state of the art gives you the capability to...

Your listeners may be thinking, "If it ain't broke, don't fix it." So in this section you need to bring out factors in the current situation that will drive a need for change. They may have known problems, opportunities for doing even better, changes that they must respond to, or underlying risks that have not been fully addressed. If you bring out any of these, you can also talk about the costs to them of not responding.

Tomorrow — where we need to go next

In this section, you build off of their current situation to talk about their needs for the future and your plans to fulfill them.

MOTIVATED SEQUENCE

Developed by Alan Monroe in the 1930s, the *motivated sequence* is a marvelous structure for a persuasive speech. It succeeds by incorporating the basic SCR structure, but then goes beyond it, painting a compelling picture that grabs the listener's imagination.

The motivated sequence is similar to the problem/solution structure, but it is much more "motivational" because it explicitly engages the listener's imagination at the end.

Attention

As with almost any presentation, you begin strong so that you can get the audience's full attention. We'll get into that in Chapter 9.

Need

The body of the presentation fits a classic three-part structure, starting with making them aware of the need. It could be a compelling business problem, personalized to the listeners. As with the problem/solution structure, you describe the problem and also point out its impact.

Satisfaction

Next, you lay out your solution and show how the proposed course of action will fill the need or solve the problem.

Visualization

This is the fun, engaging part of your presentation. Here you help them paint a vivid mental picture of the benefits. You want them to envision the happy future, in which they are enjoying the benefits of your solution.

Action

End with a focused call to action. Because you've engaged their imaginations in the visualization section, your call to action can be a little stronger than in the problem/solution format.

If you're thinking the motivated sequence seems familiar, you would be right. Martin Luther King Jr. used it to historic effect in his "I Have a Dream" speech. When he described his dream, he was inviting all his listeners to share in his vision, and it's no coincidence that the end was the most memorable part of the speech. What most people don't know is that the beginning of his speech was much different and darker. He developed the need by reminding his listeners of the riots that had occurred in the nation that summer, and left unsaid what might happen if the promissory note of full equal rights were left unredeemed.

SALES QUESTIONING MODEL

The situation-conflict-resolution structure dovetails with traditional sales questioning models used during sales calls, of which the best-known is Huthwaite's SPIN process. The general principle underlying all these approaches is that, rather than trying to motivate people to act for your reasons, it is far better to *draw out their own motivations*. They do this by uncovering gaps between the customer's current situation and an ideal state, and eliciting enough pain and tension that the customer feels compelled to act to close that gap, ideally with your plan, product, or idea.

The SPIN acronym stands for:

> **S**ituation
>
> **P**roblem/Implication
>
> **N**eeds statement

This structure can easily be adapted as a structure for a persuasive sales presentation. It also has a unique advantage: If you've gone through the questioning process during the sales cycle, *you can use the audience's own answers to your questions as the content of your presentation*. That will be pretty tough to refute!

Situation

Describe their current situation, goals, or vision. With an audience of high-level decision makers, if you begin by talking about your company and your product, you run the risk of raising their cynical defense mechanisms immediately. You have a wonderful opportunity to differentiate yourself, establish personal credibility, and get their full engagement if you begin instead by talking about *them* first: their corporate strategy, initiatives, financial goals, etc.

If it's obvious that they agree with your situation description, be prepared to cut this section short and move on. But it's always a good idea to spend at least some time on this section to confirm your understanding of the situation and to make sure all the participants in the meeting also have a common understanding of it.

Problem/Implication

Describe the challenges that keep them from achieving their goals or vision. They may be known problems, opportunities for performance improvement, changes in their environment, or underlying risks.

Next, what is the implication to the client of not solving the challenges they face? These may be tangible monetary costs or intangible consequences, such as lowered morale, damaged image, customer dissatisfaction, etc.

Needs statement

What is the underlying need and how does your solution address it? The need logically emerges from the discussion of the situation and problems as a prescription for solving the problems.

You may have noticed that the questioning structure can easily be told in the form of a story. In fact, the basic dramatic techniques in movies fundamentally follow the same structure — we get to know the characters, conflict is introduced, things rapidly reach a crisis stage, and then there is a happy ending. Why not use the same highly successful approach for your sales presentations?

STRUCTURE FOR A HOSTILE OR SKEPTICAL AUDIENCE

So far, a common element of all the structures we've seen is that you are explicit up front about what agreement you are seeking from the customer. However, this may be precisely the wrong approach to take when the audience is against your solution from the start. If you are too explicit, there is a good chance that they will close their minds to anything you have to say.

With a skeptical audience, you must begin by establishing common ground with their position, usually by making a point that you both agree with. For example, if they think your solution is too expensive, you could begin by talking about how important it is to spend wisely, because profits are critical. If you can get them agreeing with you early, you at least have a chance of keeping their attention. Only then can you begin the delicate task of gradually bringing them around to your point of view. In this example, profit and prudence have become the common ground, and you can develop the argument that your superior quality allows them to increase revenues by improving the value to their customers.

Also, don't forget to be realistic in your expectations. Attitudes are like supertankers — you can't turn them quickly. You may not be able to turn them into evangelists for your idea as a result of one presentation, but you might be able to get agreement to at least listen, or to do a trial.

THE USE STRUCTURE

When a buyer throws up an objection during a sales call, experienced sales professionals know that you can't just argue with their point of view; you have to prepare them to hear your explanation. At a larger level, the process you use in handling objections applies to a presentation to a hostile audience.

The approach that has worked well for me is called USE, which stands for:

Understand/soften

Small agreement

Explanation

In a sales conversation, the process might sound like this:

You bring up an excellent point; it is very important to save money, especially in these economic times. But I'm sure you would also agree that sometimes the true profit impact depends on more than the sticker price. By investing a little more up front, you will get a faster and more reliable system which will more than pay for itself in the form of increased productivity and user satisfaction.

Let's dissect that example and see how it would apply to a presentation.

Understand/soften

Describe their point of view and their reasons for believing as they do. Ideally, you should strive to articulate their position at least as well as they can. What you want to do in this stage is establish credibility by showing that you understand their situation and care enough about their opinion to learn from it. If you show that you are open-minded, they are more likely to reciprocate.

Without agreeing with their position, you want to show that you empathize with them.

Small agreement

Next, you have to shake their certainty a little bit. If your position is "white" and theirs is "black," you're trying to get them to acknowledge that maybe it's just a dark shade of grey. As we saw in Chapter 3, most peoples' attitudes fall within a latitude of acceptance, so you are essentially trying to shift them closer to your position.

In the example above, the customer is objecting to your higher price. Their implicit position is that paying a higher price is always bad. Before you can convince them that your higher price is worthwhile, you have to create a small opening in their minds where your explanation can at least get a grip. You do this by getting them to look at the situation slightly differently or concede a smaller point that will then lead to your position. There are several ways to do this:

Reframe. As in the example, you can get them to reframe the situation to see a bigger or different picture. In this case, instead of seeing just the price, you want them to focus on the total profit impact of your solution.

Change the analogy. They may be comparing the current situation to a similar situation they've seen in the past, which is, of course, a very natural way of thinking. As long as they cling to that analogy, you don't have a chance. Point out the differences between that situation and this one, show how the situation has changed since the original decision was made, or give them a different plausible analogy. This approach has the added benefit of allowing people in the room to save face, in case they bought the existing system.

Use verbal jiu-jitsu. Reverse their reasoning. This is my favorite approach because it uses the weight of their own argument to sell your solution. Show why your perceived weakness is actually a strength. This was the approach I used during the presentation I described in the introduction. The customer was concerned about the small size of my company in relation to my competitors, and I was able to show why being small would result in consistency of training quality and speed of customization.

Explain your solution

If you have done the first two phases well, this final phase is very straightforward. You simply tell how your solution fixes the defects in their original position.

SUMMARY AND KEY TAKEAWAYS

Structure clarifies your logic for yourself and for the audience, which goes a long way to improving your thinking.

- Structure should flow logically and incorporate the motive power of conflict and resolution.

- In most cases, it's best to signal up front your main point and what the expected decision is going to be. Use the power of three.

- Prepare the audience for your pitch by developing the need — or problem — first. The structure of your presentation will depend upon what you know about your audience.

- When you're facing a skeptical or hostile audience, you must begin from their position first, and then slowly bring them over to yours.

This table summarizes the featured structures.

	Topical	Problem/ solution	YTT	Motivated Sequence	Sales Questioning	USE
Intro	Intro-duction	Introduction and attention-getter if necessary	Intro-duction	Attention	Introduction	Introduction
Point 1	Point 1	Problem definition and cost	Yesterday	Need	Situation	Understand/soften
Point 2	Point 2	Criteria for solution and alternatives	Today	Satisfaction	Problem & implications	Small agreement
Point 3	Point 3	Chosen solution	Tomorrow	Visualization	Customer need	Explanation
Close	Conclu-sion	Describe implemen-tation	Describe next steps	Call to action	Call to action	Call to action

FIGURE 6-1: SUMMARY OF SUGGESTED PRESENTATION STRUCTURES

CASE STUDY, CONTINUED: IMS STRATEGIC SALES PRESENTATION

It took Brian several passes to decide on a structure. His first inclination, based on his prior experience, was to go with the topical approach and list the three top reasons for VI to outsource production to IMS. However, once his ideas were on paper, he thought they focused too much on themselves rather than the customer and looked too much like a brochure.

Next, he tried out the motivated sequence. Although it looked good to him, he was acutely aware of the CFO's reputation for hard-headed skepticism, and he was afraid the visionary part could backfire on him. In the end, he chose the problem-solution approach.

KEY POINTS	EXAMPLES/EVIDENCE/DETAIL
Problem Definition: The problem with the faulty power modules is only a symptom of a much larger problem	
Criteria for Solution: Must meet your quality standards; respond quickly and flexibly to change requests; and preserve profit margins.	

Alternative Solutions: Short term: upgrade production equipment to resolve individual problems as they arise Long term: Outsource production to IMS	
IMS is the right solution because we have the capability to deliver exactly what you need now and in the future; and we can best support your strategic and financial goals.	

FIGURE 6-2: MAIN POINTS ARRANGED IN
PROBLEM-SOLUTION FORMAT

7
SUPPORT YOUR MAIN POINTS

Facts are stubborn things; and whatever may be our wishes, our inclinations, or the dictates of our passion, they cannot alter the state of facts and evidence.

  —John Adams

Once you have your structure laid out, you have a solid framework of points that should be convincing — provided your audience believes your main points. That's where your support comes in. Your main points need to be buttressed with solid and compelling evidence.

Think of facts and evidence as the building materials of your persuasive structure. They must be strong enough to hold up your entire argument.

Evidence should be composed of verifiable facts and data as much as possible, but it's not realistic to expect that the facts alone will make your case for you. Even if you could line up all the facts of the situation to prove your proposal with the rigor of a geometric proof, it's no guarantee that your customer would buy your solution.

Your goal is not to prove, but to persuade; you're a salesperson, not a lawyer. That means that you do not have to prove your case beyond a reasonable doubt, as an attorney does. On the other hand, you could marshal irrefutable proof and your customer could still decide to do whatever they want. That means that any support you offer for your main points has to make logical sense, but also has to resonate with the customer's view of the world, and their values and preferences.[15]

---

[15] I'm even a little uncomfortable with the word "evidence," because it implies a legalistic approach.

The real world is too messy for facts alone, because sales propositions are essentially predictions about the future, and the future is never certain. For example, it may be a fact that your solution can shave an hour off a key process. Can you guarantee that workers won't use that extra time to relax or surf the web? Even assuming they don't, how will this process improvement mesh with other complementary processes? Getting something done faster won't help if there are bottlenecks elsewhere.

Keep in mind that while the first function of evidence is to persuade, it must also engage the audience and stick in their minds when they are ready to decide. Evidence that is not heard or remembered does not exist in the minds of the decision makers. You want the message to stick, and to be easy for them to repeat to others.

Most sales presentations are going to need much more than mere facts. We will look at about a dozen different forms of support that you can put into your toolkit for persuasive sales presentations. But first, let's keep some basic principles in mind:

SOME BASIC PRINCIPLES

Get your facts straight. A well-prepared speaker — even in a one-on-one conversation — has gathered and confirmed all of the important information. But even well-prepared speakers can be tripped up by getting the seemingly small and relatively unimportant facts wrong. A speaker gets someone's name wrong, for example, and even though it is not central to the argument, audience members pick up on it immediately. Once they start picking, it's like pulling that loose thread on the sweater — your entire presentation unravels.

Never confuse assertion or opinion with facts. There is nothing wrong with opinions and value judgments in executive sales presentations; in fact, they are a common and essential part of any sales presentation. However, it is critical that you never confuse the two in your own mind, because it's virtually guaranteed that someone will catch you on it. And never, never attempt to present opinion as fact.

Have sufficient backup. If your points are new or controversial, make sure you can back them up with appropriate evidence. Because of time constraints, you might have to leave some of your evidence out of the presentation itself, but it certainly comforts the mind knowing you can back it up if called upon. For example, you might say, "Three independent studies have confirmed these results. For example, UL showed..." Leave the other two out of the presentation, but have that information in case you're asked. (See Chapter 4 on preparing for Q&A.)

Use detail judiciously. Once again, less is usually more. As we saw in the last chapter, three very strong reasons are actually better than three very strong reasons plus three weaker reasons. Resist the temptation to show how much you know. Paradoxically, your audience expects you to have a detailed grasp of your topic, but does not want to hear all the detail. Apply the so-what test to every detail you put in. Does it advance your argument? Do they need to know this to make the right decision?

Be concrete. Two or three specific, vivid details will add credibility without boring the audience. Say you want to emphasize something like this: "The majority of respondents agreed with our point of view." You can cite a precise statistic or quote a specific respondent: "I was talking to Fred Smith last Tuesday, and he said that . . . "

Try to be original. The essence of being a consultative salesperson is that you bring new information to your customers. Every industry has its own well-known facts, and the mind tends to tune out when it has heard something before. You certainly don't want to ignore these facts, because knowing them will make you more credible to your customers, but if possible, supplement these with new information. It will perk up their attention and will bring real value. You might say something like, "I'm sure you're all aware that . . . but did you realize that a new study has shown . . . ?" Even better, if you can show compelling new information that contradicts something they have long thought to be true, you will really earn your claim to be a consultant.

A BAKER'S DOZEN OF DIFFERENT TYPES OF FACTS AND EVIDENCE

There are many and varied ways to back up your main points. Here are thirteen types, listed roughly in descending order of their persuasive strength.

Facts/statistics/metrics: Everyone respects data, especially highly analytic, data-driven decision makers. Indeed, some people go so far as to say that if you can't measure it, it does not exist. The flip side of this? If you provide measurements, the implication is that it must exist.

Besides being important in their own right, facts and hard data add an intangible legitimacy to whatever is being said. That's why you see advertisements that say things like: "Four out of five doctors recommend . . ."

Data also makes things concrete, which makes ideas more real in the customer's mind. For example, don't just say you make the process faster, say:

> *Field tests show that our solution speeds up the process an average of 38% over the next-fastest widget.*

Personal observation: When you can say you have been to the source and seen for yourself, it can be as strong as independently verified data. It can also get you credibility and respect if you can tell high-level decision makers that you have taken the time to go out into the field to see how their processes work and how your solution can impact those processes. (Toyota calls this "getting your hands dirty.") On several occasions I have ridden with account managers in the field as part of my sales process, and the observations I make during closing presentations are some of the most convincing bits of support I bring.

Appeal to authority: "Don't just take my word for it. Here is a quote from Gartner that says . . ."

Ironically, when you Google the phrase "appeal to authority," most of the entries contain the word "fallacy." That's because this appeal is often used to support a weak argument. The actor Robert Young demonstrated the power of this type of "proof" by showing that someone who merely plays a doctor on TV can be an effective spokesperson for an actual medication. Of course, you want to choose your authority appeal a little more carefully than that.

If you're careful in choosing the source of your authority, there is nothing wrong with this appeal, from a critical thinking perspective — in fact, most of human knowledge rests on previous authorities. The key is to choose sources that your audience will respect.

Some of the best sources for appeal to authority are individuals who have high credibility within the specific industries and companies you are speaking to. For example, a quote from their own Chairman pulled from their annual report — or even better, from a speech that you attended — can be extremely powerful.

Social proof: When we were kids, we would tell our parents, "All the other kids are doing it." Although it usually didn't work too well with our parents, it's surprising how well it can work with even the most sophisticated executives. There are three reasons for this. First, if other companies are doing it, there's a certain legitimacy and comfort that comes with that. Second, there is the implied risk that if they don't jump on the bandwagon they may get left behind. Finally, if you are the industry leader, social proof can be one of the best proofs of your quality and value:

> *490 out of the Fortune 500 use our software.*

Examples: Examples make things real in the listeners' minds. You've seen this in magazine advertisements for charities, in which a picture of a starving child is much more compelling than irrefutable statistics about death rates. Chip and Dan Heath call it the Mother Teresa principle: "If I see one, I will act." Here is another demonstration of an example at work:

> *One of the issues that Marketing has found with the current process is that sometimes product quality suffers. For example, they told us how Morgan Enterprises rejected an entire shipment of widgets last month because of surface delamination.*

Demonstrations: Seeing is believing. Demonstrations are excellent forms of proof to use during presentations, especially with intangible differentiators such as quality that are difficult to explain and have to be experienced to be appreciated.

Steve Jobs was a master of this. One of the best examples was when he introduced the MacBook Air. After telling the audience about how light and thin it was, he showed them by pulling one out of an interoffice envelope.

The trick to demonstrations is to do them only after the need has been established, in order to prove capability or performance. Otherwise, it's easy to lose the audience's interest, particularly as so many salespeople love their technology and want to show far more than the audience needs to see.

Common sense: Commonplaces are old sayings that have been around for years, such as "Don't put all your eggs in one basket" — statements that sound like obvious common sense on the surface. They don't prove anything; in fact, for every bit of folk wisdom you can probably find another bit that directly contradicts it. Yet they still hold persuasive power out of proportion to their actual proof content.

For example, a well-known consulting group was making a pitch to one of my clients for sales consulting. Their main premise, with which I disagreed, was that my client should replace more than half their sales force rather than training them in the skills they needed to transition to a more strategic sale. They told them, "You can teach horses to climb trees, but it's easier to get squirrels to do it." I knew they had made their point when I heard that same phrase at least three times at dinner later that night.

Many industries have their own common wisdom — accepted ways of thinking or acting that may or may not have basis in actual fact. If the common wisdom lines up with your solution, you'll be swimming with the current of thought. If it contradicts the conventional wisdom, you are certain to be challenged on it and must have solid substantiation for your position.

Questions: Questions work well because more sophisticated listeners don't always like to be spoon-fed the conclusions they should reach. By asking questions you get them to come up with the answers themselves, which can be much more effective.

> *Why do you think we're number one in customer satisfaction three years in a row?*
>
> *What would happen if there were a supply interruption to your most important component?*

Pictures: Pictures make things real and can easily clarify a point in a presentation. As we'll see in Chapter 10, they are also far more memorable than most other types of evidence.

Stories: There are a lot of excellent reasons to use stories, as we will see in greater detail later in this chapter. From a "proof" perspective, stories can make abstract ideas plausible and real. They also allow you to drop names of other companies that have benefited from your solutions and so provide additional social proof.

If you get the chance during your sales efforts to get out in the field and observe how their people do things, this can be an excellent source of stories for your presentation. Besides showing that you have been there (personal observation), they relate directly to the customer's own world.

Analogies: Analytical reasoning is one of the most common ways that executives use when making decisions. As explained in the *Harvard Business Review*:

> *Faced with an unfamiliar problem or opportunity, senior managers often think back to some similar situation they have seen or heard about, draw lessons from it, and apply those lessons to the current situation. Yet managers rarely realize that they are reasoning by analogy.*

Keep in mind that those audience members who attended business school were educated through the case method, which is essentially the use of analogies. It makes sense because most of what we know we have learned through experience, and what is experience other than viewing today's choices through the lens of situations we have seen in the past?

Analogies are especially helpful when you're presenting a new idea because they make the situation appear to be more familiar and, hence, to reduce risk.

Sometimes the most powerful analogies are those comparing your solution to the customer's own business. For example, one of my clients had to convince a skeptical audience at a tire manufacturer, who thought all mobile phone carriers were the same, that it was worth their time to shop around. She told them that carriers are just like tires: on the surface they appear to be the same, but once you learn more about them you understand that there are clear differences that are critical to their performance.

Here are a couple of other examples:

> *It's like the choice between Betamax and VHS.*

> *We are the Rolls-Royce of the industry.*

Cause and effect: Sometimes you can't prove something will work, because each customer's situation is unique. But by showing a plausible mechanism by which A leads to B, you can get people to be willing to take the risk.

> *Our active ingredient____ makes teeth whiter through its micro-scrubbing action.*

> *We invest a billion dollars a quarter in our network, which makes it the nation's fastest and most reliable.*

Because I said so: This one may seem almost ludicrous, but when you think about it, it's used all the time in business persuasion. The most likely users are high-level executives who like to wield it with their subordinates. Believe it or not, you can also use it effectively, but only after you have earned the right by proving your expertise, judgment, and integrity.

> *You can't be sure until you've tried it, but I've had twenty years in this industry, and I strongly believe this is the right way to go.*

Negative evidence: Sometimes all you might have is that no one has a better idea. This may work when status quo is not an option and there is not much time to make a decision.

This was the approach taken by Lee Iacocca when he said, "If you can find a better car, buy it."

FRAMING YOUR FACTS

There are no facts, only interpretations.

— Friedrich Nietzsche

Persuasive sales presentations require more than simple recitation of facts. You add value to those facts by placing them in proper context and helping your audience understand what they mean.

Framing is a way of presenting your message in such a way that listeners look at it one way as opposed to another. And let's not mince words here: framing can help you present your facts in the light that is most favorable to you. Just as a photographer chooses which aspects of a subject to highlight, by thinking carefully about how to frame your message, you control which aspects of the situation your listeners focus on.

Your theme as frame: The theme of your presentation is your most important frame because it will help you choose — or more importantly, discard — the facts and reasoning for your presentation. So, if your theme is that your solution will increase their profits, try to connect your facts to profit improvement. There may be other interesting things to say, but leave them out unless they tie into your theme.

Frame of reference: Facts only have meaning in comparison to other facts, so it's important to choose the frame of reference your audience will use to evaluate your message. One common example is to present bad news in the framework of worse consequences avoided: "It could have been worse."

Numbers are especially sensitive to frame of reference, as we shall see in the next chapter. Here's one example: since most executives are sensitive to their standing relative to their peers, one of the best frames of reference to use is their own industry norms and ratios.

What if you are trying to improve performance that is already above average? The phrase itself implies that average has already been chosen as the basis of comparison. Change the frame to top performers in other industries and the situation looks much different.

The audience's frames: You can also frame your message in ways that resonate with your audience. In speaking to your customer, for example, the more you know about their vision, values, strategies, and terminology, the easier this will be. At a deeper level, you should also consider the impact that the listeners' job titles and functions will have on their frames. In your preparation, ask yourself what matters most to your audience members.

Even something as concrete as a sum of money can have different meanings, depending upon context. For example, is $1 million a lot of money? Most people would say yes, but if you are a corporate decision maker and the consequences of making the wrong choice could cost billions, then $1 million is a rounding error.

A simple thought experiment can further illustrate the importance of context in money decisions. Suppose you are at a store to buy a calculator for $25, and someone whispers that you can buy the same calculator at another store five miles away for $15. Would you go? Most people would say yes.

Now, consider a situation where you are buying a printer for $425, and someone tells you they saw the same printer advertised five miles across town for $415. Would you make the drive? Most people would not, even though it is the same decision as in the first scenario — five miles for $10. Yet somehow the gain seems smaller in the second scenario.

Here is another example in a sales situation, using percentages instead of numbers. Suppose your system costs 25% more but is reliable 99% of the time, as compared to the competitor's 98% reliability. The difference between those two figures does not seem to be high enough to justify the cost difference. But if you say that their system is likely to be unavailable *twice* as often, your customer may see it completely differently.

MAKING EVIDENCE COMPELLING

The most convincing evidence you can muster will be useless if listeners don't hear it or remember it, so make your facts compelling as well as convincing.

Think of your presentation as an excellent meal being fed to your audience. Nutrition is important, and you definitely must have quality ingredients. But it also has to taste good and go down easy. This section is about how to spice it up a bit, or as Emeril Lagasse says, "kick it up a notch."

The key to making a message memorable is to engage as many senses and areas of the brain as possible. If you want them to **SAVE** your message in memory, you have four tools:

Stories

Analogy and metaphor

Vivid detail and visuals

Examples

THE POWER OF STORIES

It's important to make a distinction here between *story* and *stories*. Story is the narrative structure that underlies many successful presentations, as discussed in Chapter 6. Stories are brief anecdotes that illustrate or amplify important points in your presentation.

Stories are one of the most powerful tools for communication and persuasion that any speaker can use. They are the oldest tool in the human communications repertoire. We have all grown up listening to stories, and our brains are conditioned to hear and understand them. For countless generations, humans have used stories to impose a coherent pattern that helps to make sense of events and phenomena around them.

In addition, stories provide vicarious experience, and experiences engage emotions. Good stories are remembered longer, and even add credibility to your talk.

Probably the best thing about stories for a salesperson is that they tend to get retold. If you want to create "inside salespeople" for your solution, this is a marvelous thing.

In presentations, stories can:

Boost memory: Stories are usually remembered long after the rest of the presentation has been forgotten. I can personally attest to the sticking power of stories: I occasionally run into someone who attended a training session with me years before. Almost inevitably they bring up a specific story I told during the class.

Provide credibility: By showing your previous experience with a problem, you broadcast your credentials in a subtle way. Just be careful that you don't make yourself too much the hero of the story.

Engage curiosity: The beginning of a story compels the brain to listen for the ending, and this can help to maintain the attention of your audience.

Provide focus: The gist of the story provides focus around a key point. A well-chosen story can also transport your listeners into full attention and absorption into the situation.

Make communication efficient: Stories are a quick way to encapsulate complex information.

Promote understanding: Complex ideas and concepts can be easily grasped through the analogies provided by stories.

Develop rapport: They allow the audience to get to know you.

Inspire action: The audience becomes actively involved because as they listen they simulate the action in their brains.

Finally, one side benefit of using stories is that they are easy for you to remember, so you're much less likely to have to look at your slides or your notes to remind you what to say.

One important caution: stories should be the type that invite listeners to imagine themselves in that situation. In other words, make it about them, not you. How many sales presentations have you seen that insist on telling the seller's story — as if customers really care about how they grew so quickly from such humble roots?

TIPS FOR TELLING STORIES

Make them relevant. A story without a point might be entertaining, but that is not why your audience is there to hear you. In my own experience of twenty years in front of audiences, this can be the hardest thing to do, because when you have a fascinating story, you want to share it. However, because stories are so memorable, they will crowd out some of your important points — unless they tie directly into those points.

Keep them short! Leave out irrelevant details. Usually you have to tell the story a few times before you can figure out what to leave out.

Be specific. Vivid and relevant detail engages the audience and makes the story more believable. Name names and provide details about the setting, for example. Detail will help you stimulate several senses at once, which will make the story much more real to the audience. While logic thrives on generalities, emotion responds to specifics.

Stories succeed with the right balance of familiarity and novelty. If you are not the protagonist in the story, try to make your protagonist as similar to the audience as possible. The more they can empathize with the hero of the story, the more they will get involved. At the same time, if you can introduce a new twist that gets them to look at the situation in a slightly different way, that's going to keep their interest and possibly advance your sales opportunity.

ANALOGIES AND METAPHORS

We've seen how analogies can strengthen your argument. They can also make your content more compelling. Like examples, analogies and metaphors engage listeners by making abstract ideas more concrete and more familiar. Familiar objects are easier to remember. People instinctively look for similarities with familiar objects and patterns, so analogies and metaphors can provide instant understanding of your point.

When listeners accept your analogy, it guides them to pay attention to the specific aspects of the issue that you want to stress.

Metaphors can also be used to "borrow" emotional impact. By making a valid comparison between your message and another idea that carries emotional weight, you can give your own idea added emotional impact.

In the 2007 Berkshire Hathaway annual report, Warren Buffett said: "You only learn who has been swimming naked when the tide goes out — and what we are witnessing at some of our largest financial institutions is an ugly sight."

Analogies are particularly helpful in putting statistics and numbers into context. For example, $1 billion sounds like a lot of money, but it sounds like a *huge* amount of money when you explain that it is equal to 20,000 pounds of $100 bills!

Anchor and twist is a technique described by the Heath brothers that taps the power of analogy and adds to it. They explain that analogies (what they call "anchors") help explain new things by grounding them in something familiar. But then you need to explain what is new about them, and that is the twist. So, for example, if you say your solution is like a laptop on steroids, you show the familiar part and then introduce the part that makes them so powerful.

Take special care in selecting the right metaphors for your presentation. Be imaginative — new metaphors hit home by creating a vivid image, but clichés shut down thought.

Choose metaphors that fit your audience. Some of the best analogies are those taken from the customer's own business. For example, one of my clients selling to banks compared the security of their network to the bank vault.

Be careful with one of the most common sources of analogies: sports. A sports analogy won't work with an audience that is not familiar with or interested in the sport you choose.

You may find apt metaphors and analogies in:

- similar choices made by the listeners in the past

- local or current events

- historical parallels

- their particular functions and responsibilities (*like a government bond* when speaking to finance, for example, to emphasize the low risk)

VIVID DETAIL AND VISUALS

When your decision makers decide, they will review everything they know about your solution, and probably about competing solutions also, so you want them to remember as much as possible about your presentation. The facts that come most readily to their minds tend to be those that are most vivid. It would be nice if all your important facts were easily remembered, but it's not always necessary; small but vivid details can be powerful memory aids, if they are associated with the important points you make.

Studies conducted using mock jury trials have shown that vivid details are remembered, and given greater weight than they might logically deserve.

In one drunk-driving case, the prosecutor had to convince the jury, based on circumstantial evidence alone, that the defendant was impaired.

In one version, the testimony said:

> *On his way out the door, Sanders staggered against a*
> *serving table, knocking a bowl to the floor.*

A second version went this way,

> *On his way out the door, Sanders staggered against a*
> *serving table, knocking a bowl of guacamole dip to the floor*
> *and splattering guacamole on the white shag carpet.*

When the subjects of the experiment judged the cases immediately after reading the testimony, there was no significant difference between the two versions. However, when they had to judge the cases two days after having read the evidence, those who read the second version were much more likely to find the defendant guilty. The guacamole splattered on the white carpet was not relevant to the case, but it reminded the jurors of the stagger, which *was* relevant. It probably also magnified the stagger in their imagination.

Memorable detail is the stuff of mental pictures. Help people envision a situation, either the dire consequences of the current threat or the promised happiness of your recommended course of action. Besides being more mentally engaging, verbal pictures make communication more efficient because listeners can color in your sketch with their own detail.

The trick is to choose your details carefully and sparingly. Too much detail will confuse your listeners.

At this point, we're just considering verbal and mental pictures, but real pictures can be extremely powerful as well. We cover those in much more detail in Chapter 10.

EXAMPLES

If a picture is worth a thousand words, the same could be said for a relevant example. Examples work because they are concrete and can be visualized, thus engaging more of the senses.

Real people to whom your listeners can relate are excellent examples, which is why presidents always have a few people sitting in the gallery during a State of the Union address, and why charities like to use real people in their appeals. It goes back to the Mother Teresa principle, "If I look at one, I will act."

Examples are also great for social proof. Giving examples of other customers who have benefited from your solutions gives you credibility and your listeners confidence.

One final benefit of using examples is that it puts a name and sometimes a visual on the idea or concept, which makes it tangible and concrete.

CHOOSING THE APPROPRIATE MIX OF EVIDENCE TYPES

With all these different persuasive tools, how do you go about choosing the appropriate ones for the occasion? There is no clear answer to this; it's definitely a judgment call. However, here are a couple of principles to keep in mind.

Variety is important. A presentation full of statistics and metrics may have airtight logic, but it may also put the audience to sleep. On the other hand, if all you have is stories, your audience may be fully engaged, but when the time comes to make a decision and the good feeling has worn off, they may find little solid backing to your message. Someone in the audience may remind everyone else: "The plural of anecdote is not data."

Tailor the evidence type to the decision makers' social and work styles. As we saw in Chapter 3, individuals in your audience have different preferences for the type of evidence that they find convincing.

In addition, companies have their own cultures that dictate the types of support and evidence they will respect. Google is known as a highly analytic culture, so make sure you lead with data and use stories as support, rather than the other way around.

SUMMARY AND KEY TAKEAWAYS

When it comes to expensive, complex, and risky investments, decision makers need solid and compelling evidence, whether to be persuaded themselves or to justify their decision to others.

- Collect as much evidence and support as you can find, and then choose only the most compelling.

- The four most credible types of evidence are data, personal observation, appeal to authority, and social proof.

- Supplement the "big four" with a variety of other forms of evidence to make your presentation more compelling.

- Use analogies, examples, pictures, and stories to engage the audience and make your information memorable.

CASE STUDY, CONTINUED: IMS STRATEGIC SALES PRESENTATION

Here is Brian's first draft in which he lists the examples, evidence and detail that will flesh out his main points. At this stage, the body of his presentation is substantially complete. It is not a script, but a thoughtfully structured list of talking points.

KEY POINTS	EXAMPLES/EVIDENCE/DETAIL
Problem Definition: The problem with the faulty power modules is only a symptom of a much larger problem	Problem description: We were called in to consider a proposal for providing HBT substrate subassemblies. Our investigation and analysis traced the root cause to design for manufacturing issues (evidence: quotes from interviews; photos and actual damaged modules; Pareto analysis) This problem may become more common and more severe as production demand increases and product life cycles continue to accelerate. (Chart showing projected smartphone demand for the next three years; quotes from Gartner Group study)

	Cost: Direct financial cost is that scrap and re-work costs can impact COGS. (Use benchmark figures and confirm agreement) Long term possible impact on quality reputation and capacity as growth continues, and Top customer relationships are at risk (evidence:
Criteria for Solution: Must meet your quality standards; respond quickly and flexibly to change requests; and preserve profit margins.	-cost per unit less than 8% of total -able to be implemented with low disruption to existing production schedule -reduce or eliminate complaints from top customers -design turnaround time of 3 months or less
Alternative Solutions: Short term: upgrade production equipment to resolve individual problems as they arise Long term:	(table listing weighted decision criteria and relative solution scores) Upgrading your production equipment is relatively inexpensive and can be implemented with little disruption to existing production, and is also favored by plant operations manager.

Outsource production to IMS	
IMS is the right solution because we have the capability to deliver exactly what you need now and in the future; and we can best support your strategic and financial goals.	We have the capability to deliver exactly what you need and grow with you: -track record (statistics, Behemoth Industries white paper; CEO testimonials) -lean six sigma certifications -projected capacity growth The benefits to VI are very compelling: -cash flow engineering (reduced CapeEx and JIT inventory) -free up your resources to focus on core competencies of user design, innovation, and quality -speed to market (Chart of projected demand vs. capacity; Gartner study citing CSFs for SmartCall)

FIGURE 7-1: DETAIL ADDED TO SUPPORT THE MAIN POINTS

8
POLISHING

Presentations are like diamonds: they have to be cut and polished to achieve their full value. You can skip the polishing step and still have a good presentation, but you'll never have a great presentation without it.

You are more likely to ignore the advice in this chapter than any other. You will probably agree with its key message, but as an extremely busy sales professional, you will feel like you have to cut corners somewhere — and this is the part most people leave out.

I know because I've done it myself a few times. Sometimes I've gotten away with it, and "good enough" really was good enough. But I've also had occasion to regret skipping this step, and it was usually during the most important deals, in front of the highest-level audiences.

That is because nothing comes out perfectly the first time. Your first effort can *always* be improved, and most of the improvements come in the form of clarity and conciseness.

BE CLEAR

Speak properly, and in as few words as you can, but always plainly, for the end of speech is not ostentation, but to be understood.

—William Penn

Above all, senior executives are looking for clear thinking. If you have settled on a clear theme and have decided on a logical structure, you're well on your way to a successful executive presentation. The next necessary step is to ensure that your expression is as clear as your thoughts.

You can't persuade your audience if they don't understand you. Sometimes it's easy to forget how complicated some of the material is that you take for granted, and if people don't follow what you're trying to say, they're not likely to admit it by asking for clarification. Make the complicated simple, and speak plainly.

One of the points that emerged from my interviews with senior executives is that plain speaking — using words that are straightforward and do not obscure the truth — shows that you're confident in your message and clearly understand it.

You can ensure clarity by paying close attention to your word choice, avoiding some common errors, and making your structure explicit.

CHOOSE COMMON, SHORT, AND CONCRETE WORDS

Broadly speaking, the short words are the best, and the old words best of all.

—Winston Churchill

Eliminate sesquipedalian obscurantist vocabulary! (Translation: don't use big words when small ones will do.) Use simple words — your audience appreciates plain speaking.

Use common words. Some people seem to have an internal thesaurus that they switch on when talking to a higher-level audience, and it generally pumps up the number of syllables they use. Trying hard to seem sophisticated, they employ pretentious, puffed-up language, or rely excessively on business cliché.

This is a mistake for two reasons. First, using big words does not make you look smarter; in fact, research has shown that it can make the audience perceive you as *less* intelligent. If they don't understand you, they can either decide that you are much smarter than they are, or that you don't know what you're talking about. In the case of senior executives, which do you think is more likely? Second, if you sound like one person during the sales cycle and another person when you present, you're going to make them wonder about your authenticity.

Use concrete words when possible. Typically, the higher the level of abstraction, the harder it is for listeners to understand. This can become a problem when you are a specialist in your topic, because the more you know about something, the more you tend to speak in abstract generalities. Make it easy for your listeners to envision what you are saying by using concrete words when possible; you will get a double payoff in both clarity and in emotional impact.

For example, one of the most common words used in sales presentations is "productivity" — as in our solution will improve yours. How do you take a word as abstract as that and make it more concrete? Express it in real-life terms: Productivity is simply more output for less input. More output may mean happier customers, more widgets sold, higher prices, and so on; less input might mean less hours, fewer bodies doing the work, etc. So you might say, "By the time she finishes with her fourth patient, Sally Smith will be able to visit one more instead of having to head home to fill out paperwork."

You may have noted from that example that concreteness also makes you much more credible because those details only come from knowing the details of the customer's processes.

On the other hand, it may be possible to take concreteness too far; if all the audience members are as knowledgeable about the situation as you are, being too concrete can make your point sound simplistic. It can be a tricky balancing act that, quite frankly, requires a bit of experience and judgment to get right. It all goes back to knowing your audience.

Use their words as much as possible. During your sales cycle and your research and analysis phase, you will probably encounter common words and phrases that your customers use in their internal conversations. Using these will resonate with your audience members and will give you added credibility. Someone in one of my classes told me that his own company's vogue phrase was "value-added," and he purposely used it several times for an internal presentation. As he said, "It worked like a charm."[16]

---

[16] It may be a cliché, but it was *their* cliché.

Think about the implied meaning of your words. Words have meaning beyond their dictionary definition. For example, in his book, *Words That Work*, political expert Frank Luntz describes how two industries have managed to clean up their image partly through verbal makeovers. The *gambling* industry now calls itself the *gaming* industry, and *liquor* is now called *spirits*. In sales, most experienced salespeople know that the competitor's solution is *cheap*, while their own is *economical*; you *spend* to buy theirs, *invest* to buy ours, and so on.

IT'S EASY TO CONFUSE YOUR LISTENERS

Jargon: The use of jargon, or specialized language, is one of the trickiest minefields to navigate. Mistakes can happen when you try to use their jargon to appear smart and can't quite pull it off, or when you unknowingly use your own jargon that your audience does not understand.

Jargon gets a bad reputation because it usually only becomes noticeable when it leads to miscommunication, but it can actually be a very efficient and credible form of communication. Complicated concepts can be communicated quickly with just a short phrase or even an acronym. It's possible to do because members of the same in-group have enough shared experiences to be able to develop shortcuts for expressing them. Over time, however, the shortcuts get so ingrained in their way of speaking, they forget that others don't know what they mean, just like a fish is not aware of the water it swims in.

It's because of that shared meaning that people who use the jargon correctly can have instant credibility. You probably have to know your audience or your customer well enough to use the jargon correctly, so if you can pull it off, the right jargon can be a tremendous asset.

The absolutely key word in that last paragraph is *correctly*. There are two risks. It's easy to hear a term used once and think you have grasped its meaning, but you may run the risk of sounding slightly off-kilter when you use it. In that case, your use of the jargon can backfire, and your listeners could turn against you. The second risk is that you could get it right, but some devious audience member may decide to test you a bit and find out how well you really know it, either by asking additional questions or one-upping you on the use of jargon to put you in your place.

To ensure that neither of these happens, ask someone you trust from the target in-group to advise you on the use of the term. Make sure you're totally comfortable with it before you use it in conversation or a presentation with others. Also, be a little hesitant and humble the first time you use it. "If I understand the term correctly..."

When it comes to using your own jargon, sometimes there is no elegant way to avoid it. If you have to use jargon:

- Ask listeners how familiar they are with a term the first time you use it

- Give a paraphrase with the term if necessary

- Pay attention to ensure they understand

References that don't make sense to your audience: Know your audience to ensure that your analogies and references resonate with them. One of the most common issues might be the use of sports analogies; not all audience members are into sports, and even those that are might see their use as too clichéd.

Your references should also be age-appropriate. Beware of the potential for a generation gap between you and your audience.

I used to use Columbo as a positive example for the value of asking questions until I figured out that fewer and fewer of my students knew who he was. I've also used a picture of George Costanza on one slide, but I'm starting to get quizzical looks.[17]

On the other hand, look at it from the reverse point of view. A lot of the people you're trying to convince or impress with your presentations are senior-level executives who are, quite frankly, in the older age group. Are you using terms that they don't understand? Have you made a reference to a musical group or actor they've never heard of? How did it work out for you?

---

[17] If you need to look up either of these references, I've made my point.

Finally, be extra careful to eliminate references that a specific audience might find offensive, such as when a colleague told a training class of copier reps that they should "Xerox" their call plans for the next workshop.

Euphemism, excessive political correctness, or excessive tact: While you want to play it safe by not offending anyone, this can lead to sacrificing frank, candid discussion of the issues at hand.

Corporatespeak: These are the kind of clichés that get people in the audience playing buzzword bingo:

- End-to-end, scalable, 24-7 solutions

- Best-in-class, leading-edge technology

- Synergistic partnership

Vague language: These non-specific phrases send a signal that you are not confident or don't have a firm grasp of the details:

- Approximation: "about," kind of," "like"

- Indeterminate numbers: "a couple," "a bunch"

- Possibility and probability: "not necessarily," "sometimes," "probably"

Lack of fluency: One marker of confidence and credibility is your fluency, or how smoothly your words flow together. Try to stay away from these:

- Filler words: "umm," "and," "like," "sort of"[18]

- Lack of clear enunciation

- False starts: "What I'd like to say is . . ." "Of course, you may already know . . ."

---

[18] In Chapter 14 we discuss ways to reduce the use of filler words.

CASE STUDY IN PLAIN SPEAKING: HOW WARREN BUFFETT DOES IT

Annual reports can be dry as dust, so it's instructive to see how Warren Buffett makes them clear and compelling through candidness, plain speaking, and audience focus.

Candidness: *Most annual reports, Enron notwithstanding, are not technically dishonest. They don't lie outright, but they do make it difficult to figure out the truth, especially when that truth reflects unfavorably on the leadership. Buffett's self-effacing candidness actually increases his credibility.*

And now a painful confession: Last year your chairman closed the book on a very expensive business fiasco entirely of his own making. (2009)

During 2008 I did some dumb things in investments. I made at least one major mistake of commission and several lesser ones that also hurt. I will tell you more about these later. Furthermore, I made some errors of omission, sucking my thumb when new facts came in that should have caused me to re-examine my thinking and promptly take action. (2008)

Plain speaking: *This is a close cousin of candidness — you always know exactly what the words mean. Buffett himself weighs in on why plain speaking is so rare:*

We sometimes encounter accounting footnotes about important transactions that leave us baffled, and we go away suspicious that the reporting company wished it that way. (2006)

But I'll make more mistakes in the future—you can bet on that. A line from Bobby Bare's country song explains what too often happens with acquisitions: "I've never gone to bed with an ugly woman, but I've sure woke up with a few." (2007)

Audience focus: *Buffett always tries to make things as easy as possible for his audience to follow. He also makes you feel like he's chatting with you in a personal conversation, not speaking from a podium above you, bathed in lights.*

To build a compatible shareholder population, we try to communicate with our owners directly and informatively. Our goal is to tell you what we would like to know if our positions were reversed. (2009)

Before you read further, let me underscore the obvious: Berkshire has a dog in this fight, and you should therefore assess the commentary that follows with special care. (2009)

If Warren Buffett can demonstrate plain speaking in something as bland as an annual report, there is no reason you can't in your presentations.

USE VERBAL OUTLINING TO MAKE YOUR STRUCTURE TRANSPARENT

You should have already designed your presentation so that your arguments and key points are logically arranged. It's also helpful to make your structure explicit through *verbal outlining*, which means using phrases to help the listener keep track of where you are in the conversation and where you are going next.

Signposts point the way ahead for the conversation, which helps the listener organize the information to come. "I'm going to tell you about a problem we are facing in our market today, explain why it's important that we address it immediately, and propose a cost-effective solution." This is the old "Tell them what you're going to tell them."

Boundaries and transitions mark the start and end of specific topics. "That's the first reason. The second reason is . . ."

Highlight specific pieces of information. You can say things such as: "It's very important that . . ." "Don't forget . . ." Two other useful highlighting tools are *repetition* and *pauses*.

Link subtopics to each other. Also link them to things that are familiar or relevant to the audience:

- Examples
- Analogies
- Experiences
- Knowledge

Questions are a useful way to signal a change in direction in your presentation:

> *What alternatives do you have?*
>
> *What happens if the problem is not addressed?*
>
> *Why is our solution better?*

Acronyms can also be excellent memory aids and organizers. For example, we talked in the previous chapter about how you can make your presentations more compelling by remembering SAVE. (See if you can recall what it stands for, or check back in Chapter 7 to refresh your memory.)

BE CONCISE

"If it takes a lot of words to say what you have in mind, give it more thought."

—Dennis Roth

We like to think that our fast-paced world poses unique challenges to presenters because of the audience's impatience, but actually the need for brevity has been respected for thousands of years. If you think senior-level audiences can be tough, imagine being an official from the city of Samia having to ask the Spartan authorities for aid after being driven from their city by the Persians. The Spartans, besides being fearsome warriors, were also renowned for their love of brevity. When the delegation first spoke, they spoke so long that the Spartans said they had forgotten what they heard at the beginning and didn't understand the rest. The Samians tried again the next day, this time bringing an empty sack and simply saying: "This sack needs barley meal." The Spartans applauded their brevity and approved the request, although they did say the word "sack" could have been left out.

Anytime you talk to someone, either individually or in groups, you are competing for a share of ever-shrinking attention spans. Try to send your message as efficiently as possible. Your listeners may not be Spartans, but they'll never complain if a meeting runs too short.

A concise message is efficient *and* effective because it:

- Shows you know your stuff
- Communicates confidence

- Demonstrates respect for everyone's time
- Makes it easy to follow
- Accommodates attention span
- Allows time for listeners to ask follow-up questions

Brevity has the added benefit of forcing you to figure out what is truly meaningful. The mental discipline that you go through to figure out your main point can only help to clarify your message. This is why busy leaders like Churchill and Reagan insisted that any issues presented to them had to be contained on one sheet of paper. Think about it: *Should we invade France in 1943, or 1944? Negotiate with this fellow Gorbachev?* One sheet of paper.

HOW LONG IS A HALF-HOUR PRESENTATION?

This may sound like a silly question, but it's actually a key question for your preparation and planning. Sales presentations should *always* last longer than the time allotted to their delivery. If they don't, you're in trouble, because no interruptions and no questions at the end are clear signals that the audience doesn't care enough to engage.

You should always plan your speaking points for less time than your specified time slot; if all goes well, you're going to have questions, digressions, and changes. This is especially true if your presentation is just one item on their agenda.

HOW DO YOU TRIM YOUR MESSAGE?

Establish your purpose before building the message. Be absolutely clear about what you want to accomplish and what you want to say. The thought process and template we have been following so far will ensure that you are clear in your own mind about what you want to say.

Front-load your message. Give them the main point and then supporting information, if necessary. Often you'll find the supporting information is not necessary in the body of your talk. It can be saved for the take-home materials or for Q&A.

Focus on the meaningful few. Don't commit the common sales-pitch error of telling everything possible about your solution. Many of your features can be matched by competitive alternatives, so focus on the major differences *that matter to your customers.*

Use the appropriate level of detail. Although it's difficult to specify what level of detail is appropriate, it's better to err on the side of less detail than more. Again, you can always supply more information in written material or in the Q&A.

HOW TO PRESENT NUMBERS

It's pretty hard to give a sales presentation without numbers. But if you think words can be tricky, numbers present their own special challenges. It would seem that there could not be anything more precise than a number — after all, 100 is 100 no matter what language you use. Yet, just like words, they mean different things to different people.

COMPARISON AND CONTEXT MATTER

Numbers represent quantity, but quantity is a perception that depends on context. Numbers gain meaning through comparison and context, and it's up to you to control the context. For example, in the figure on the following page, the interior circle on the right appears to be larger than the one on the left, despite the fact that they are the same size. The perception of size is affected by the context surrounding the dot.

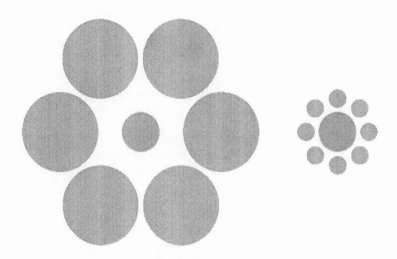

The illusion (called the *Ebbinghaus illusion*) works because the things being contrasted are similar. If each circle were surrounded by triangles, the effect would almost disappear. So, if you're using the contrast effect to present numbers, make sure they describe similar things.

Because numbers are meaningless except in relation to something else, the only way to make sense of a specific figure is to compare it to another familiar figure. Financial ratios are an excellent example of this. A 10% net margin may sound impressive, but not if the margin for the previous year was 15%, or if other companies in the same industry have 30% net margins.

Anchoring is another surprising and curious phenomenon that affects how we perceive numbers. To demonstrate, write down the last two digits of your cell phone number on a scratch sheet of paper. Now, write down your estimate of what percentage of countries in the UN are in Africa.

Without realizing it, your first answer probably affected your second, through the phenomenon called anchoring. Daniel Kahneman and Amos Tversky first discovered anchoring in 1974 in experiments using a roulette wheel. Participants were asked the same question, but first were asked to roll a roulette wheel that was secretly rigged to land on either 10 or 65. Participants who landed on 10 estimated the number of countries at, on average, 25%, and those who landed on 65 estimated an average of 45%. (The answer is 23%.)

Besides affecting estimates, anchoring also affects our choices. In an experiment described by Dan Ariely in his book *Predictably Irrational*, an audience is first asked to write the last two digits of their social security numbers, and, second, to submit mock bids on items such as wine and chocolate. The half of the audience with higher two-digit numbers would submit bids that were between 60% and 120% more. The simple act of thinking of the first number strongly influences the second, even though there is no logical connection between them.

The first information we receive — the "anchor" — has a disproportionate influence on our thinking.

One of the most surprising things about anchoring is how powerful it is even when we're on guard against it. Even when we know the initial number is totally arbitrary, or way beyond anything reasonable, it still has an effect. If we're given a high number to begin with, we adjust our own estimate downward, but we don't adjust it enough.

Even well-informed professionals such as real estate agents are not immune to the effect themselves. In one experiment, four different groups of agents were given 10-page packages describing a specific property. The only difference was in the listed price. When asked to appraise the property, the median value correlated to the listed price, even though each denied that it had any effect on their decision.

Surely professional economic forecasters with serious quantitative training are protected from anchoring? Wrong again — the Federal Reserve studied professional economic forecasters and found that they exhibit anchoring bias toward previous forecasts. In another study, bank loan examiners who know the previous rating given to a loan end up closer to that rating, on average, than those who begin with no prior knowledge.

Numbers Also Have Emotional Impact

Numbers carry meaning beyond simply quantifying something. The mere use of numerical data in a presentation sends important signals to the audience. It tells them that you are competent — you have solid information to back up your sales pitch. It tells them you are prepared, because you have taken the time to gather the data.

Numbers would seem to be the ultimate expressions of rationality, but in fact we also process numbers emotionally.

A surprising statistic can make an impression on someone's mind during your presentation. If they have to rely on memory a few days later to make the decision, they are far more likely to remember the impression than the number itself. In fact, researchers have shown that they may actually rely on the memory of the impression and then reconstruct a number in memory that matches what they *felt* when they heard the number!

With Context and Emotion in Mind, Go Forth and Use Numbers

Keeping these points in mind, here are some ideas that will enhance the use of numbers in your presentation.

Provide the context first, and then the numbers. Because numbers make sense only in relation to something else, that's what you want to present first. Without the appropriate context, you have no control over the initial impression the number will make on your listener's mind — and then it may be too difficult to change it.

Believe it or not, an annual report provides an excellent example of this. You don't get to the numbers section until way back in the annual report. The first sections are devoted to management's explanations in the form of the Chairman's Letter and Management's Discussion of Results.

Choose well-scaled comparisons. Numbers only have meaning in comparison to another number. A number can appear small or large depending on what number it is being compared to. Figuratively, you can choose the size of the outer circles. For example, if your solution costs $50,000, when you list alternative solutions you might want to begin with a solution that costs $60,000.

Relate the numbers to the customer's business metrics. The most compelling so-what for any fact is how it relates to their own most important concerns, in most cases the key performance indicators and metrics they pay attention to.

> *Boosting outputs by 15% would be more than half of the increase you said you had targeted for this year.*

> *Our solution averages out to four cents per unit you produce, which puts it in the top quartile for your industry.*

Relate the numbers to meaningful standards. You should know the key financial and process measurements relating to your customers situation.

State the number in human scale. People have difficulty understanding large numbers; it's best if they are on a human scale. For example, which explanation do you find most convincing?

> *Our system is so accurate, it would be like throwing a rock from the earth to the sun and hitting within 1/3 of a mile.*

> or

> *Our system is so accurate, it would be like throwing a rock from New York to LA and hitting within 2/3 of an inch.*

When these statements were put to the test, 58% of respondents thought the first statement was very impressive, but 83% thought the second statement was very impressive. Here is a statement that uses the precise scale of the customer's business:

> *Our solution averages out to three dollars per employee per quarter.*

Adjust the time scale if necessary. Another way to make numbers more "human" and personally meaningful is to adjust the time scale. You can shorten the time scale to make a number appear smaller:

one of the most common sales tactics is to take a very large number and make it seem much smaller by breaking it down into a daily cost.

> *Over the life of the system, it will end up costing you just $10 per day — which is less than you spend in tips.*

On the other hand, if there is a slight chance that something risky can happen, you can magnify the perceived risk by expanding the time scale.

> *Over the next five years, there is a greater than even chance that could happen. Can you deal with the consequences?*

Percentages vs. real numbers. Another choice is to decide whether to express your numbers as real numbers or as percentages. In general, real numbers have greater impact, as demonstrated by research as well as sales common sense. Research shows that people generally find percentages easier to understand, but numbers have more impact. For example, in a study that sent postcards out asking for support for cancer research, a statement saying that cancer could strike thirty million Americans got more contributions than one that said it could strike 10% of the population.

From a sales perspective, there is another good reason that real numbers might have greater impact. You can only use real numbers if you know specifics about your customer. For example, it's possible to be able to say that your solution can improve some measure of a process by 10%, because that is something that you could have observed with previous installations with different customers. But the only way you could say what that 10% translates to in dollars is to know your customer's own numbers. (By the way, even if you know the answer, sometimes it might be better to let the customer give you the answer themselves during the presentation. See *questions as proof* in Chapter 7.)

Speak the language of their numbers. Senior-level decision makers have a scorecard they follow very closely. At top levels, the scorecard may measure financial results such as revenues and profitability; at operational levels, they are going to pay attention to process metrics such as throughput, cost per ton, etc. For credibility and impact, make sure you use these numbers in your presentation. Going back to Chapter 3, one of things you should seek when you analyze your audience is to understand the personal measurements they each care about.

Financial presentations, of course, have their own specialized language, including payback and return on investment. Those measurements are beyond the scope of this book, but you should be familiar enough with them to know how to use them correctly. For example, don't say, "Your payback is 30%," because payback is measured in terms of time. If you do plan to use these terms, but are not totally comfortable with them, make sure you pass your presentation by one of your own financial analysts to double-check it.

Decide whether to use hard or soft numbers. Hard numbers are those that are directly measurable; soft numbers are difficult to measure or too intangible to really count. There are people who will tell you that only hard numbers count in sales — that if it can't be measured, it does not exist.

That advice may have contained more truth in previous days, when value in the economy consisted principally of things, but in today's knowledge economy, following that advice will cause you to leave huge amounts of value on the table. We've reached the point in our economy where the value of intangible assets is almost equal to that of tangible assets.

Value is perceived in the eye of the customer. Will they value such things as time to market, employee engagement, innovation, and security, even if you can't put a hard dollar value on them? Of course they will. It's your job to affect that perception; don't preemptively surrender by leaving out intangible benefits.

"Soft" numbers have the disadvantage of being much easier for people to challenge, but that can also be an advantage, because your customer might put a higher value on an intangible than you would dare to claim for it.

Frame numbers to your advantage. Numbers that are mathematically equivalent can appear different depending on how they are presented, or framed. For example, your system may be 99.9% reliable as compared to your competitor's system which is 99.8% reliable. Presented that way, the difference appears negligible. However, you could equally make a case that yours is twice as reliable as theirs: yours is down .1% of the time as compared to .2%. In this same example, if your system is used in online transactions that the customer depends on for their revenue, and if they run a million transactions a year, the difference could be 1,000 more lost transactions.

Learn the special language of pricing. If numbers have an emotional impact, that is nowhere more true than with price. Here's William Poundstone, author of *Priceless*, on the emotion of pricing: "Though a price is just a number, it can evoke a complex set of emotions — something now visible in brain scans. Depending on the context, the same price may be perceived as a bargain or a rip-off; or it may not matter at all." To illustrate the importance of context, imagine this scenario:

> You are lying on a hot beach and decide that you are really thirsty and would love a cold beer. The only place to get one is a fancy beach bar 100 yards away. You walk there and find that they want $6 for a beer. Do you get one?

Now here's a slightly different scenario:

> You are lying on a hot beach and decide that you are really thirsty and would love a cold beer. The only place to get one is a small convenience store 100 yards away. You walk there and find that they want $6 for a beer. Do you get one?

Most people would say yes in the first scenario and no in the second. The only difference? Context.

That's just one illustration of why you have to put a lot of thought into preparing the right context — the right frame — before any price numbers come out of your mouth.

Double-check your calculations. This is even more important than avoiding typos. Any mistakes will throw everything else you say under a cloud of suspicion.

Use numbers sparingly. I'm a very numbers-oriented person, but even I tend to skip over some parts in books that contain a lot of numbers, unless I'm really motivated to pay close attention. Using too many numbers can cause your audience members to tune out.

At this point, you may be thinking that numbers can be easily manipulated to show almost any result you want, and you would be partially right. If it makes you feel better, keep in mind that in order to show statistics you have to have real data. That's one way of keeping people honest. As Chip and Dan Heath say, data enforces boundaries.

EXPLAINING TECHNICAL MATERIAL

The old joke about asking what time it is and then suffering through an explanation of how to build a watch applies especially to high-tech solutions. Sometimes you have to explain how something works, but often it's a just a salesperson (or, worse, a sales engineer) getting carried away with their enthusiasm for their product.

Keep in mind that if the audience consists of high-level executives, you are probably far more interested in how your product works than they are. They care much more about what it does and why that's important, and will leave the *how* part to their own technical staff.

It's possible both to overestimate and to underestimate an audience's ability to absorb your information. If you overestimate it, you will speak too fast or in too much detail and lose their attention. They may be intimidated by the complexity of the material, afraid to look stupid by asking questions. As a result you think they understand even when they don't.

If you underestimate it, you may bore them or turn them off by appearing condescending. You can improve your chance of hitting the sweet spot by asking questions and setting ground rules up front. If the group is small enough, you can ask questions to gauge their knowledge levels and find out how much detail they want. One useful line of questioning is to find out why they need to know the information, and then tailor your talk along those lines. (Of course, this is best done before your presentation.)

Begin by putting yourself in the place of your audience. Only include what they really need to know to understand the material or to accomplish your purpose.

Err on the side of less detail. One way to do this is to speak like a journalist — give the headline, followed by the gist of the story in a lead paragraph, and then tell the story if the detail is needed.

You can set ground rules, such as letting them know you will cover material in less detail to begin with but will be open to questions as you talk. If there is a range of technical sophistication in the audience, err on the side of less technical, and offer to add detail in written form or Q&A afterwards for those who want it.

Overcome your ego. It's easy to fall into the trap of showing off your knowledge, especially if there are other technical professionals in the audience. Remember to focus on the needs of the audience, not on your own.

Use analogies to connect difficult concepts to the familiar. These analogies don't have to be perfect, but they do have to be effective.

SUMMARY AND KEY TAKEAWAYS

No communication comes out perfectly the first time. You can take your presentation from good to great by clarifying, rewording, and trimming.

- Be clear. People respond best to common, short, and concrete words.

- Avoid confusion. Try to eliminate specialized jargon, obscure cultural references, and meaningless buzzwords and clichés.

- Be concise. It takes time to make presentations shorter, but it pays off in increased clarity and attention.

- Make numbers meaningful and real by comparing them to familiar concepts and situations.

- If you're very technical, make sure you know *why* your audience needs the information so you can decide *what* to tell them.

9
ADD THE OPENING AND THE CLOSE

By this point, you should have a solid and compelling pitch put together; now you just have to make sure that people will listen to it and act on it. That leads us to the final two steps in putting together your presentation — writing a strong opening and close.

THE IMPORTANCE OF A STRONG OPENING

The most important time in any sales presentation is the first sixty seconds. (It actually starts *before* any words come out of your mouth, but we'll get to that later.) By the end of the crucial first minute, most members of your audience have already formed important judgments that will affect how they will receive your message, or even if they will pay attention to you at all.

People form first impressions very quickly, so your introduction has to show you and your message at your best. Just as in competitive diving, your entry will have a disproportionate impact on your score, except that in presentations your goal is to make a large splash rather than a small one.

FIRST, DO NO HARM

Remember when we talked about the anchoring effect as it applies to numbers? Anchoring also applies to first impressions, especially if the first impression they get from you is negative. If they don't like you to begin with, they're much less likely to pay attention enough to have their minds changed.

Unfortunately, the first sixty seconds is also the time during which most speakers are at their worst. They tend to be nervous, boring, and sometimes even offensive, and it takes far more time to recover from a bad impression than it does to create one. Here are the top three mistakes speakers make:

Mistake #1: Starting off slowly and predictably. You will probably not have the audience's full attention when you begin. Unless you're first on the agenda, listeners are still thinking about the previous presentation, or have taken a few moments to check messages or talk to their neighbors. That's why the first ten seconds of the first minute are the most critical of all. You need to grab your listeners by the shirt collar and get them to look into your eyes and pay attention. So what do most speakers fill that first ten seconds with? "Good morning, my name is Joe Fizzlewhait, and I'm delighted to see you all here today . . ." Get rid of the boilerplate fluff. As Churchill said, "Opening amenities are opening inanities."

Mistake #2: Not giving them a clear reason to listen to you. Sales lore tells us how important it is to have a "hook" that captures the prospect's interest and makes them willing to listen. Whether you call it a unique selling proposition, a value proposition, or a "WIIFM" (What's in it for me?), you need to have one. They are not there to be entertained; they are there for clear business reasons and you can't assume they already know the reason when they're sitting there.

Mistake #3: Making it all about yourself. Self-introductions, as we've seen, waste the most precious time during the presentation. Many speakers compound this by going on at length about their background or credentials to establish credibility. If you've earned the right to present at this level, you have already established your credentials to a large extent.

The ironic thing about credentials is that the more time you spend talking about yours, the more defensive you sound. Credentials are important, of course, but there are better ways to establish them, as we shall see.

WHAT YOU NEED TO ESTABLISH IN THE INTRODUCTION

Avoiding a bad impression is a good start, but there's so much more you need to get done during the first minute:

>   *Interest:* Make them want to listen.
>
>   *Rapport:* Get them to like you.
>
>   *Credibility:* Get them to believe you.
>
>   *Structure:* Provide a road map.

GRAB THEIR ATTENTION

Think about your own state of mind when you last attended a presentation. Were you thinking about something else? Were you unsure whether this presentation would be of any value? This is precisely what will be going through the minds of your audience. Your introduction needs to break through and grab their attention immediately.

Attention is the most elusive and precious commodity you can have in any communication. There is so much competing for your audience's attention, especially in this age of constant and instant connectedness. You can lose a listener in less than a second, and it can take much longer to refocus their attention once that has happened.

It's important to ensure the right kind of attention. You want your audience to be involved and actively following your argument with interest. You don't want them listening critically and reactively, looking for ways to counter your points.

If you want to get your listeners' attention, you have to make them *want* to know what you are going to say next. Attention travels down two paths, *self-interest* or merely *interesting*. To use a familiar analogy, we choose what we want to eat either because it's good for us or because it tastes good, or both.

PIQUE THEIR SELF-INTEREST: "IS IT IMPORTANT TO ME?"

We'll start with this first question for the simple fact that your audience in a strategic sales presentation is not there to be entertained. They are there primarily to learn how to improve their business or personal situation

; make it in their self-interest to listen to you.

Charles Hand, who recently retired as Region President of a major telecommunications company, told me that one of the most important bits of advice he would give to presenters is to structure your introduction to concisely state why they should listen to your presentation.

Here's a dramatic example from a tax lawyer, who told a room full of senior executives:

> *I realize that tax law is not the sexiest topic for anyone in this room, but I will guarantee you this: ten minutes of listening to me just might keep you out of jail.*

Self-interest is especially important when you're trying to drive change. In Chapter 2 we learned that people will tend to default to a lazy mode of thinking, which generally supports sticking with the status quo. However, they will engage their critical thinking faculties if their interests are clear. So, if you're trying to sell them something new, you definitely have to engage their self-interest.

Engage their self-interest using a value proposition that answers the question that is uppermost in the audience's mind:

> *Why should I listen to you?*

The value proposition must be focused specifically on this meeting or presentation. It tells the audience what's in it for them.

Your value proposition should not be some generic statement about your own company, such as "We are the leading provider of . . ." It is about how your customer's situation will improve as a result of listening to you today, right now.

Make sure your value proposition matches the interests of the highest-level people in the room and is specific to them and their situation. It goes back to what we talked about in Chapter 3, the Three Ps of Process, Problem and Profit. If you make the mistake of making your value proposition about product or price, you will shut down attention immediately.

Here are two examples:

For an initial presentation, you might want to get the group interested in a concept, and this can be posed either as a problem that must be solved or an opportunity they can seize:

> *Social media is radically changing how companies compete for market share; our purpose today is to explore ways to ensure that you can protect your market share and take advantage of new channels to increase revenue...*

For a closing presentation, you may focus on specific benefits or what you uniquely bring to the table:

> *We've spent the past three months working closely with your supply chain staff to identify process improvements and we've identified an approach that can lower inventories and speed up customer fulfillment...*

USE YOUR VALUE PROPOSITION TO DIFFERENTIATE YOU

If all your value proposition does is get their attention, you've only accomplished half of what it can do. It should also be used to differentiate you, to dictate the aspect of the situation that they need to pay attention to, one that aligns with your competitive advantage.

If you are in a closing presentation, you're probably one of several companies chosen for the short list. At that point, you and your competitors are seen as reasonably similar to each other; you've all met the minimum requirements and you're all seen as plausible solutions to the problem the customer faces. So telling the customer they have a problem and you have a solution is not as compelling as it would be earlier in the sales cycle. What they want to hear instead is *why you*?

For example, if you compete against much larger companies, you may run into the attitude that bigger is better. So, in your value propositions, you have to say something that opens their minds to the benefits of being smaller, possibly by stressing some aspect of their situation that calls for flexibility, quick response, and individualized attention.

MAKE IT INTERESTING

Just because your message is good for your listeners, there is no reason it can't also be "good tasting." We can pique their interest through surprise and curiosity.

Surprise is an excellent way to engage your listeners' full attention. Our minds are exquisitely attuned to the unexpected. We tune out the ordinary but become instantly alert when something breaks a familiar perception or pattern. You can exploit this in your opening; when your audience expects you to say something familiar and you surprise them with the unexpected, they have no choice but to pay attention.

Curiosity is just as powerful because humans are naturally curious; we love to learn new things and explore the unfamiliar. Here are some effective ways to surprise your listeners and engage their curiosity:

Tell them something new. Some communities have found that a good way to get people to pay attention to speed limit signs is to post an unusual speed limit, such as 37mph. It works because novelty is an excellent way to achieve surprise. Just be careful, though; it should be new enough that it will seem different, but should be related to something they already know so that they don't tune it out completely.

Tell them something that contradicts either common sense or an opinion commonly held in their industry. Contradiction is a particularly effective form of novelty.

Ask a question. Questions that force your audience to ponder in order to give a valid answer will engage and keep their attention, especially if they include paradox or contradiction. "Does anyone know what the leading cause of customer dissatisfaction is today?"

You could also ask a rhetorical question that will set up your premise. For example, if your theme is that it's important to be the industry leader, you could ask them the name of the world's second tallest mountain, or the second person to fly across the Atlantic solo.

Challenge them. A challenge can be risky, as it might put your audience into a critical and reactive mindset, but if you've got a strong case it can work very well. In a class I teach for senior-level executives who are giving outside speeches on behalf of their companies, I begin by saying: "Welcome to the most important class you will take in your career with this company." The instant I say it, you can almost hear every eyeball in the room locking onto me.

Do something different. An easy and effective way to break the familiar pattern is to launch right into your value proposition, pause, and *then* introduce yourself.

Tell a story. As discussed in Chapter 7, anyone who hears a story's beginning has to hear the ending. One way to exploit this is to begin with a partial story — and keep them waiting for the ending.

Regardless of which approach you take, there are two caveats to keep in mind.

First, if you set out to surprise your listeners during your opening, you run the risk that you may go too far. The line between compelling and cheesy can be a thin one. My own experience is that what sounds good to you when you're thinking of your opening late at night may not sound quite so good in the light of day. You might want to test it on a colleague just to make sure.

Second, make sure it's relevant. It's important to make your surprise part of your core message and not just some gimmick that will make them feel cheated. People appreciate a relevant surprise, but they will feel manipulated if it turns out to be a transparent ploy.

ESTABLISH RAPPORT

Rapport is important for two reasons. The general reason is that people are more likely to trust — and be persuaded by — people they like. You must let them know you like them and have their best interests at heart. The second reason is that a big-ticket system purchase usually leads to a close working relationship between the seller and the buyer. Buyers need to feel comfortable with the people they are going to be tied to for what may possibly be a long time. One SVP at a major technology firm related a specific instance where a lead presenter came across as too aggressive, and even arrogant; he immediately thought that if she were this way during the courtship phase, she would be very difficult to work with.

Thin-slice research, in which researchers show short video snippets of people presenting, has shown that people make extremely quick and generally accurate judgments about other people, sometimes in as quickly as five seconds. Elements of rapport are the easiest and most accurate judgments that people make very quickly, so you have to start off on the right foot.

How do you establish rapport in the introduction? Some people try to "break the ice" by telling a joke, but I strongly recommend against it. This is one of the oldest suggestions in public speaking, and one of the most harmful. It supposedly breaks the ice, and helps you connect as a regular person. In my experience, this is the surest way to dig yourself a hole that you might not be able to climb out of.

First, even if the joke goes perfectly, the audience knows exactly what you're trying to do. Second, unless you're a professional comedian, chances are that it won't come off perfectly. In today's oversensitive society, you also run the risk of offending at least one person in the audience. This doesn't mean there's no place for humor in presentations, but just don't make it the first thing you do.

One possible exception is self-deprecating humor. I love this opening line from former Senator Alan Simpson: "I know you want to hear the latest dope from Washington. Well, here I am."

Don't misinterpret this: stories are an excellent way to begin a presentation. Sometimes a story can make you seem relaxed and confident, but make sure the story directly leads in to your value proposition.

So, if you can't break the ice with a joke, how do you establish rapport? First off, by not trying too hard. People will like you if you provide value and don't waste their time. You can acknowledge some of the people in the room, but don't spend too much time doing this. (Most of your presentations will be informal enough that you will have time to do some of that before you begin your presentation.)

One way to get people interested in you is to show your interest in them. Having a good value proposition helps, especially if you personalize it or make it directly relevant to them — possibly by referencing something you read about them recently in the news.

ESTABLISH YOUR CREDENTIALS

Credentials are the first contributors to your credibility because they are generally the first things your audience sees. In fact, depending on how the meeting is set up, they can project credibility even before you appear in front of your audience.

Credentials are defined fairly loosely to go beyond formal credentials, such as position and education, to include less formal signals such as your appearance, experiences, and achievements.

If you have strong credentials relative to the subject being discussed, they can be even more effective if you're not obvious about them. The best way to do this in front of a group is, if possible, to have the person who introduces you tell a bit about your background. You can also do some amount of casual name-dropping, but be careful not to overdo it. It's important not to overstress your credentials, as it can make you sound defensive.

The best way to gain credibility is to say things that demonstrate your knowledge. A more subtle, and no less powerful, method of signaling your credentials is to give examples or tell stories that highlight your experience with the matter in question.

Credibility is highly dependent on your appearance and demeanor, which we cover in Chapter 11, "Executive Presence."

LET EVERYONE IN ON THE PLAN

The fourth task of your introduction is to provide a road map of your upcoming content, lending clarity and context to what you are going to say. This is where you *briefly* "tell them what you're going to tell them."

As noted in Chapter 6, a verbal map makes it easier for your audience to organize the incoming material in their minds.

Your structure can be presented verbally, or you can provide a formal agenda, either as a slide or a handout. In Chapter 15 you will learn to use an interactive agenda to pull your audience into your way of thinking.

HAVE A POWERFUL AND FOCUSED CLOSE

When Martin Luther King ended his famous speech on the national mall, he did not say, "Well, I see our time is up. Thanks for taking the time to listen to my dreams, and please let me know if you have any questions. If not, enjoy the rest of your time in Washington."

His ending was far more memorable and inspiring, of course, and we can take from him and other great historical speakers some lessons that will do the same for our speeches and presentations.

Although the two most memorable moments of any presentation are the opening and the close, most speakers pay far more attention to the opening and tend to neglect their ending. There's a good reason to pay more attention to the opening, because first impressions can be very powerful. Yet there are also excellent reasons to be just as careful with the preparation and delivery of your close. The close is the last impression listeners have of you; do you want it to be weak? Do you want listeners to begin tuning out before the final words are out of your mouth?

You began preparing for your executive presentation by selecting an overriding theme, which is the main point that you want your listeners to remember. When you close your speech, it's your last and best chance to sum up your points and hammer home your theme. Use your closing remarks to call your listeners to action or remind them of your message.

Make your close memorable and put just as much thought into it as into your beginning.

WHAT ARE THE MOST COMMON CLOSING ERRORS?

Just as we began the introduction section, we will first focus on avoiding the most common closing errors.

Slow fades: Songs on the radio fade in volume toward the end, but presentations should never end that way. Ending with "That's about all I have to say on this, does anyone have any questions?" is all too common. Your listeners can sense the fadeout and begin turning their thoughts to checking email or thinking about something else.

Long summaries: Some people will argue with this. After all, the most venerable presentation structure is the Three Ts, which ends with, "Tell them what you told them." There are good reasons to end this way: repetition is generally a good thing. The problem is that an executive audience, whose members pride themselves on being quick studies, is going to feel patronized by that. They will begin tuning you out as soon as they know that the summary is coming. If you feel you must give some sort of summary, keep it brief.

Ambiguous or tentative call to action: "Thank you, and I hope I'll have your support." There should be no question what you want from them, so give them a clear path to agree

Pushy call to action: On the other hand, if you try too hard to close, you can easily blow up any credibility or goodwill you have built up during your presentation. Besides, they may have their own procedures for discussing the presentation and arriving at a decision, and you have to respect those. Always remember that when you put people under pressure for a decision, especially important people, the easy answer is no.

Talking past the close: One of the most common mistakes in selling also applies to presenting. If you've clearly made your case and confidently asked for agreement, anything you say afterwards can only hurt. It will either show a lack of confidence or give your listeners reasons to change their minds.

When Andrei Mikhalevsky, CEO of California Dairies, was a young salesman starting with Campbell Soup, he and his new boss visited a customer to make a presentation. Andrei was so concerned about making an impression on his new boss that he worked extra hard on the presentation. They arrived at the customer's warehouse, and Andrei told the customer up front why they were there and what they hoped to sell. The customer said, "OK, I'll buy." But Andrei was so focused on delivering what he came to say that he began presenting anyway. After about five minutes, his boss interrupted him and said, "We've got the deal. Let's go."

Being surprised by your own ending: This is the opposite of talking past the close. Too many speakers ramble early and then freak out when they realize they're running out of time. They speed up or leave out important material.

Adding something new: Don't bring out something new that you hadn't already covered; it will confuse your audience and possibly negate everything that was said before.

WHAT CAN YOU DO WITH YOUR CLOSE?

Unlike the introduction, where there are four things you *must* establish, there are four things you *may* accomplish in your conclusion (you don't have to aim for all four):

1. Amplify your points.

2. Summarize your facts and arguments.

3. Rouse the appropriate emotions in your audience.

4. Call to action.

Amplify and summarize: These two are listed together because you don't need to spend too much time summarizing your points, unless it was a very long presentation. Senior-level people will find it unnecessary and condescending. Instead, put everything you told them into context by reminding them why the topic is important to them, and use your conclusion to tie together your main points into a repetition of your key theme.

Rouse the appropriate emotions in your audience: Senior executives are people too, so emotion will work with them, but you have to be subtle in your appeal.

As long as they are not overdone, appeals to emotion can be very powerful, and their power can be amplified even further by contrasting negative and positive emotions.

The two principal emotions that will move an audience to action are fear and confidence. If they fear the consequences of not acting, and have confidence that the course you recommend is the right way to go, they will probably decide in your favor.

Churchill gave an excellent example of this in his "Blood, Toil, Tears and Sweat" speech on May 11, 1940. Just before his final words, he said,

> . . . *without victory, there is no survival. Let that be realized; no survival for the British Empire; no survival for all that the British Empire has stood for, no survival for the urge and impulse of the ages, that mankind will move forward towards its goal. But I take up my task with buoyancy and hope. I feel sure that our cause will not be suffered to fail among men.*

Of course, in a sales presentation you're not going to be that overt in your emotional appeal. There are many variations that can be much more subtle. Instead of fear, you can appeal to loss, dissatisfaction, inconvenience, or competition, to name just a few. For positives, you can appeal to satisfaction, or profit, or paint an exciting picture of the future.

Let's apply the spirit of Churchill's closing to a business setting:

> . . . *failing to keep up to industry standards will make it harder and harder to maintain your share in a market that you are used to dominating. But I'm confident that the solution we've outlined will not only solve the immediate problem but will also put you back in your familiar position as the industry leader.*

Call to action: Because you are there to achieve your sales call purpose, it's generally a good idea to ask for it at the end of your presentation. If your speech purpose is to compel action, you must close on the actions you targeted during your planning. Don't be afraid to "ask for the order."

Similar to the caution about emotions, you want to be direct but not pushy about it. Around half of the senior executives I interviewed for this book stressed that they prefer the presentation to be more about providing information than about trying to sell them.

Churchill's call to action in his May 11 speech was:

> *At this time I feel entitled to claim the aid of all, and I say, "Come, then, let us go forward together with our united strength."*

In a business situation, your call to action will be a bit more restrained:

> *If we can have a contract signed by the end of this month, I can commit to having the solution in place by Q3.*

How to Close a Presentation with Style and Punch

Chances are you won't be called upon to deliver a speech to save western civilization, so you will sound ridiculous if you try to match these levels of grandiloquence:

> *. . . and so my friends, it is your solemn duty to remember your obligation to future generations of shareholders by investing in these widgets . . .*

Yet your ending has to match the importance, quality, and impact of your presentation, and you can achieve this by thinking about how you want your listeners to feel and what you want them to do as a result of your talk.

You won't go wrong if you summarize and amplify, rouse the appropriate emotions, and call the audience to action. Yet, you can add style and punch to your close with a few simple techniques.

Leave no doubt about what you want your audience to do. If it's agreement you want, ask for it. If you want action, make your call for it clear, decisive, and confident. You can even end with a challenge: "We've put this decision off long enough; this is our last chance; the time to act is now."

End with a question. Get the audience to close for you, by asking them a direct question that forces them to make their intentions clear:

> *What do we need to do to make this happen?*

> *What do you think?*

Use a tagline. Give them a tagline or sound bite that sticks in their minds. Say what you will about Johnnie Cochran's defense of OJ Simpson, his closing was effective and memorable:

> *If it doesn't fit, you must acquit.*

End with the headline you want the press to write about your presentation. Your tagline can play off your corporate motto, or even better, play off the customer's.

Wrap a bow around it. Tie back to your opening for a neat and memorable way to close the presentation. For example, if you began with a story or a question, you can tell the ending or the answer in your close.

How *did* King close his great speech?

> *Free at last, free at last, thank God almighty, we are free at last!*

Now *that* was an ending!

SUMMARY AND KEY TAKEAWAYS

Audiences are likely to remember more of the first and last things you say during your presentation, so you must take extra care in making sure you start and end strong.

- Above all, avoid a weak start!

- Grab their attention through self-interest and/or surprise.

- Develop rapport by being yourself and showing interest in your listeners.

- Establish your credentials without being too overt.

- Give your listeners a road map of what you're going to say.

- Use your close to:

    - Amplify and summarize your points

    - Rouse the appropriate emotions

    - Call to action

CASE STUDY, CONTINUED: HYPOTHETICAL STRATEGIC SALES PRESENTATION

As you can see from Brian's introduction, he chose to begin with a story. It was calculated to be informal, but to leave no doubt about his theme that the customer faces an important and urgent decision.

In his close, he came back to the same theme, and then ended with a subtle yet unmistakable call to action.

BUILDING THE PRESENTATION

Introduction

Last year, my brother-in-law had to go to the emergency room when he hurt his shoulder playing softball. It turned out to be the luckiest injury he ever had, because while he was in the hospital they discovered a potentially fatal problem with his heart, and fortunately they were able to take care of it relatively easily because they caught it in time.

Your problem with faulty power modules might just be the lucky injury you needed at this time.

We are here today to propose an outsourcing partnership that will best position Visionary Industries to continue your stellar growth. I'll begin by describing the circumstances that led us to discover...

Close

To sum things up, it may be tempting to solve your immediate problem and put off these bigger decisions for later. But the best time to dig a well is before you're thirsty.

As your name implies, Visionary Industries has proven to be a company that can see the big picture and move quickly to give the market what it wants before it knows it wants it. I believe this is one such moment, and we look forward to being a valuable part of the Visionary team.

FIGURE 9-1: INTRODUCTION AND CLOSE

10
VISUAL PERSUASION

In 2001, scientists played a dirty trick on some of the world's foremost wine experts. They gave them samples of white wine to taste — but these samples had been turned red with food coloring. We all know that wine experts have a language of their own, which baffles those of us who are less sophisticated. Actually, they have two languages — one used for reds and one for whites — and their respective vocabularies are meant to be totally distinct. Yet every one of the experts described the white wines using the specialized language for reds. Their highly educated and finely calibrated senses of taste and smell were overridden in their brains by their visual sense. That's how powerful a visual impression can be.

If a visual can convey false information so strongly, imagine what it could do in support of a true message. The visual sense is generally underused or misused in business communication, and that's a shame because it means that salespeople are leaving a lot of money on the table.

How Pictures Can Help You Persuade

The first point about visual persuasion is that we are *all* visual. There is a common misconception that people have clear preferences for auditory, visual, or kinesthetic learning, but the fact is that all of us depend heavily for learning on our visual sense. About half of the processing capacity of our brains is devoted to the visual sense. As John Medina says in *Brain Rules*, "Vision is probably the best single tool we have for learning anything."

It's a tool that can help increase your persuasiveness in many ways:

Get attention. You can't persuade them if they're not paying attention. When people are expecting yet another series of text-filled bullet-point lists, well-chosen pictures can reach out and grab the attention of your audience.

Help them remember. When you make a sales call or a presentation, the people you talk to may decide later, or they may talk to others who will influence their decisions. So it's important that they remember your message the way you want them to remember it, and pictures can be a huge help. When information is presented orally, people remember about 10% three days later. When pictures are used, retention goes up to 65%. Even more impressive, subjects have looked at 2,500 pictures and remembered them with 90% accuracy several days later, and 63% *a year* later.

Make it real. Pictures "prove" something actually exists. Seeing is believing. Subway's Jared holding up a pair of pants that he used to wear is a powerful testimonial to his weight loss.

Stir emotions. A picture of a polar bear marooned on a small bit of ice can convey a far more powerful impression than reams of statistics. While the experts debate the extent and causes of climate change, powerful images settle the argument in the minds of millions.

Help you say a lot in a short time. Pictures can be grasped in one glance; often one truly can be worth a thousand words. If your listeners are pressed for time, pictures can help you cram more meaning into less time.

Clarify. Pictures can make relationships between concepts easier to follow and understand. They can make difficult quantitative comparisons visible and thus easier to grasp.

With all these benefits, the use of slide presentations, because they can project visual information so easily, should be a slam dunk. Yet we all know that most slide presentations are anything but clear, persuasive, or memorable. To see why this is so, and what we can do about it, we first need to understand a little about the limitations of information transfer.

LIMITATIONS OF INFORMATION TRANSFER

The unspoken assumption of most presenters is that if they transmit the information to the audience, it will be received, remembered, and applied, but the sad truth is that most of what you say is forgotten almost immediately. Think about it: How many PowerPoint presentations have you attended during your career? How many of those do you remember?

We'll look at why this is so and what you can do about it.

It is possible to transfer vast amounts of information from one mind to another, but there is a very narrow bottleneck through which it must pass: the visual and auditory channels and working memory. There are three critical mental activities occurring at the same time at this interface:

1. We must *capture* the appropriate signals.

2. We must *process* them into meaningful information.

3. We *integrate* this meaningful information with what we already know to create new knowledge and ideas.

IMPROVING THE CAPTURE OF INFORMATION

Our visual and auditory channels have limited capacity. Too much information overloads our capacity and, as a result, meaning is lost. So when incoming information exceeds our capacity, we pick and choose what we pay attention to.

One of the main culprits of information overload is the tendency to put a lot of words on our slides and read them to the audience. It's a common misconception that redundancy is good. Most think that if they can both hear it and see it, it's better than either one alone. In reality, the audience can't read the slide and listen to you at the same time. When they begin reading, they are not listening, and vice versa. In other words, the channels are actually overloading each other.

In one study, it was found that using pictures and taking most of the words off the screen aids the retention and transfer of the message. The research showed an average increase in retention of 30% and transfer of 80%. Retention refers to their ability to remember the information. Transfer is the ability to apply that information when they need to., You want them to be able to apply the information you imparted during the sales presentation as they make their decision, so anything that almost doubles transfer is a huge advantage.

Another interesting finding is that extraneous material on slides — that which does not directly contribute to your message — limits the audience's ability to grasp the material. Removing extraneous material was found to improve retention and transfer of information by 105%.

IMPROVING THE PROCESSING OF INFORMATION

Although your executive listeners are no doubt pretty intelligent, they still suffer from normal human limitations of their processing capacity. Too much information at one time will overflow the processing capacity of even the smartest person. That's because incoming information must first be processed in working memory, which is kind of a mental scratch pad we use to make sense of new information and connect it to what we already know.

A well-known study, published in 1956, pointed out that most people can only hold approximately seven items in working memory at any one time. However, that study actually focused more on immediate memory, which can be used to remember something like a phone number until you need to use it. When you consider *working memory*, which is used to manipulate and make sense of ideas in order to integrate them into long-term memory, it has been shown that the number is probably even smaller, probably as few as three or four items.

Even though working memory can only accommodate a few chunks at one time, you can transmit an awful lot of meaning by grouping information into chunks that are meaningful to your audience. For example, it might be difficult to remember everything on a twenty-item shopping list, but if you were asked to bring back the ingredients for a breakfast omelet, a peanut-butter-and-jelly sandwich lunch, and a spaghetti dinner, it would probably be easy for you.

Of course, the person giving you the shopping list instructions would have to know that you are familiar with these common menu items, or they would only create more confusion. Similarly, a speaker has to know the audience's knowledge level in order to find the right balance between simplicity and complexity, and to identify the best opportunities for chunking.

In order not to exceed the audience's processing capability, give them new information in small gulps, with a little bit per slide. You can put more on each slide if you separate information into visual chunks that can be processed individually.

Our content carries two types of cognitive load: *intrinsic load* has to do with the difficulty of the material itself, and *extrinsic load* is related to how it's presented. Your goal with your visual aids is to simplify them as much as possible to reduce the extrinsic load. By reducing the audience's extrinsic cognitive load, you free up resources, which makes it easier for them to absorb complicated content. And if it can't be simplified, at least give it to them in digestible chunks. By making it easier for them to follow, you actually become more persuasive.

Simplification does not mean "dumbing down." In fact it's quite the opposite, because it takes a deep understanding of the material to know how to simplify it for presentation.

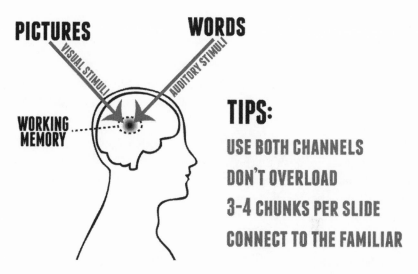

FIGURE 10-1: INFORMATION TRANSFER LIMITATIONS AT A GLANCE

With these thoughts about the audience's cognitive capabilities as context, let's turn our attention to the most ubiquitous visual medium we have in business today: PowerPoint slides.

THE PROS AND CONS OF POWERPOINT

Now that you have confidently planned what you want to say, and have polished your content, it's time to get it ready for the big screen.

A small, albeit growing, band of holdouts and rebels dares to suggest that it's still possible to stand in front of a group of business decision makers and just talk to them, sharing ideas through conversation as humans have done for millennia. (According to his latest biographer, Steve Jobs was particularly contemptuous of slides.)

After all, before PowerPoint was introduced in 1987, speakers somehow managed to move their listeners to action without slides. Dr. King did not have a huge screen set up in front of the Lincoln

Memorial with pictures of the red hills of Georgia or of Lookout Mountain in Tennessee, but he somehow communicated a compelling vision to millions.

Salespeople sold the ideas, machines and equipment that built the modern American economy long before presentation software graced our lives.

But it is a new millennium, and the reality is that PowerPoint slides are ubiquitous in business presentations today. You will probably use them, and your customers will likely expect to see them. The goal of this chapter is to give you ideas to ensure that your presentations increase, rather than decrease, your chances of making the sale.

The first step is to take care of the obvious weaknesses and then build off the strengths of this medium. Let's begin by looking at what's wrong with most slide presentations and then consider ways to fix those wrongs and turn your slides into assets.

WHAT'S WRONG WITH SLIDE PRESENTATIONS?

Most people who have sat through mind-numbing meetings would agree that the average slide presentation is too wordy, too boring, and too complicated. When you add up the hundreds of millions of daily meetings multiplied by the number of attendees and their costs, the result is billions of dollars wasted annually. I want to make sure that your meetings don't contribute to this economic sinkhole.

But it's not PowerPoint's fault. It's a poor workman who blames his tools. I do not believe PowerPoint is evil, or even that it dumbs down thinking. Most bad presentations can be traced to three main causes: incomplete or unclear thinking about the message, trying to do too much with the tool, and the fact that the software is so easy to use.

Incomplete thinking: If you have taken the time thus far to go through the steps outlined in this book to create and refine your message, you know that coming up with good ideas requires solid analysis and thinking. The next step, figuring out how to communicate those ideas in the clearest and most compelling way so that others understand them as you do, is even harder.

In *Speaking PowerPoint*, Bruce Gabrielle says, "Complex slides are often a clue that the slide designer didn't know what they were trying to say. They poured data onto a slide, but didn't do the hard analytic work to figure out what message they were trying to convey."

If you're writing out your presentation, it's hard enough to get things down concisely; the task becomes several times harder when you need to get the ideas down to the number of words that fit comfortably on a slide.

Trying to do too much with the tool: A hammer is the best tool for driving nails but it doesn't do too good a job opening beer bottles (trust me; don't try it at home).

Similarly, PowerPoint is an excellent tool for some tasks but not for others, and it's important to limit its use to its specific strengths. Remember that it's a *presentation* tool, not a writing tool. Although many people can and do use it successfully as a document creator, those are documents that are meant to be read and can stand on their own. In your case, you will do most of the work and the presentation will be there for support.

If you think of an executive sales presentation as a "show and tell," slides are an excellent tool for *showing*, but they are poor tools for *telling*. Telling is *your* job. There is an additional task: *documenting* what was said so that audience members can refer back to the information when they are ready to decide. PowerPoint can be used for that too, but not the version that is projected on the screen. That's an important distinction: there may be a document that is produced, such as a detailed proposal or implementation plan, but there is no law that says what is on paper has to exactly match what is on the screen.

Too easy to use: The third reason for poor presentations derives from one of PowerPoint's greatest strengths: it's speaker-friendly. It's so easy to outline your topic that you tend to take the path of least resistance, which makes it difficult for you to think carefully about how best to structure your argument. You begin with a weak structure that is further watered down by the default style of headers and bulleted lists. The resulting series of lists that you read to the audience robs your presentation of any originality or personality. Executives want strong reasons delivered in a confident conversational style, not generic laundry lists.

The ease of use makes it too easy to throw every detail into your presentation to ensure that the audience gets it, and most speakers inevitably feel compelled to cover everything that is on their slides. In doing so, they make it difficult for the listener to focus on and remember those parts that are key.

It also makes it easy to turn the presentation into a set of speaker's notes, which is why it's so common for someone to be able to deliver someone else's deck; they don't have to know the material, because it's all in the deck.

It does not have to be that way. Used properly, PowerPoint can add clarity and impact to your executive presentation.

MAKE YOUR PRESENTATION LISTENER-FRIENDLY

Bad presentations implicitly assume that it's your job to transmit and the audience's job to receive. However, meaning derives from the exchange of ideas, which is much more than the simple transmission of information. Therefore you need to take responsibility for whether and how the message is received.

In this chapter, we have already stressed the importance of framing your message in terms that make it easy for your audience to understand and relate to. Good presentations take into account how people capture information, process it in their minds, and integrate it with what they know.

You are the best visual aid

Most presentations are so detailed that they can almost stand on their own. They do most of the work and leave very little room for the presenter to add value. PowerPoint does a great job as a visual aid, but it is still far inferior to you.

Think about it this way: if you had the choice to deliver the presentation without slides, or to deliver the slides without you being there, which would you prefer? I hope you chose the former because otherwise you are just a projector operator, not a sales professional. If the document can stand on its own, why do your customers need to attend a meeting to hear you present? Why not let the proposal writers earn all the commission bucks? (And reduce carbon emissions while you're at it.)

People come to listen to you, not to see your slides. They come to see you because you can add interest, connect with them on an emotional as well as logical level, and vary your presentation to suit the audience and situation. They want to be able to look into your eyes and gauge your confidence and sincerity as you urge them to a decision; they want to know about the person they might be entrusting their business to.

Presentation success ultimately comes down to trust, and trust rests fundamentally on a human connection. Slides don't provide that. Slides can't anticipate and pre-answer all the questions and concerns the audience will have; they can't listen or empathize or reassure.

Everything should have a point

Make each slide count. Every element on the slide should add to your message, or it should be removed. The discipline of deciding what's essential will be a huge gift to your audience. It will also help you by forcing you to think critically and clearly about your message, and the clarity that emerges is one of the most important assets of any persuasive message.

CREATING YOUR PRESENTATION

If a strategic sales presentation could be made into a movie, the two stars would be you and your audience. Slides would only be the supporting actor. That means that you write your part and the audience's part first, and then you turn your attention to creating your slides.

Message first, then medium

Because PowerPoint is easy to use, it's tempting to use it to begin writing your presentation. Resist the temptation — make sure you know what you want to say first, before you open the application.

When Leonardo painted *The Last Supper*, he did not begin by slapping paint right on the wall. He first had to think very carefully about what he wanted on the wall of Santa Maria delle Grazie in Milan, and then he spent hours drawing his ideas on paper. Only when he was satisfied with the general outline did he begin to transfer the figures on paper to the wall itself. He made changes and adjustments as the final picture began to take shape, but most of his thinking was done first.

Why can't you just begin writing and clarifying your thoughts in PowerPoint? The problem is that it's hard to separate the expression from the presentation. While your mind is trying to figure out the best way to sharpen your message, it may also be distracted by fiddling with font sizes and colors — or even worse, animations.

You should take Leonardo's approach with your own masterpiece. Figure out your theme and then choose the supporting points using the templates provided in this book and in Chapter 6.

Once you have your structure figured out, you can begin creating the slides. If each of your main points is a single sentence, you can easily create a new slide with each sentence at the top as a headline. Start with the big picture first so you don't get lost in the detail of each individual slide. This will help you make sure your speech flows logically. There are several ways to do this:

- In PowerPoint, you can use the outline view to write your slide headlines, then switch to the slide sorter view to see if the headlines flow logically.

- You may find it useful to print the 3-slides-per-page handouts view at this point. There is enough room on the side to write the main points that you will make for each slide, or to fill in the supporting detail. If you find that your main points don't fit in the small space provided, consider whether you are trying to accomplish too much with one slide, and possibly break it into smaller gulps.

- There is a lot to be said for a low-tech approach: use 3x5 index cards to design each slide. It will allow you to rearrange the cards to ensure that your points flow properly. More importantly, it will discipline you to ensure that you don't put too much on each slide.

- Design and rehearse simultaneously. There's no rule that says you have to design the entire presentation and then rehearse it. Design a bit, rehearse the presentation of the slide, and make adjustments to the design as necessary. Hearing your words out loud will often cause you to go back and tweak what you've written.

Design for interactivity

Good presentations support your intended structure, but you also have to prepare for the almost inevitable fact that the audience might refuse to cooperate. They may take you off track by challenging your points or requesting additional detail, or open up a totally separate line of thinking.

That won't be a problem if you've anticipated the possible digressions and have designed your slides accordingly. You can put in as many hidden slides as you think you might need, and be prepared to bring them up as necessary.

If you do this, however, there is a right way and a wrong way to get to those slides during your presentation, and we'll cover that later in this chapter.

DESIGN MAKEOVERS

Before diving into some practical ideas for designing slides, it's important to remind you that these tips are meant for the typical sales presentation, which is at least somewhat interactive and is meant for an audience of 4-15 listeners. This is important because there is no one best practice for the design and content of slides; it will vary depending on audience size and purpose.

At one extreme, think of Steve Jobs introducing the iPhone at MacWorld: a very large audience, huge screen behind him, and no interactivity with the audience. For these types of presentations, text should be minimal and pictures should be large and memorable. At the other extreme, you might be sitting in front of one or two people reviewing a business proposal. In this situation, you might not even use a screen at all, and your slides can have much more text and detail.

Most sales presentations fall between those extremes, and that's where the ideas below will be most effective.

Could they read it a 70mph?

Think of most of your slides as highway billboards. Long before slide presentations were invented, the outdoor media industry has had almost one hundred years to master the art of getting a message across to readers quickly and effectively. They do this by making their point concisely, making it easy to read, and making it memorable.

One of the ways billboards make it easy to understand is that they make it easy for the eye to follow. Every element has its place for a reason. When someone is in a speeding vehicle, you don't want their eyes wandering all over searching for the main point.

Not all of your points can be made that quickly, however, and there will be times you might have to spend several minutes on one slide, so don't take this idea to extremes.

Still, the idea of making your slides as easy as possible to understand carries a lot of merit. As Daniel Kahneman tells us, *cognitive ease* carries its own rewards. When something is easy to understand, it feels familiar, which makes it feel more true. When it's effortless, it makes more sense and actually makes people feel good. As we said, even highly intelligent and engaged executives like to conserve cognitive resources, which basically means they don't want to have to think too hard.

Reduce clutter

We saw earlier that removing extraneous visual elements can double retention and transfer. What are the most common extraneous visual elements on sales slides? Look for overly fancy decorations embedded into the slide template, corporate logos, fine print disclaimers about confidentiality on the bottom, etc.

I realize that your marketing and/or legal departments may give birth to a half-grown cow if you tell them you're going to take those things off, so you need to decide what's best for you. Just remember two things: there is a cognitive cost to keeping them in, and an image on a screen is not permanent.

Three-part slide structure

The structure and content of a good slide resembles the structure of the presentation itself: *theme* — *support* — *illustration*. On a slide, it's *main point* — *supporting detail* — *picture*.

Main point: Use headlines instead of titles

Probably the most popular suggestion I make in my classes is to use headlines instead of titles in PowerPoint. By headlines, I mean either a complete sentence, or a headline-type sentence which may not be grammatically correct but makes a point or tells a story.

Most slides you see have a title at the top, such as "Recommendations," followed by a laundry list. If newspaper headlines were written this way, the day after the Super Bowl you would see a headline reading "Super Bowl Results."

Complete sentences and headlines are easier for the audience to process because they bring your logic to the surface; they get to the point right away. In writing, they are called *advance organizers* because they help audience members organize their minds to receive the incoming information. If you give them the meaning first, the details make more sense and are easier to follow.

The discipline of writing headlines also makes you think very carefully about the point of each slide. The question you want to answer for each slide you include should be: "What is the main point of this slide?"

It should not be that hard to come up with your headlines — if you follow the steps in this book, each of your main points is a headline.

Supporting detail: The use and abuse of text

The first rule of text that is projected on a screen is that it is there to support the spoken word, not to stand on its own. (There's a tool that works great for text that stands on its own — it's called a document.) It makes your spoken words easier to follow by providing structure and by guiding the audience's attention to what you are talking about. In a sense, they can serve as an overlay, similar to Google Maps.

Let the bulk of the meaning come from your spoken words, with the on-screen words as support. As we saw earlier, narration plus pictures significantly improves retention and transfer.

So the first radical makeover to your slides is to take out words. Be as concise as possible. They should be getting meaning from your talk, not from the slide itself.

Taking out words may make you feel like you're working without a net, as many presenters use a lot of words on their slides as a substitute for really knowing their material. If you need that much help, maybe you should reconsider the speaking opportunity.

On the flip side, having few words can definitely improve your presentation of the material itself. First, you will probably sound a lot more spontaneous because you won't have to try to align your words with every single bit of text on the screen. Second, it will force you to really know your material because you won't be using the screen as your cue cards.

Are there times when it makes sense to add more text to your slides? The answer is yes, but it depends on the situation. If you plan to be in a discussion meeting, which has a small audience and is intended to be very interactive, it might help to have a more document-type look and feel to your presentation. In that situation, audience members will probably have a printed copy that they can refer to as you talk. This type of meeting is more likely to take place in the middle stages of the typical sales cycle. For example, you might have to present findings of your analysis of their business operations or technical procedures to suggest improvements.

In that case, there is good reason to have a lot of text, but make it easier for them to follow the discussion by bolding or highlighting key words. Even better, put the supporting text in gray and key words in dark blue or black.

If you're presenting to a larger group, make sure your words can be read by the people in the back of the room. The simplest way is to ensure that the text is large enough for everyone to read, but also make sure that the text color contrasts well with the background.

Reduce your use of bullet points: they are so common that eyes automatically glaze over when they appear. If you can figure out a different way to say it, do it. Despite the near-religious fervor with which some pundits excoriate them, there is nothing inherently wrong with bullets. The problem is that every text box in PowerPoint begins in bullet format by default, so slides eventually all look the same. You need to break the pattern to keep things fresh.

The best reason to use bullet points is to provide structure to your listeners so that they can see the relationship between what you are presently saying to the main point of the slide. Go ahead and use them, but try to limit them to as few words as possible. One expert recommends three words or less; that may be a little extreme, but it will force you to think carefully about the point of each, and will allow you to have attention focused on your explanation rather than on reading the screen. When you have too many words on the screen, you almost force yourself into reading them.

One of the easiest ways to sap your credibility is to display a slide with typos on it. Spell-check is your first line of defense, but don't rely on it exclusively. It would not find fault with the line: *Their our fore weighs two right you're name.* Get someone else to proofread your presentation, preferably by beginning at the last slide and working backwards, which helps the mind focus more on the spelling of the words than their meaning.

Don't get carried away with too many different fonts. Fonts should be consistent and easy to read.

Pictures

Pictures are one of the best reasons to use slides because they can illustrate ideas so efficiently and add impact to your talk. The following tips will help you get the maximum benefit out of your pictures:

Make sure images are relevant. If a picture is worth a thousand words, make sure those words match your message. This will allow you to take advantage of the listeners' dual channels. When pictures complement the spoken word, comprehension and retention increases.

Eliminate irrelevant visual elements. Logos, most footers, disclaimers, fancy templates, references, and citations are all distracting. Put them in the handouts.

Use high-quality pictures. Why detract from the quality of your message by using cheesy clip art? For one thing, it's probably been seen before. Picture quality indicates that you took special pains for your audience — like the difference between serving a meal on paper plates or fine china.

Keep words and pictures close together in space and time. It prevents split attention. If you're showing a diagram of your product, place labels close to the parts they are naming, for example.

Charts, graphs, and tables

When you have a lot of numerical data to present, you almost always have to do it with some chart or table. Charts and tables can be extremely effective or laughably ineffective.

To make sure they are the former, follow two simple but powerful rules:

Show the data. Edward Tufte, the leading evangelist of what he calls a high *data-to-ink ratio*, says, "Above all else, show the data." While this may sound obvious, too many presenters get carried away with decoration. There is far more ink or pixel count devoted to the structure, background, and decoration of the charts than to the data itself.

Make them easy to understand. Most charts can be difficult enough to decipher, so audience members won't make the effort to read charts unless they need the information to make sense of what you're saying.

At the risk of belaboring the obvious, I have to stress that you don't begin with a graph and build your presentation around it; graphs are created as a means of properly displaying the evidence you need to support your main points. Think first about what you want the numbers to show before you show the numbers.

Make sure the chart makes a clear point that supports or advances your argument, and make sure the audience gets it quickly.

Give them a headline instead of a title. One of the best ways to help your listeners to make sense of the chart is to tell them what the chart shows by using headlines instead of titles, just as you do with your slides. For example, rather than a title that reads *Comparison of total lifetime costs,* your headline can read *Our solution has the lowest total lifetime cost.* And, if you can't think of a good headline, think hard about whether you need the chart at all.

Select and highlight the important data. Chances are you won't be at a loss for data to display; your challenge will be to select the relevant data that advances your argument and drop the rest. Then, highlight the data points that are important.

To help the audience take in the information at a glance, draw their eyes to what's important and try to eliminate or subdue the rest. For example, if you're making a point about how your product's performance compares to competitors', use neutral colors for each competitor, and a reasonably bright or bold line for yours.

Organize and show it properly. The main purpose of a chart is to show a picture of the data. A great way to test whether your chart is doing this effectively is to apply the squint test. Squint your eyes so that the numbers are too fuzzy to read: can you still grasp the gist of the message? For example, something is growing much faster than its peers, or something changed significantly at a certain time. Graphs are meant to be processed through the visual channel, which means you tend to take in the information at a glance.

Choose the right type of chart. This is not always easy, and is beyond the scope of this book, but in the notes section I list some resources that can help you figure out the best way to show your data.

Reduce clutter. As we discussed earlier, removing extraneous visual elements more than doubles retention and transfer.

Extraneous elements include the obvious, such as decorative pictures or elaborate effects, which don't clarify anything. If you're creating charts in Excel, there's a temptation to get all fancy with the possible effects. One of the most egregious offenders is the use of 3-D, which rarely adds valuable information and frequently distorts the information you have. There are other, less obvious extraneous elements, such as excessive grid lines, too many numbers along the axes, or too many zeros for large numbers, etc.

You can make it easier to read a graph by placing labels as close as possible to the information, or by putting in pointers to call attention to a certain data point, etc.

Tables follow a different principle than charts. They are meant to be processed in the verbal rather than the visual channel, which means that instead of taking in the message at once, you process the data sequentially.

Rather than showing the shape of the data, they are used for precision. For example, you might want to compare the performance of several different locations along various measurements. This means that a table often cannot and should not be simplified too much. You need the detail, but that's also a reason to have a paper copy that audience members can look at up close.

Animation

Most animation is irrelevant, silly, and downright distracting, so it's tempting to advise you to stay away from it entirely.

In certain limited circumstances, however, judicious use of animation can lead to enhanced clarity and improved understanding. It's useful for directing attention to a specific section of the slide you are showing at the time. If you have a complicated flowchart, for example, you can trace steps or movement through it by drawing attention to each section of the chart as you discuss it.

Animation may on certain occasions be used to build text as you discuss it. There are differing opinions on whether it's best to build your bullet lists one by one as you discuss them, and I haven't seen research which comes down on one side or the other. But if handouts can help comprehension, then there's no reason to think that you should hide text.

Some people advocate building text because it lets you control the pace of the presentation. That may actually be the best reason to show all the text at once. Based on my interviews, most senior executives prefer to ask questions as the presentation is going on, and putting all your bullets on the screen at one time gives you flexibility to vary the time you spend on one or another point, depending on the audience's reaction to the information.

If you want the best of both worlds, you can show all the text at once and then highlight each bullet as you talk about it, but be prepared to flex with the discussion.

Notes pages can be used as handouts

If you have done everything recommended in this book, you may have some good reasons to give your audience additional documentation. Although PowerPoint is not meant to be a document creator, the Notes Pages view can be used for this purpose. There is a half sheet of room for your supporting detail, which may be necessary for audience members to refer to later.

In fact, most existing slide presentations would benefit from being pasted into this view, with the slides themselves reserved for the main headline and illustration, supported by your narration.

Should you give handouts at the beginning of the presentation or save them until the end? The argument for waiting is that if you hand them out before, you run the risk of losing the audience's attention, as they read ahead. It's a valid concern, but there are good reasons to give them out beforehand.

First, research shows that when audience members can control the pace of instruction, they learn more. Classroom studies have shown that printed handouts increase test scores. Second, if they are flipping pages it can serve as an early-warning signal indicating that your audience is not interested in what you are saying at the moment. Finally, sometimes you have to drill down into detail, and it's often easier for people to follow something on paper in front of them as you talk. I've noted this in presentations I've attended — to the extent that even the speaker was not paying attention to the screen and the discussion advanced several pages beyond what was on the screen.

By the way, if you took off those extraneous visual elements on your screen slides, it's probably a good idea to put them in the handouts.

DELIVERING YOUR SLIDE PRESENTATION

Unlike a written document, a slide deck used in support of a sales presentation should not be able to stand on its own. If they ever get that good, our days as professional salespeople are numbered, and the graphic designers will begin earning all the commissions.

Effective slide presentations are like a dance between the presenter and the screen, with the presenter firmly in the lead. Remember that you are the one having the conversation with the audience, not the deck. You bring the personality, your personal perspective, and substantive detail not available on the screen.

Never forget that you are the best visual aid to bring to an executive sales presentation. Slides can complement your message, but make sure that you never let your presentation control you. You've probably seen it countless times: someone gets a decent conversation going with the audience and then is sidetracked by a slide that interrupts the main point, or forces them to go through a long list of irrelevant points just because they're bulleted up on the screen. Sometimes they're taken by surprise when their time is cut short and they are unable to adjust their presentation because they're chained to the slide order.

The best way to demonstrate confident mastery of your topic is to stay in synch with your slides. When you know what's coming next, whether it's the next bullet point or the next slide, and you can make seamless transitions with barely a glance (if that) at the screen, you absolutely radiate competence.

Synchronizing with your slides does *not* mean reading the text on the slides word for word. As we saw in the section on information transfer limitations, getting words off the screen and speaking them instead can almost double the audience's retention and transfer of the material, plus it also shows that you know your stuff. Instead, *paraphrase* the bullets, incorporating the key words in each, so the audience can follow where you are.

How do you get to the point of being in synch with your slides without reading from them?

The most obvious answer is to know your material thoroughly. That's a lot easier to do, of course, if you keep your slides simple, clean, and concise. You should also practice your transitions.

If you can't get the time to really learn your material and practice the transitions, there are several workarounds. Try to position your laptop where you can see it at a quick glance while speaking to the audience. In presentation mode in PowerPoint, with most computers you can even project a filmstrip of upcoming slides on the bottom of your laptop screen that does not show on the main screen, which will help you anticipate the next slide.

Another option is to print your slides in handout format, with six slides per page, which you can also set up directly in front of you as a reminder.

If you designed your presentation with hidden slides, you will blow away your audience with your mastery of your material by knowing how to get to the right slide instantly and then return to where you were before the interruption. There are two ways to do this in PowerPoint.

The low-tech way requires knowing your presentation thoroughly. Suppose you know that the supporting detail to a question is on slide 15, which is hidden. In presentation mode, you can punch in the number "15" and then hit *Enter*, and it will take you right to it. Of course, you will have to remember the number of the slide you were on to return to it, so this does take a bit of work and practice.

The high-tech way involves building navigation buttons into your presentation so that you can hyperlink to the appropriate slide and then return to the previous one. You can actually build these hyperlinks into your text so that they are not obvious to the audience.

Depending on the room setup, you can interact with your screen, for example standing to one side and pointing to various aspects you're talking about. Try to point at the screen while maintaining eye contact with your audience, like a TV weather announcer.

If possible, use a remote control to advance the slides so you don't have to keep walking back to the computer. Whatever you do, stay away from the laser pointer feature! If your slide is so busy that you need a pointer to orient the audience, you're definitely in trouble.

There's no law that says you have to have an image projected on the screen the entire time you are presenting. If someone asks a question that is not germane to what's on the screen at the time, it can be a distraction to leave an unrelated image up there. In situations like this, you can blank out the screen by pressing the letter "B" on your keyboard, which will turn the screen black. If you're in a dark room, press "W" for a white screen.

SUMMARY AND KEY TAKEAWAYS

The visual sense is a powerful route to persuasion — if used properly. It's critical to remember that your customers are relying on you personally to sell them, to answer their questions, and provide the credibility and trust essential to a favorable decision, so your visuals should definitely be in a supporting role.

When you design your visuals, keep these principles in mind:

- You are limited by how much visual and verbal information listeners can process at one time.

- You are the best visual aid; slides should support your talk, rather than the other way around.

- Do your thinking before you begin creating your slides.

- Emulate a billboard: use headlines, limit text, and add relevant pictures.

- Stay in sync with your slides, but do not read from them.

CASE STUDY, CONTINUED: IMS STRATEGIC SALES PRESENTATION

Based on his preparation template, Brian "storyboarded" ten slides with the following headlines:

1. *Introduction*

2. *Initial problem: Your "lucky injury"*

3. *The problem will only grow*

4. *The problem will have financial and strategic impact*

5. *Criteria for solution*

6. *A short term fix is possible*

7. *Long-term prevention vs. treating symptoms*

8. *IMS can meet your immediate and long-term needs...*

9. *...and support your strategic and financial goals*

10. *Dig your well before you're thirsty*

Brian also has twelve backup slides and supplemental handouts to be used only if necessary to answer specific questions.

PART 3: STAND AND DELIVER

If you have carefully planned and prepared your presentation according to the ideas in the previous ten chapters, that should be enough to make the sale. You've studied the needs of the buyers, have tailored a solution that meets those needs better than any competing alternative, and have crafted a message that makes perfect logical sense and is reinforced by compelling evidence. If the world were completely rational and fair, all that hard work should be guaranteed to succeed.

But the world isn't, and you could still fail.

Your audience may be sophisticated, data-driven, and logical, but they will still factor your presence and your delivery performance into their decision. "Will this expensive investment succeed?" is a difficult question. "Is this person believable?" is an easier one.

11
EXECUTIVE PRESENCE

What is executive presence? On the surface, it may seem difficult, if not impossible, to define exactly what executive presence is. We may be left in the position of Justice Potter Stewart when he said of pornography: "I know it when I see it."

Yet by defining it properly, it then becomes possible to deconstruct and examine the elements that contribute to executive presence. The earliest definition comes from Aristotle's *Rhetoric*, in which *ethos* is one of the three pillars of persuasive argumentation. Ethos is a quality of the speaker that determines whether the audience believes and trusts them. It is the impression created by your reputation, behavior, and appearance that adds to the persuasive power of your presentation.

Ethos is also specific to the audience; every audience has a different view of what constitutes credibility. Mitt Romney would be very credible to an executive audience, but probably not so much if he were to speak to Occupy Wall Street protesters.

Putting those two ideas together, we will define executive presence in this chapter as reputation, behavior, and appearance that creates a positive feeling of credibility and trust when you are among an audience of senior-level decision makers.

That definition allows us to create a model, shown in Figure 11-1, that captures the ideal elements of executive presence.

FIGURE 11-1: EXECUTIVE PRESENCE MODEL

On one side of the chart is competence: *do you know what you're talking about, and do you apply that knowledge and ability with my best interests in mind?*[19]

Competence is not enough, though, if you can't communicate effectively. Here we see five qualities that make a difference in how executives perceive you: *conviction, candor, confidence, genuineness, and curb appeal.*

We'll break down each one into its component elements.

---

[19] You will note that these questions are similar to Howard Stevens' questions in Chapter 3 (p. 64).

COMPETENCE

Audience members want to know their time in the presentation will be well spent. They're not there to be entertained; they want to know if you will bring them information that is worth listening to and that will improve their situation in some way. That boils down to two critical questions:

> *Knowledge:* Do you know what you're talking about?

> *Motives:* Do you have my interests at heart?

KNOWLEDGE

Ultimately, consultative selling requires that you bring new knowledge to your customers, so we have to turn an old sales saying on its head:

> *They don't care how much you care until they know how much you know.*

Knowledge should be the least of your worries because the very fact that you've been asked to speak indicates that you will be the most knowledgeable person in the room on that particular topic at that particular time. The trick, however, is to quickly make your competence apparent to your listeners.

An audience's perception of your competence should stem primarily from your mastery of the topic, but you can add to it by the other evidence you present. As with everything else, there is a happy medium in the task of marshaling evidence of your competence: it's possible to err on either side of giving too much or too little.

Those who are the most secure in their own competence may underestimate the need to tout their expertise and competence. If this is you, keep in mind that there is nothing wrong with tooting your own horn a little. You can't take for granted that your listener will immediately appreciate your competence, especially when they are less knowledgeable about your field.

Those who are less secure often make the opposite error and spoil the effect by trying too hard. Excessive talk about credentials can make a speaker seem either arrogant or defensive. The most effective speakers convey competence without talking too much about their credentials. Here are three useful techniques:

Personal background: Interject references to experiences that demonstrate that you've "been there, done that." The issues at hand may be new and alarming to your listener, but you've dealt with them before.

Stories and examples: When illustrating a point in your explanation, the use of stories and examples can be a great way to proclaim what you have done or seen without calling attention to yourself. In a sales presentation, the most effective ones come from the two areas that are most relevant to your audience: their own company, or similar companies facing the same issues. If you spent time in the field studying their operations, examples drawn from your time there can give you enormous credibility — sometimes you will know more than your audience does about their own operations.

Questions: A subtle way to show you understand their issues, jargon, etc., without explicitly stating the point. For example, you may ask how they are adapting their strategies to respond to the new regulations in their industry.

If you do feel you need to make your credentials explicit, try to have your sponsor do that for you.

MOTIVES

Knowledge is essential but not sufficient to establishing trust. You can be the smartest person in the room, but if the audience doesn't trust your motives, anything you say will be immediately suspect.

We turned the old cliché on its head in the last section, but it's still important that your listeners trust what you tell them, so we'll bring it back in its original version:

> *People don't care how much you know until they know how much you care.*

The best situation is to have no motives other than the good of your listeners. If you are completely disinterested — you have nothing to gain if the listener does as you advise — your credibility goes sky-high. But of course, that's not possible to do as a salesperson. They know you're there to sell them something and that you benefit if they buy.

And yet, audience members in general want to know that you are not there just for your own selfish ends. According to psychologists Valerie White and Ann Demarais, "People are highly attuned to others' interest in them. They feel it when it's there, and they feel it even more when it's missing."

You may recall the survey cited in Chapter 3 that asked senior-level executives what they valued in sales professionals. Of seven behaviors or characteristics, two of the top three were: *Will you take responsibility for my results?*, and *Will you be on our side?* In other words, potential or current customers always want to feel that you sincerely care about them. If you can get that sense across to them in your presentation, you will go a long way toward establishing trust.

You can show you care by making the presentation much more about them than it is about you. Don't fill the early part of your presentation with your corporate story or glossy pictures of your headquarters. Begin by talking about them, focusing on their situation and business improvement opportunities. Show that you've done the research and that you have created a presentation specifically for their own situation, needs, and interests. Remember the quote mentioned in the introduction: "Not tailoring your message to the audience is like addressing a love letter to whom it may concern."

Make it as personal as possible, using examples from their own industry or company. Use their names. Link back to conversations you had during the sales cycle. Get them engaged. Above all, pay attention to their reactions and adjust your presentation as necessary.

Your goal is to make every individual in that room feel as if they are personally important to you. The ideal is encapsulated in a quote by a young woman in England who said, "When I dined with Mr. Gladstone, I felt as though he was the smartest man in England. But when I dined with Mr. Disraeli, I felt as though I was the smartest woman in England."

You can also acknowledge your own interests, by bringing them out into the open. You might say something like, *Obviously, I'm biased, but I sincerely believe this is the best course for you to take. Here's why . . .*

Finally, being candid about your weaknesses contributes to a positive perception of your motives, as you will see in the next section.

COMMUNICATION

Competence is critical, but without the ability to effectively communicate your message your presentation will be like a bicycle with a flat back tire. Pump it up with these five qualities: *conviction, candor, confidence, genuineness,* and *curb appeal.*

If you can project these qualities, you should easily be able to project executive presence, even if you aren't tall, grey-haired and square-jawed.

Let's go into each quality in detail.

CONVICTION

Conviction is probably the most important element of all in projecting credibility. Your listeners may not agree with you, but they will respect and appreciate anyone who clearly and strongly believes in the proposal they are presenting. Don't be afraid to let your conviction show through.

Conviction is not the same as passion. A common theme among most presentation books is the importance of having and displaying passion for your topic. We're told that passion excites and engages audiences and furnishes you with the fire to be strong and credible. And they're mostly right: when you're trying to instill a vision, motivate your listeners, or inspire them to act on their beliefs, your passion may be the crucial ingredient that makes the difference.

But too much of a good thing comes with a cost, and too much passion can damage your credibility and effectiveness, especially for selling a complex business solution to a key customer.

The first problem is that passion makes it all about *you*, and one of the key principles of persuasive communication is that it's never about you — it's about the other person, the one you are trying to persuade. If you focus too much on why you care about the topic and how important it is to you, there's very little room for what's important to your listeners. In fact, the more passion you bring the less likely you will be to make it about the other person.

Persuasion is about reaching common ground with your listeners by building bridges from their point of view to yours. Too much passion can make it difficult for you to take their perspective and figure out where and how that bridge can be built. Too much passion can blind you to opposing points of view.

Being too wrapped up in your own point of view will also hurt you during the Q&A, first because it makes it difficult for you to prepare by thinking of any reasons someone could be against you, and during the questioning itself it can be a barrier to listening to their questions and empathizing with their objections.

Passion also smacks of emotionalism. While emotions can be contagious, they can also create their own defenses. That's why passion is especially dangerous when your audience is made up of senior-level decision makers. They have attended so many presentations in which passionate proponents have tried to sway them that they're professionally immune to passion. In fact, they've created mental antibodies that react negatively against it. They will either tune you out or take an extra-hard look at the evidence you bring to support it.

I attended a Fort Lauderdale City Commission meeting where residents were trying to fight a large building planned for construction on the edge of their neighborhood. As each speaker came up and got progressively more emotional, you could see the listeners on the dais withdraw into themselves to the point where only the mayor was making a pretense of paying any attention.

There's nothing wrong with bringing and displaying strong belief in your presentations, but make sure it's grounded in solid facts and is soundly reasoned, while being open to the other person's point of view. The word for that is conviction.

CANDOR

Politicians are notorious for answering any question with whatever spin they want to put on it, and are masters at evading direct questions. Salespeople are held to a higher standard.

Studies have shown that intelligent and sophisticated audiences respond best to appeals that recognize both sides of an issue. In these situations, it is all right to acknowledge the strengths of the opposing side. If there is a significant weakness in your own position, you will be more credible, if you bring it out rather than be perceived as trying to hide something.

Answer questions directly and honestly, without trying to skirt the central issue or concern of the questioner. Your audience will take your candor as a sign of general trustworthiness.

CONFIDENCE

As social beings, humans are exquisitely attuned to the relative power between individuals, and confident language and demeanor are our principal tools for expressing our power, so it's important to be aware of how your speech patterns affect your persuasiveness. You also need to consider the company you are in and adjust your speech patterns up or down accordingly.

Avoiding "power leaks"

We all have an interest in being perceived as credible and sure of ourselves when we speak. Of course, the best way to sound confident is to *be* confident, which comes from preparation, research, and thinking. That having been said, it's not always enough. Sometimes that which sounds so good in your head loses power as it comes out of your mouth.

For example, you may feel yourself in a subordinate position, and you might signal that feeling by "mitigating" your speech, unintentionally draining confidence out of your speech patterns.

These signals have been studied extensively by researchers in the courtroom, where persuasiveness may be a matter of life and death. They have identified five principal forms of powerless speech which sap a speaker's forcefulness:

Hedges: these are minor additions to your sentences that undermine your position.

> Prefaces: *I think that... It seems to me...*
>
> Appendages: *you know, like*
>
> Modifiers: *kinda, sort of*

Hesitations: otherwise known as filler words — *um, er, well.* We'll address filler words in more detail later in Chapter 14.

Excessive politeness: too much use of *sir* and *please* puts the speaker in a subordinate position. You want to respect your customers without sounding subservient.

Uptalk: this is a form of speech where your sentences end in rising intonation, so that a declaration sounds like a question.

Excessive Intensifiers: Using too many words like *very, definitely,* and *really* dilutes their power and may make you seem as if you're trying too hard.

If you use any of these forms of powerless speech, they're probably deeply ingrained into the way you normally talk, so it's not an easy matter to change. The first step is to practice awareness, so that you catch yourself using them. Listen to yourself, or enlist your peers to help; ask them to let you know when they hear them.

Increasing forcefulness

Now that we've looked at what not to do, let's look at positive steps that we can take to pump up the forcefulness of our speech. This hinges on verbally doing what you focused on in Chapter 8, being clear and concise.

Be clear. Einstein commented that if you can't explain it simply, you don't understand it well enough. People who are easy to understand sound like they know what they're talking about.

Be concise. Salespeople have long been taught not to "talk past the close," because once the listener is convinced, further talk makes you seem unsure of yourself. Make your point and shut up.

Finding the sweet spot of confidence

There are times when confidence can be taken too far. Mitigating your speech may lead to others to believe you are unsure of what you want, but the person who is always completely direct gets tiresome very quickly. Being too forceful may make you look defensive or shrill. Or, in a room full of big egos, someone will have a go at taking you down a peg or two.

You don't have to be forceful and direct to be persuasive; we all know people who are very persuasive and soft-spoken at the same time. Quiet speech can convey confidence by showing that you have enough faith in yourself, or in your position, that you don't need to force it.

Humility can foster deep and productive conversations. If you go in too passionate, too assertive, or even arrogant, you can easily shut down communication. Audiences that feel like they are part of the conversation will be more engaged.

Some good evidence for this comes from outside the business environment that a softer approach can be a stronger approach. In a study that tested the reactions of mock jurors to testimony from expert witnesses, it was found that medium-confidence witnesses were judged to be the most credible.

When to dial down your forcefulness

Situational factors will help you decide when it is better to tone down the forcefulness in your presentation:

When your credibility is already established. If your credibility or authority is already established, you can afford to mitigate your speech through "quiet leadership." You have earned the right to be indirect — just be sure that you are not misunderstood.

When you need input to improve your thinking. People who are assertive all the time may close off challenges to their thinking because they do not realize the chilling effect it can have on full and frank discussion. A person who dismisses doubts as negative thinking, for example, may close out valid concerns that could expose flaws in his thinking. It's especially important that you surface potential objections and concerns early in the sales cycle because they only get bigger with time. Someone who feels like they can't voice their opinion in a meeting with you will work behind the scenes to undercut your position.

When you're trying to encourage diversity of thought. There are times to persuade and times to listen. For example, when the right decision is not yet clear it helps to have a diversity of opinions, so it is important to make the atmosphere safe for people to express themselves. At these times, dial down the confidence and turn up the humility.

The best way to strike the right note, just as the best way to find the right approach in any communication, is to pay close attention to your intended audience. Know your listeners, approach them accordingly, and then pay close attention to how your message is coming across. Be direct and clear in your expression, but ask questions to understand their reaction and their thinking.

GENUINENESS

As we saw in Chapter 1, one of the key themes of this book is to be genuine, but what does that mean exactly?

It does not mean letting it all hang out or even being completely transparent and honest. It means presenting your best self for your particular situation.

You are always choosing which aspects of yourself you want to show to the world. You talk to your friends differently than you talk to your spouse or your children. You probably talk to your sales VP differently than you do with your peers. In other words, you adjust to the person you are interacting with, and that's a good thing.

Call it strategic authenticity, which is choosing how you want the world to perceive you. In other words, you do have to care about what others think. The process of caring what others think is what is going to make your messages more powerful and more persuasive. Caring about what others think and adapting your behavior and message accordingly is the one of the fundamental skills of persuasion.

There are two important limits to the practice of calculated authenticity. Most importantly, I am not advocating lying or dishonesty. Secondly, I also think it's important for your long-term credibility that the best self you present to your customers should be reasonably consistent. Be strategic, but never dishonest.

Rapport

As we saw in Chapter 2, people are more apt to agree to requests from people they like. You don't need a scientist or a book to tell you that. In fact, my main point in this section is to urge you not to rely on rapport too much in your presentation.

Rapport helps, but it's best to let it develop naturally. Don't spend too much time trying to establish "common ground" before the presentation. After my presentation in New Zealand, I heard that one of the presenters before me in New Zealand came into the room wearing an All Blacks jersey (for the NZ national rugby team). Presumably his intent was to stress his commonality with the audience, but all it did was turn them off.

Also, don't begin with a joke to "break the ice." It's too much like the stereotype of the glib salesperson. Besides, they will feel that their time is too valuable to waste with getting to know you.

The best way to get people to like you and to develop a good relationship is to take a genuine professional interest in the people in your audience and show how you can improve their lives. Believe me, they will like you better for that than for any joke you might be able to tell. As one crusty old executive told me, "If you want a friend, get a dog."

Having said that, it doesn't hurt to manage the way you come across to the audience in ways that improve your likeability. Curiously enough, research has shown that there are differences in the way men and women are evaluated on their likeability. Viewers who saw male presenters in silent videos rated them as more likeable when they used *outward-directed cues*, such as gesturing or nodding toward the audience, and of course smiling. Women were rated as more likeable when they had animated and spontaneous facial expressions.

Energy

Act like you are excited to be there. Roger Ailes, who wrote speeches for Ronald Reagan, among others, said: "An ounce of energy is worth a pound of technique." He goes on to explain further that focused energy is "an inner flame that we display when we sincerely believe something and we talk about it."

Contrast this demeanor with the perky artificial enthusiasm that a lot of corporate facilitators like to project. That's a sure way to turn off a sophisticated and, dare I say, jaded audience. Leave the fake enthusiasm at home, and instead bring a real focused energy that says you have conviction that your message brings real value to your listeners.

CURB APPEAL

We're all familiar with the old saw that you can't judge a book by its cover, yet we all do it anyway. In fact, in our increasingly distracted society, we are probably less likely to take the time to look past the cover if it does not attract us.

It's the same with your presentations: the world is not a fair place, and the unfair fact is that attractive people are more likely to get their way.

Even if they forget your words, they will retain the impression of the professionalism and authority you project. First impressions are the most important of all, as we will see in Chapter 13.

While you can't do much with what you were born with, you can improve your appearance through your dress and grooming, and by paying attention to detail.

It's tougher than it used to be to decide what to wear to a sales presentation. It used to be easy; you always wore a dark, conventional suit. Nowadays that can actually hurt you in some companies that might have a more casual approach to dress.

If you're unsure how to dress for the presentation, ask your sponsor. If that's not possible, it's better to err on the side of formality and conservatism. There's a downside risk to being dressed too informally, and very little upside. On the other hand, if you're dressed more conservatively than your audience, it paradoxically sends a signal of respect and of authority at the same time. Respect, in that you acknowledge their importance, and authority, because well-dressed people tend to be seen as more authoritative.

Regardless of how casual the dress code is at a customer site, a jacket is always a good idea. Dressing up a little gives your confidence a boost. If wearing formal business dress is unusual for you, you will probably feel special when you do put it on. There's just something about putting on that suit of armor that puts steel in your backbone and a spring in your step. Clothing has a potent effect on how competent or authoritative others judge us to be.

You can always shed that jacket or tie if you need to, but you would sure look awkward trying to put on a tie just before you begin.

SUMMARY AND KEY TAKEAWAYS

Executive presence is difficult to define, but it is real. Pay close attention to your knowledge, motives, communication style and appearance and you will be treated by even the highest-level audiences with respect and close attention.

- Don't trumpet your credentials; signal your knowledge through stories, examples, and questions.

- Show the customer you have their best interests at heart, without hiding your biases.

- Be candid and direct by admitting weaknesses and disadvantages.

- Conviction beats passion in executive presentations.

- Find the right level of confidence.

- Be genuine by being energetic and likeable.

- Appearance counts towards authority. Dress professionally — you can always adjust it down — and pay attention to details.

12
DEALING WITH NERVES

The mind is a wonderful thing. It starts working the minute you're born and never stops until you get up to speak in public.

—Roscoe Drummond

Confidence is a key element in establishing trust with a senior audience, but there's a catch. You don't always feel confident before a presentation, and even when you do, you can still feel nervous tension. In fact, chances are that you *will* be nervous, because just about everybody is when they have to make a big presentation. On top of general presentation anxiety, you're also going to be contending with the high stakes riding on the outcome (both personal and business), as well as the possible intimidation factor associated with the high rank of your audience.

If you're nervous before an important presentation, good for you! As long as you don't let your nerves overwhelm you, they can make for a better presentation. In fact, nerves are a sign that you care, and nervous tension can boost your performance.

The trick is not to try to completely eliminate your stage fright, but instead to harness it to create focus and energy for your talk. We'll look at various ways to do this, but first we need to understand a little about why it's natural — and positive — to get nervous.

THE PSYCHOLOGY OF STAGE FRIGHT

Deep in our brain are little bits of tissue, about the size and shape of an almond, collectively called the amygdala. The amygdala functions like an overly sensitive alarm system in a home, poised to detect — and instantly react to — any hint of a threat from the environment. It's automatic, decisive, and amazingly fast, causing us to react before our conscious minds are even aware of what's going on. That's why we can swerve so quickly when a car pulls out in front of us. It's also autocratic: it can override our best intentions and command our body to fight, flee, or freeze.

When the amygdala detects a threat, it triggers a flood of hormones that mobilize your sympathetic nervous system for action: the proverbial *fight, flight, or freeze response*, raising your heart rate (shallow breathing, heart flutter), redirecting the blood from your extremities to your major muscles (cold feet), and shutting down your digestive system (butterflies, dry mouth).

The amygdala is a fantastic asset in a physically dangerous environment, where threats can kill us before we can analyze the situation and devise a response. Unfortunately, it can't tell the difference between an actual physical threat and a stressful situation such as the few minutes before a presentation.

By priming your body for action, the amygdala turbocharges your capacity for action. That extra juice is what's going to propel extraordinary performance. The key is to use the boost without letting it take control of the performance — that's the difference between chokers and champions.

There's a big difference between nerves and anxiety. Nerves are caused by the physical sensations we feel when our bodies and minds are aroused for extraordinary performance. Anxiety is caused by our conscious minds *misinterpreting the physical sensations as a negative*.

So if you're feeling anxious, the first thing you have to do is change the interpretation. If you can see your nerves as a welcome gift that nature has given you, it can make all the difference. In fact, your goal is not to "relax" before a big presentation; you *want* the energy that nerves give you. Your task is to channel that energy into your best performance.

As John Eliot, expert on peak performance, reminds us:

1.   *Everything that your body does to you when the pressure is on is good for performance.*

2. *Pressure is different from anxiety; nervousness is different from worry.*

It's not about eliminating the pressure; it's about performing at your best *because* of the pressure. After all, as the philosopher Thomas Carlyle said: "No pressure, no diamonds."

TWELVE TECHNIQUES FOR PERFORMING UNDER PRESSURE

Here are a dozen tried and tested ideas and techniques to help you perform at your best in spite of your nerves — and possibly even because of them.

These ideas come from my own experience (and I have a *lot* of experience with being nervous before presentations!), from the ideas of some of the top speakers around today, and from field of sports psychology.

Some of these contradict each other, but that's because different people react in different ways.

1. Realize that you are the expert.

Remember that you have been asked to speak because you know more about your topic than anyone in the room.

People in the audience may have greater technical knowledge and they certainly know more about their own business than you do, but as the account manager, you know the big picture better than anyone else in the room. You know more about how your particular solution helps this specific customer with their unique situation at this particular time.

You should also feel good knowing that your solution is going to improve your customer's situation — it's going to make their lives better in some way, right? You know it's the best thing for them and you're excited to get started.

Finally, please take the time to reflect that your mind has made this out to be a bigger problem that it actually is. As renowned baseball coach and consultant H.A. Dorfman put it:

Fear is a monstrous liar. It tells us that situations are more threatening and harder to handle that they truly are, and it tells us we aren't capable of dealing successfully with these situations...The Monster, fear, breaks down our confidence, brainwashes us, makes us play losing mental games. And we built the Monster!

2. Be extremely well prepared.

Know what you are talking about, do your homework, and rehearse your speech. Thorough preparation equals total confidence. If you've taken the steps to shape the conditions for success, you are as well prepared as anyone could be. You know what is important to each person, you have crafted a presentation that addresses their needs better than any alternatives, and you probably have strong supporters who will help you succeed — all because of your superior preparation.

Remember the story about Jack Welch's preparation in Chapter 1? That's the best way to deal with nerves — be so excited by your preparation that you *can't wait* to get there and deliver your presentation.

If you're nervous because you did not prepare, you deserve to be.

3. Practice realistically.

No matter how good steps one and two make you feel, your body may still show signs of nerves. Even the best-trained athletes feel this when they show up for the game. This is where "muscle memory" that comes from practice can take over until you get going.

Try to practice under stress if possible. You can't exactly simulate the nerves you will feel in practice, of course, but you should try to make your practice as close as you can to the real thing. Practice in front of peers, if possible. A lot of the salespeople in my classes tell me they actually find this more intimidating than speaking to customers, so getting through the practice makes the real thing seem like a breeze.

Other people get incredibly nervous when they see a video camera pointed their way, so you might find this to be another helpful way to introduce stress to your practice. Of course, it has the added benefit of allowing you to evaluate yourself and make improvements.

4. Understand that your audience does not want you to fail.

In almost every case, the audience wants you to do well; they truly want to you to succeed — unless your success is going to harm their interests in some way — and even then, it's usually not personal. Also, they know how hard it is; most executives have seen more than a few high-pressure situations themselves.

Even if they are not actively pulling for you, they probably don't care that much. They are there to evaluate a purchasing opportunity for their company, not to watch you perform. To you, that presentation may be the most important thing going on in your life for quite some time; to them, it's business as usual. The point is that they are usually not paying that much attention to you as a person, and they're definitely not wasting too much time focusing on what you're feeling inside. Sorry, but it's the truth.

Because of that, they are not as aware of your jitters as you think they are. They're not mind readers. Although your own internal state is uppermost in your mind, it usually does not show to the audience.

5. Bond with your audience.

Unless it's an initial introductory presentation, you will probably already have at least one champion and several allies in the room whose interests coincide with yours. If you've shaped the conditions for success, it's practically guaranteed.

Keep the audience on your side; help them to help you. It can start even before the presentation. Make it a point to introduce yourself to audience members as they come in. Then, pick a few friendly faces and talk directly to those folks. Make eye contact with supportive people in the audience. Remember, you don't speak to an "audience"; you speak to real people in the audience.

Honestly work to value your audience and show them respect and gratitude for their attention and time, and they will do the same for you.

6. Focus on the process, not the outcome.

Self-help gurus constantly tell us to envision success, and success will somehow happen. Visualization is an extremely beneficial practice to improve your performance, but only if you envision the actual steps you will take to ensure success, not just the success itself. As Heidi Grant Halvorsen tells us in her book, *Succeed,*

> *Mentally simulating the process of achieving the goal, rather than the hoped-for outcome, not only results in a more optimistic outlook, but in greater planning and preparation. Picture yourself doing what it takes to succeed, and you will soon find yourself believing that you can.*

7. Focus externally.

If you spend too much time dwelling on how nervous you feel, it will only make you even more nervous. Shift your attention to the audience, to your surroundings, to your notes — anything but your own internal state of mind. This has the added benefit of making you appear confident.

Instead of focusing on how you are feeling, notice how the audience is feeling and reacting to your message.

8. Reframe: "Welcome, my familiar friend."

Despite what FDR told us, fear itself is nothing to fear. You can choose how to interpret it.

Embrace your nervousness as a natural and a positive feeling. It shows that you care. In my own experience, in the rare times when I was not nervous at all, my performance came across as a bit flat. Nerves are a manifestation of the fight or flight response that your brain and body go through to gear up for superior performance.

When you see your jitters as an asset instead of a liability, you will be better able to deal with them. I generally get them a few minutes before the presentation, and I tell myself, "Here they are, right on schedule!"

Another way to reframe is to view this presentation opportunity as a can't-lose situation. If you did not make the presentation, you would not get the sale. Just like a lottery, you can't win if you don't play, and your odds are infinitely better because you control them. If you don't get the sale, you're no worse off than you were before you went in. In fact, you're better off no matter what because you have faced your fears and you have learned something.

9. Label your feelings.

Labeling is one of the newer techniques for calming yourself that has not been covered much yet in presentations literature, although I believe it will be because it can be so effective and because it has solid scientific validation behind it.

The essence of labeling is to put into words (mentally, not out loud), what you are feeling when you are nervous, anxious or even on the verge of a panic attack.

It works because excessive nerves are the result of your amygdala being on the verge of hijacking your nervous system. When you face a condition of extreme danger, it's useful for your primitive brain to take over. It can respond much faster than conscious thought and allows you to perform physical feats you would ordinarily have no chance of doing.

But in other stressful situations, and certainly in presentations, it's critical to keep your logical faculties in control. Labeling, by forcing you to form the words in your mind, engages your prefrontal cortex (PFC), and this helps put it back in control. Studies conducted using functional MRI machines actually show the blood in the brain flowing from the amygdala to the PFC when subjects are put under stress and try the technique.

When you use labeling, you have to be honest with yourself. Self-affirmation, the old advice that the motivational types always push on us (*I'm not nervous. I feel great. I'm totally confident.*), is bogus and can backfire. Your brain knows you're lying; it won't be fooled and will probably leave you feeling less confident.

10. Breathe deeply.

A few deep breaths can have a wonderful calming effect. Without getting too technical, breathe from your diaphragm. Your deep breath should puff out your belly, not your chest; that way you know you are pulling the air deep into your lungs. Just don't be too obvious about it.

Follow that with a long, slow breath. Making your exhale longer than your inhale has the opposite effect of hyperventilation. It's both calming and energizing.

11. Fake it 'til you make it.

Your nervousness will be far more apparent to you than it will be to observers. If you act confident, your psychology will follow your physiology. Believe it or not, your mind often takes cues from your body to determine how it's feeling. By adopting an expansive pose for two minutes before a presentation or an important meeting you can increase testosterone levels (women too) and decrease cortisol levels, which will cause you to feel more powerful and reduce your stress, helping you present a more confident and relaxed demeanor to the listener.

As we will see in Chapter 14, behaviors that project confidence include taking up space, defying gravity in the form of erect posture with head raised, and having an open stance. Just remember what your mother told you: "Stand up straight, speak up, look people in the eye, and smile." This will do wonders for your state of mind. It will also put others at ease. Confidence is an emotion, and if they feel confident in you they will project that back to you and it can become a positive feedback loop.

When you're introduced, walk confidently to wherever you will speak from and look at your audience for a moment with a friendly and confident smile before you begin speaking. That momentary pause and gaze will project a tremendous amount of confidence.

12. Start strong.

It's a good idea to memorize your introduction. It will give you the confidence of knowing that you can operate on autopilot during the first stressful moments. Once you get going, you will most likely be so focused on the audience and the presentation that you won't even think about being nervous.

A strong start is so important that it's the subject of most of the next chapter.

SUMMARY AND KEY TAKEAWAYS

Nerves are normal before important presentations, and in fact can be harnessed to improve your performance.

1. Realize that you are the expert.

2. Be extremely well prepared.

3. Practice realistically.

4. Know that your audience does not want you to fail.

5. Bond with your audience.

6. Focus on the process, not the outcome.

7. Focus externally — that is, on your audience.

8. Reframe by welcoming your nervous energy.

9. Label your feelings.

10. Breathe deeply, with a long, slow exhale.

11. Fake it 'til you make it.

12. Start strong.

13
PERFORMING: FROM REHEARSAL THROUGH THE FIRST SIXTY SECONDS

He has little or no patience for anything but excellence from himself or others.

—Mike Evangelist

The above quote is from an ex-Apple employee, describing Steve Jobs' famously perfectionistic approach to presentations (and life). Your presentation is a performance that can be improved through careful attention to the details at each step. This chapter is about everything you need to do to ensure a smooth and effective production.

REHEARSAL

This is one of the most important — and most-often-skipped — activities in all of executive sales presentations.

The rehearsal step is most often skipped for three reasons. The reason most often given is the least valid: you don't have time. That answer is totally unacceptable and unworthy of a true professional. Your time in front of high-level decision makers is the most highly leveraged use of your time that you can have. If you don't have time to make sure you're at your best, how do you find time for all the other things you do in your work life?

The second reason is complacency. Maybe it's an established customer that has been with you for a while, or you think your offer is so good that it can't fail. Trust me, it can. No matter how strongly positioned you think you are, a little healthy paranoia never hurt any sales professional.

The third reason is that you think you're better on your feet. You haven't gotten to where you are by being slow on the uptake; you know you can do well in unscripted situations. You may actually be right: you can do well in unscripted situations. But you can always do better when you have planned and rehearsed.

Things always sound better in your head. Until you've actually said something out loud, you just don't know for sure how it's going to sound, and how it's going to come across to your listeners.

Besides, if you don't care enough to practice, why should they care enough to listen?

When you do rehearse, try to make it as close as possible to the real thing, from the type of room, to the number of people.

Begin rehearsals early. You may find out that there is a gap in your presentation or a need for additional information, and getting an early start gives you time to fix it.

Time yourself. In addition to helping you be concise, strict time limits impose discipline on your presentations. If your presentation rehearsals vary widely in their timing, it's a clear indication that your structure is too loose. You may be leaving things out or overexplaining other parts, and you have no idea of how it's going to go when you do the real thing. When you stay within a narrow window, it shows that your content is well-organized and that you know it.

If you really want to go the extra mile in your rehearsal, try giving your presentation at least once without slides. It won't be perfect, but it will either give you the confidence of knowing your material or it will expose areas where you might need to learn it better.

As painful as the prospect seems, you should also videotape your rehearsal and then look at it. Outside feedback is very important, but sometimes you need to see and hear yourself in action to make the necessary improvements.

Steve Jobs was a master presenter, and such was his effect on audiences that he could probably read the phone book for fifteen minutes and get a standing ovation. Yet Jobs would typically begin rehearsing two days before each presentation. The first day would be relatively informal, with Jobs testing various approaches. The day before the presentation would have at least one and often two full dress rehearsals. Of course, your sales presentations probably won't move the stock market to the tune of several billion dollars, but I'll bet they're pretty important to you.

WHEN YOU ARRIVE

One absolutely ironclad rule is to get there early. Murphy's Law can strike at any time, and by definition it will at the worst possible time. You can't escape it, but the best way to mitigate it is to have time to recover when things do go wrong.

Make sure you have time to set up properly and deal with unexpected contingencies, such as projectors that don't communicate with your laptop, incorrect room setup, understanding the lighting system, extension cords, etc.

Having a few minutes in the surroundings can also make you more comfortable. Getting there late, on the other hand, can get you flustered as you race to get everything prepared and connected properly.

BRING SPARES

Always assume that something will break or get lost or not connect at the worst possible time. If you're delivering a slide presentation, have backups — and not all in the same luggage, either. If you've ever arrived at a hotel in China only to find out that your laptop somehow gave up the ghost somewhere over the International Date Line, it's a lesson you'll never forget.

GREET PARTICIPANTS AS THEY ARRIVE

It's good practice to arrive early and have everything set up properly, with enough time before the formal part of the presentation to greet and get acquainted with people as they come in. Learn their names if possible. Besides helping to create a personal connection, it can also ease your nerves a bit.

As we've seen, getting to know audience members as people before your speech is one of the most effective ways to alleviate stage fright. It gives you friendly faces to speak to. You can even develop common ground with your audience if you are speaking to a group.

If you have a chance to talk to individuals as they arrive, show interest in them: who they are, what they do, what they might be looking for from your presentation, etc. It's a great way to build rapport and to get information that might be useful during your presentation.

HAVE A STRONG OPENING

Most audiences spend the first sixty seconds sizing up the speaker and making a judgment about them that will affect the entire program.

People form unconscious opinions about your competence and trustworthiness in that first minute, and because of quirks in the way the mind works these opinions are very resistant to modification. The first impression you make is in effect a filter through which they evaluate the rest of what you say.

THE SCIENCE OF FIRST IMPRESSIONS

Let's go back to see what psychology tells us about first impressions:

Halo effect

There's a scene in the movie *Moneyball* that wonderfully captures one of the most important hidden influences that affects our judgment and decision making. The Oakland A's manager, Billy Beane, is presiding at a meeting in which his scouts are discussing prospects they like. The discussion is heavy on references to looks, such as "He has a strong jaw" — as if that has any correlation at all to the real question: can he produce runs? Another does not like a prospect because he has an ugly girlfriend; it tells him the player lacks confidence.

The scouts were showing a bias called the *halo effect*, and it has a powerful influence on the success of your persuasive efforts. The halo effect means that we have a tendency to let a judgment of a particular trait affect our judgment of other unrelated traits. For example, attractive individuals also tend to be perceived by others as more competent or likeable.

Because of the halo effect, we may perceive individuals differently depending on the situation, or may perceive the situation differently depending on the individual.

In *The Halo Effect*, former Harvard Business School professor Phil Rosenzweig told the story of two executives. One was described as "charismatic, bold and visionary." The other was seen as "arrogant, imperial, and resistant to criticism."

Who were they? "They" were the same person, Percy Barnevik. As the CEO of Swedish multinational ABB in the mid-1990s, when his company was turning in stellar performance, he was widely seen as one of the best business leaders in the world. Several years later, the company ran into difficulties, and Barnevik's traits were then seen in a totally different light. I suppose it's possible that he had undergone a fundamental change in his personality during that time (maybe all the adulation went to his head). But it's more likely that one obvious external characteristic, company performance, fundamentally affected how others saw the less obvious internal traits.

The halo effect (and its less positive corollary, the *horns effect*) is why first impressions are so important. When you meet a customer for the first time, or during the first moments of a presentation, the impression they form will color their perception of any additional information they hear.

Anchoring

In Chapter 8, we saw how anchoring can skew the perception of numbers. The same effect also applies to judgments about people.

Here's a simple demonstration from an experiment by Solomon Asch:

> **Alan**: intelligent, industrious, impulsive, critical, stubborn, envious
>
> **Ben**: envious, stubborn, critical, impulsive, industrious, intelligent

Most people would rate Alan more favorably than Ben because the initial positive descriptors affect the perception of the others.

If the first judgment your audience makes about you is that you are nervous, weak or unorganized, it's going to drag down any other perceptions that follow.

Thin slices

First in Chapter 2, and then again in Chapter 9, we alluded to studies demonstrating that people form remarkably accurate impressions of certain characteristics with very short exposures to other people. In fact, they can't help it; the impressions are made automatically without conscious effort. The few studies that have been done with salespeople confirm the effect. In one, involving professional purchasing managers who viewed videotapes of sales role plays, it was found that brief exposures led them to form impressions of believability, based on such cues as eye contact and hesitations.

The science of first impressions means that it is critical not to leave your first impression to chance. Your audience's attention is at a peak. You have only one chance to make a good first impression.

YOU CAN EASILY AVOID A BAD OPENING

It's nice to have a strong start, but it's not essential. What *is* critical is to avoid common mistakes that guarantee a negative impression on the audience. Negative initial impressions are difficult to recover from, especially in the time you have. That's because your listeners will be less disposed to pay attention to anything positive you might do or say. It can take many positive behaviors to overcome the impact of *one* initial negative behavior.

Here are the top three easy-to-avoid paths to a bad opening:

Starting late. A late start either shows disrespect, incompetence, or disorganization.

Apologizing. Have you ever heard a speaker say, "Sorry, I didn't have too much time to prepare, but..."? Instant bad impression.

Inappropriate story. If you haven't figured out by now that I oppose starting with a joke, it may be too late. But seriously, even if you begin with a true story, make sure that it is relevant and appropriate to the topic and the occasion.

GET THINGS STARTED OFF RIGHT

Here are some ways to break out of traditional weak patterns and start strong:

Memorize your introduction. I don't advocate memorizing your presentation, but I do make an exception for the introduction. This does not mean that you should recite it mechanically as if reading from a script, but you should know it well enough so that even if you get a momentary mental hiccup you will be able to start strong. It will ensure that you begin strongly and confidently.

Don't begin with opening amenities. Most speakers begin with a brief self-introduction, or greetings to the audience, followed by little courtesies such as thanking them for taking the time. Remember in Chapter 2 where we talked about the qualities of messages that make them memorable? One of them is surprise. When you break an expected pattern people take immediate notice.

Why not just start talking? They will already know who you are, because it is on the meeting agenda. If you're not comfortable omitting these opening amenities entirely, you can begin with your introduction, then take a momentary aside to say hello or introduce yourself if you think you need to. You usually don't.

Begin with the screen blanked out. This way all eyes will be on you. Launch into your opening remarks, and then bring up the first image you want to present.

Begin with a question. Questions engage the brain and beg for an answer. If you ask a question for which you expect an answer in return, don't be afraid of silence as people ponder the question and decide who is going to answer it.

A HOSTILE OR SKEPTICAL AUDIENCE

Those techniques work well when the audience is neutral or favorable to your point of view, but when they are skeptical of your position to begin with, or downright hostile to it, the game changes.

Consider the skeptical audience's state of mind as they're waiting for you to begin. They already hold a point of view on the topic that is opposed to yours. Because people have a strong tendency to ignore or actively oppose information that contradicts their beliefs, the natural reaction against someone who states an opposing idea right up front is to shut down attention, or to listen only with the intent to refute. That's not a good place for your audience to be when you are speaking to them. The result is not a dialogue, but two competing monologues, the one you are delivering and the one in their heads which is arguing against yours.

Politicians have a lot of experience talking to skeptical audiences, so I would like to share an example from that arena that will illustrate the approach you should take to get their attention.

In 1983, Ted Kennedy accepted an invitation from Jerry Falwell, the leader of the Moral Majority, to speak at Liberty Baptist College in Virginia. It could have easily been a disaster — one of the most liberal members of the Senate speaking to a group that was actively opposed to most of what he stood for.

Kennedy may not have changed many minds that day, but he did accomplish something very important: he got his audience to listen to him.

Your first task is to get them to lower their guard enough so that they will pay attention to your message.

How did Kennedy get his audience to lower their guard? Although I don't normally advocate opening a speech with humor, I make an exception with a skeptical audience.

> *Actually, a number of people in Washington were surprised that I was invited to speak here — and even more surprised when I accepted the invitation. They seem to think that it's easier for a camel to pass through the eye of the needle than for a Kennedy to come to the campus of Liberty Baptist College.*

Humor can help to disarm their defenses, especially if you direct it at yourself. Humor works by putting the audience into a good mood and shows you as a real person. It's harder to dislike a person than a position. Notice that Kennedy not only poked a bit of fun at himself, but also, by using a reference from the Bible, used the language of his audience.

When you view a video of his speech, you see the audience laughing and clapping, and I'd like to imagine that you can see their minds and ears opening slightly. Sometimes the smallest gap is enough to get a handhold so that you can make the difficult climb to agreement.

What Kennedy said next pried open their minds just a bit more. He went on to say,

> *I know we begin with certain disagreements; I strongly suspect that at the end of the evening some of our disagreements will remain. But I also hope that tonight, and in the months and years ahead, we will always respect the rights of others to differ, that we will view ourselves with a sense of perspective and a sense of humor.*

In this second passage, Kennedy accomplishes two things. By telling the audience that he expects disagreements will remain, he makes it "safe" for them to listen to his point of view. In effect, he's saying, "Relax, put your guard down; I'm not going to hit you." He then appeals to a larger principle that they will find it hard to disagree with, that they should respect the right of others to differ.

The third passage demonstrates another way to disarm them: acknowledge their position and concerns.

The separation of church and state can sometimes be frustrating for women and men of religious faith . . .

Kennedy validates their frustration without agreeing with it. You may want to go even further: make their case for them; describe their position and reasoning, and even amplify it.

This does two things. It shows them that you are open-minded and took the time to study and understand their position, and they will tend to reciprocate your open-mindedness. It also surprises them a little because it is not what they expect. It shows you to be an intelligent, fair-minded individual.

By the time Kennedy gets to this third passage, he is already well into his speech, without yet trying to state his position. While I've said frequently that you should front-load your message, it can actually be the wrong approach to use when your audience already holds a different point of view. When they hear a challenge to their side before they're ready, they're likely to tune out the rest of what you say.

The final step is to find common ground between your position and theirs. Show them where you both agree. Change the color of the argument — instead of black and white arguing against each other, move the discussion into the neutral grey zone where agreement is possible.[20] Kennedy does this by showing that Dr. Falwell himself had been attacked by groups further to the right than his, and then he appeals to his and the audience's common heritage as Americans.

Get them to put down their guard, open their ears, and at least be willing to listen — then and only then will you have a chance to sway skeptics to your side. It requires tact, timing, and nuance, but it's the ultimate challenge that lets you know you've arrived as a speaker.

---

[20] It's the "small agreement" you saw in Chapter 6 (p. 115).

SUMMARY AND KEY TAKEAWAYS

The most finely crafted presentation still depends for its success on your performance in front of your audience, and great performances don't happen without painstaking attention to preparation and detail.

- Adequate and timely rehearsal provides confidence and improves the expression of your ideas.

- Arrive early and set up, so that you can be relaxed and professional.

- Because first impressions are so important, you must have a strong opening.

- If your audience is skeptical to begin with, your most important task is to get them to listen.

14
PLATFORM SKILLS

Stand up straight, look people in the eye, and smile.

—Mom

Your mother probably told you something like the quote above when you were quite young. It was excellent advice then, and it summarizes this chapter quite nicely.

There is no magic to platform skills. Some people seem to think that body language is the most important aspect of speaking in front of groups. Presentation trainers and books repeat the myth that 93% of communication is nonverbal. That statistic was based on one very narrowly focused study that was conducted years ago and somehow became "common knowledge." If it were true, we wouldn't need to learn foreign languages, but then we wouldn't get too much out of listening to the radio, either!

Without a strong proposition and a well-structured presentation, the best gestures in the world won't make your sale for you.

That said, the fact remains that we influence via both System 1 and System 2 thinking, and your physical presence sends cues that your listeners' minds are hardwired to take into account when evaluating your overall message. Remember that the substitution principle states that when we are faced with a difficult question, our mind often substitutes an easier question. Instead of answering the question *Will this large investment pay off?*, we may unconsciously answer the question *Do I trust this person who is telling me it will?*

Your platform skills send messages about your candor, confidence, and conviction, helping them answer the easier question,.

THE SKILLS

If you have to think about everything you do during a presentation, there are a lot of different skills to keep track of. Fortunately, as an intelligent and articulate adult, you already do most of these competently. The four principal skill areas are:

- Voice

- Face

- Gestures

- Posture and movement

VOICE

Your voice should portray friendliness, honesty and authority. While you probably already convey these characteristics in everyday conversation, the challenge of speaking in front of groups can rob your voice of its normal qualities. It's important therefore to be aware of how you sound, and to practice modulating your voice. Pay attention to:

Variety: Vocal variety is the best way to keep the audience engaged and to show your personality and energy, while a monotone is the best way to have your audience nodding off or heading for the exits. You can vary your volume, pitch, and speed to create a dynamic and interesting effect.

Volume: Most sales presentations are going to be in front of reasonably small audiences, so you're probably not going to have to worry too much about projecting your voice. Just pay attention to the size of the room and speak loudly enough so that those furthest from you can hear you. An exception is when you want to gain the audience's rapt attention: speak at a volume just above what they can hear.

Speed: Most speakers err on the side of speaking too fast, propelled by nervousness. Be aware of your speed. Slow down individual words, the speed of sentences, and the pauses between phrases.

If you naturally talk fast, that's not necessarily a problem. In fact, faster talkers can be seen as more believable, more sure of their information. But you should pause occasionally for emphasis and to allow listeners time to process important points.

Pauses: Well-timed pauses can be your most effective tools for controlling your rate of speech, emphasizing important points, and projecting confidence. They also help to avoid the use of filler words, about which more below.

Articulation: Speak clearly, without slurring or clipping your words. Pronounce words fully, which may make you sound slightly more formal than in ordinary speech, but will sound normal in front of an audience. This becomes especially important when you speak to international audiences. Even with domestic audiences, it is increasingly common to encounter people in the audience for whom English is not their first language.

To work on your voice,

> *Practice all or part of your speech delivery.* You'll soon find that the more times you practice, the more natural it begins to sound.

> *Record your voice and listen to yourself.* It will sound funny at first, but it is what you actually sound like to others.

> *Practice words that you normally clip or mispronounce.* Articulate them fully, exaggerating the movements of your mouth.

Fluency: Many people, when they get nervous during a presentation, will fall back on filler words or crutch words such as "ah" or "um" when trying to gather their thoughts.

I don't generally believe in zero tolerance for filler words; they're a natural part of conversational speech because they serve as useful signals to your dialogue partner when they can speak without interrupting. But because presentations are more one-way than conversations, they can become distracting to an audience. If the habit becomes too strong, they can drain the power from your speech (as we saw in Chapter 11), and your entire presentation can be jeopardized.

The first cure for filler words is awareness. Ask someone to keep track during your practice, or watch yourself on video, because you're not always the best judge of how often you use them.

If you know you're using them, learn to be comfortable with silence. It is far better to pause for just a second, to buy a moment to collect your thoughts and get back on track. The silence will seem to be about three times as long to you as it does to the audience — don't let it intimidate you. When you pause, keep your eyes on the audience.

Crutch words are another sort of filler; they are specific words that a speaker gets "hooked" on and will repeat over and over again throughout the presentation. Some common crutch words include: *basically, actually, honestly, frankly, well, to be honest, okay, you know, as a matter of fact,* and the current favorites, *like* and *so.*

The key to avoiding crutch words is to develop a wide array of different transition words that you can interchange throughout your talk.

EYE CONTACT

Turning to the visual aspects of platform skills, we begin with eye contact because it is the single most important aspect of body language. Research has shown that listeners pay far more attention to the speaker's eyes than to any other part of the body: 43% of the time, compared to the second-most, the mouth.

Even without the research, we instinctively know this to be true. To stress the importance of eye contact, think of what you infer about people who don't look you in the eyes when you talk to them. You wonder if they're ignoring you, are lying, or maybe just lack confidence.

There's a good reason listeners pay so much attention to your eyes: they can be incredibly expressive and brutally honest. They are quite literally windows into your brain as you speak.

Eye contact makes you more persuasive. It's easier to ignore someone if there is no eye contact, which is why we tend to avert our eyes when a panhandler approaches us on the street, and why people sitting next to a vacant middle seat on Southwest Airlines look away when you walk down the aisle looking for a place to sit.

It makes you more credible, even with people who are not the target of the gaze. Courtroom research shows that witnesses who look at the cross-examining attorney are perceived as more credible with juries.

It can make you seem more powerful. You assert power by looking at others while talking to them and looking away while listening to them. I don't advocate the latter, but the former will definitely make you seem more dominant.

The eyes can be very expressive of genuine emotion. At least unconsciously, listeners are calibrating the emotional content of your words against the message conveyed by your eyes.

Finally, eye contact also helps you maintain your audience focus and awareness. How are they responding? Are they listening, or tuning out? Do they look confused? Do they agree with your message?

With so much riding on your eyes, you can't leave it to chance. The most important rule is to look your listeners in the eyes when you speak to them. Although that seems obvious, too many presenters violate the rule either out of sheer nervousness or by spending too much time looking at their own slides. Keep your slides uncluttered and make sure you know your material.

To ensure that you keep the visual connection, think of your listeners not as an audience, but as a group of individuals, each of whom is critically important to the success of your presentation. Most sales presentation audiences will be small enough that it's realistic to try to make direct eye contact with everyone.

Scan the room, but make sure you look at one person for a second or two and then move on, or you'll look like a human sprinkler. Your gaze can linger on one person immediately after making an important point, but don't lock on for more than about two seconds or it can get uncomfortable.

You can also kick up the level of personal engagement by providing "customized eye contact" — when you make a point that is most relevant to a particular person in the room, look directly at that person. Some of the best moments in sales presentations occur when you seem to be momentarily having a private conversation with one person, and you are rewarded with a nod of agreement. (Of course, you can be even more overt about it and use their name).

Finally, be aware that it's possible to err on the side of too much eye contact. There are two likely scenarios where this can happen. The most common mistake salespeople make is to focus too much on the most important person in the room. Since their opinion counts for so much, it's natural to be more concerned with their reactions, but it can cause you to ignore others in the room. The other problem is to spend too much time monitoring the reactions of the one skeptic or opponent in the room. If it's not going well, it can make you uncomfortable or throw you off your message. Unless they have veto power over the decision, your eye time would be better invested with the other influencers in the room.

FACIAL EXPRESSIONS

Your face can be very evocative and communicative, especially if you make effective eye contact. We saw in Chapter 11 that, especially for women, people perceive you as more likeable when your facial expressions are animated and spontaneous.

The best facial expression is a *sincere* smile.

Keep your expressions natural, although it's alright to exaggerate slightly so that those in the back of the room will not miss your nuance.

If you want to work on facial expressiveness, you can watch videos of your own rehearsals or actual presentations, or practice in front of a mirror.

GESTURES

Gestures and hand movements can help you tell a better story and be a more effective communicator.

There was a FedEx commercial where a low-ranking employee suggests opening an online account to save shipping costs. No one responds. A few seconds later, the boss says exactly the same thing, only this time using emphatic gestures. Everyone cheers and adopts the solution. When the young guy points out that he suggested the same idea, the boss says, "But you didn't use the chop," as he karate-chops the air.

That scene may be a bit exaggerated, but the fact is that many speakers unconsciously disarm themselves by imprisoning their hands while they speak. Gestures are performance boosters for almost any presentation: they add information, help you think, and help to convey authenticity and energy.

Gestures supplement your words with visual information. Here's a simple experiment you can do yourself to demonstrate the difference. Try giving someone complicated directions (go three blocks, then take a left and veer right at the fork…) without using gestures. It's hard for you to do, and harder for them to understand the instructions, because the added clues provided by your gestures make it easier for them to envision spatial information.

Research results are unclear on whether gestures make it any easier for your audience to understand your message, but there is no evidence that gestures interfere with understanding.

Gestures actually improve your ability to think while speaking. In *Hearing Gesture*, researcher Susan Goldin-Meadow says, "Giving an explanation while gesturing actually takes less cognitive effort that giving an explanation without gesturing." In experiments, speakers given more difficult speaking tasks gestured more, and they recalled more information.

There's also evidence that it can help you be more fluent, although it's not conclusive. Goldin-Meadow cites studies in which speakers who were told to restrain their hands had more pauses. If that's true, gesturing might even help you limit your filler words.

Certain gestures can indicate high confidence on the part of the speaker, such as the forceful chopping gesture and steepling of the fingers. Conversely, there are some common gestures speakers use that indicate a lack of confidence — wringing hands, and touching the neck and face, for example.

Keeping the hands, and especially the palms, visible indicates openness. Body language expert Joe Navarro says: "When the hands are out of sight or less expressive, it detracts from the perceived quality and honesty of the information being transmitted." Research in courtrooms indicates that jurors find lawyers and witnesses less credible when they can't see their hands. This makes evolutionary sense, as there is clear survival value in being able to see a potential adversary's hands. It seems we're hardwired to pay close attention to hand movements.

Gestures add energy. Speakers who actively gesture are more dynamic and hold the audience's attention for longer. Gestures also have the effect of taking up more space in the room, which is perceived as a sign of confidence and dominance.

There's a paradox, though. The more you think about your gestures, the worse off you may be. If you make an active effort to incorporate strong gestures into your speaking style, you're probably going to make a mess of it unless you have a *lot* of practice. This is because you can't completely separate verbal and nonverbal communication. Gestures are not separate from speech. In fact, spontaneous gestures tend to begin *before* the words come out.

Without enough practice to make them automatic, scripted gestures are guaranteed to be ever-so-slightly mistimed. Your listeners will perceive them as fake, even if they can't consciously tell you why they feel that way. For a very clear demonstration of this, watch Tiger Woods' first press conference after his very public marital scandal. His movements were obviously rehearsed (for example when he placed his palm on his chest to indicate his personal responsibility), and his apology seemed forced and unnatural.

Trained actors with years of experience can do it, but you have a lot more important things to do with your time.

Free your hands

Since you don't have all that time, there is one simple thing you can do which will take you most of the way there: just *free your hands*. Let them find their own natural level while you talk. When your hands are free to do what they want to do naturally, they get in synch with your words, and you come across as natural because you are natural. Whether you use large, sweeping movements or small subtle ones, they are part of who you are.

There are several ways that nervous speakers imprison their hands. Do you clasp your hands at crotch level in front of you? That's called the fig-leaf. Maybe you clasp them behind you, making you look like you're handcuffed. Hands folded across your chest make you look nervous and defensive, and hands in pockets are worst of all, especially when you start jangling coins or keys.

It's OK to rest your hands in these positions briefly during a talk, but be sure you don't do it too long. This might take a little practice (you can't get away from that, can you?).

Free your hands and let them do what they want to do while you speak — they will definitely add power to your words. You look more confident, and you add life and fluency to your talk. If the eyes are a window on the soul, the hands help to open the front door.

Eliminate negative gestures

Besides imprisoning your hands, you may send messages to your audience that you are nervous or anxious if you do any of the following:

Self-touching: These movements, such as touching your hair or your face, are also called *adaptors*. Women tend to cover their throats with their hands when they're nervous.

Fidgeting: This includes anxiously pacing back and forth, swaying, etc.

Nervous hands and fingers: Especially when you're holding something such as notes or markers, your digits can really get going. I used to do a lot of training using flipcharts, and I would uncap and cap the markers repeatedly, which I only noticed at the end of the day because my outspread fingers resembled a rainbow.

Holding the lectern with a white-knuckle death grip: Pretty self-explanatory. If you're speaking from a lectern, use it to support your notes, not your hands.

POSTURE AND MOVEMENT

There are three major rules to follow with regard to posture:

1. Be open. Facing people squarely and openly sends a message that you are not hiding anything and that you are willing to be vulnerable.

2. Take up space. Confident and dominant people tend to take up a lot of space. They have expansive gestures, their feet are spread apart, their arms are away from their bodies, etc.

3. Defy gravity. Have an erect posture, smile, keep your head up.

Whether you stand behind a lectern or move around in front of the audience may be answered for you already depending on how the room is set up and whether you have a microphone that is fixed in one place.

If you have a choice, speaking without a lectern can help you project confidence and add variety to your speech, but keep the following tips in mind:

Have a purpose for your movements. Nervous pacing back and forth will only distract your audience.

It's best to keep still while delivering complex information or in the middle of a point. Move during transitions between points.

Make your movements decisive. Don't just shuffle a few nervous steps.

Stand solidly on both feet; this will keep you from shifting or rocking back and forth.

SUMMARY AND KEY TAKEAWAYS

Good platform skills won't make up for a bad presentation, but bad platform skills can kill a good one. While it's important to be yourself, this chapter provides tips to ensure that you present yourself and your ideas in their best light.

- Eye contact is critical for ensuring a personal connection and for monitoring the reaction of the audience.

- The two main factors for effective use of your voice are variety, which shows personality and energy, and articulation .

- Stand up straight, chin up, and smile.

- Free your hands.

- Avoid nervous distractions — have a purpose for your movements.

15
MAKE IT INTERACTIVE

In some ways, it's easier to plan a presentation in which you simply talk for your allotted time. That way, you can think about and rehearse exactly what you are going to say, how to say it, and when to say it, and there are no surprises.

There probably would be no sale, either. If the audience does not engage with you during and after your presentation, you are probably in trouble. It most likely means they have no interest in what you're saying, either because they don't see a need or because they have already made up their minds.

These broadcast-type presentations are efficient, but not always effective. If you're willing to sacrifice efficiency and risk some unpredictability, you can take your sales presentations to a higher plane of effectiveness by planning to make them more interactive.

Being interactive means that you are moving towards the dialogue end of the scale. By doing so, the presentation takes on more of the character of a real-time conversation. The benefit of this is that your listeners feel like they are involved in formulating a mutual plan to improve their business situation rather than simply being dictated to.

When listeners feel involved in describing the problem and constructing the solution, there is a sense of shared ownership that makes for stronger agreements. And whose opinions do listeners trust above all others? When you can draw statements out of the audience, they are much more credible.

With senior-level audiences, you're probably not going to have a choice in the matter. Even if you don't plan to make it interactive, it's almost a guarantee that they will, so you might as well jump in front of the parade and interact on your own terms and timing. Besides, if they're interrupting, it shows they care.

The ideal situation in any sales conversation is to *get the customer to tell you what you want them to hear*.

PLAN TO MAKE IT INTERACTIVE

Interactivity can be managed through your agenda, by asking questions of the listeners, using various techniques to engage them personally, using visuals interactively, and finally through productive Q&A.

INTERACTIVE AGENDAS

The audience wants to know where the presentation is going. Use your agenda to tell them. However, there are better ways than presenting a prepared agenda to get your audience fully involved. A nice change of pace for your audience is to get them involved in setting the agenda, while you still keep control of the content.

One simple way to get audience involvement is to present an agenda (either on paper or as a slide) that has a couple of blank lines on the bottom. Ask them if they have anything they would like to add to it. Or, ask your listeners which topics they would like to spend the most time on.

An even more interactive method is to get the audience to help you prepare the agenda "real-time" on a flip chart or whiteboard. The trick here is to keep control of the items by asking good questions. You can make sure your key points are covered by asking:

> *To what extent is* _____ *important?*

Continue this until each of your points is on the agenda, while also adding others that come up. At the end, you will have the agenda you planned, while the audience thinks it was their idea!

ASKING QUESTIONS

Questions are a great way to get people engaged.

Rhetorical questions can serve as advance organizers, to help prepare their minds to hear the answer. For example: "What is the major factor that determines the success of a CRM implementation?"

Occasionally, you can check to ensure that they are listening by asking questions such as, "Does that make sense?" When you do, pause long enough to check for agreement before moving on. You can also ask more open-ended questions, such as "What impact would a faster response time have on your customer satisfaction?"

If you know your audience well enough (and you should), you can direct a question like that to the specific person in the room who cares most about that particular topic. That type of question is particularly useful for getting audience members to provide evidence for your presentation.

Questions are particularly helpful when you are selling intangible benefits; you can't give a hard number but you can usually draw one out of the person who is most concerned with the issue.

You can even structure your entire presentation around questions. As we've seen, stories are wonderful tools for getting audiences engaged, and you can get them to tell you the story by asking questions. The standard story structure is SCR — Situation-Conflict-Resolution — and you can ask questions designed to bring each of those out. For example, you might ask a couple of questions to confirm your understanding of their current situation. You would then draw out the conflict, by asking questions about problems, opportunities, or risks. Build additional urgency to act by asking questions that quantify the costs of the problems that are identified. Finally, ask questions that draw out their needs.

Finally, you can use questions at the end of the presentation to close, lock in agreement on next steps, or gauge the listeners' acceptance of your message. You can do this without being too pushy by asking simply, "Do you like it?"

VISUAL INTERACTIVITY

The three most important persuasion tools you have at your disposal are stories, questions and visuals. If you put those three together, you have a chance to create something special and powerful during your presentation.

By asking questions during a sales presentation or call, we said you can get your listeners to *tell you what you want them to hear*. Use a whiteboard or flipchart to add visuals created in real time during your presentation and you can also get the customer to *show you what you want them to see*.

Slides are wonderful for putting together professional-looking, elaborate visuals, but they also have a bit of a "take it or leave it" whiff about them.

The key difference between a whiteboard drawing and a prepared presentation is that it is created in real time, sometimes with the help of your audience. This does several things for you:

- It shows that you know your stuff. For example, suppose your solution improves one of their current processes. Drawing out the process, with its steps, inputs, outputs, etc. shows how well you know it, as opposed to a nice flowchart that could have been designed by your marketing department.

- It allows you to adjust on the spot, especially based on input from the audience. They feel that their input is valued. You could outline a process, ask the audience a question, and use their answer to fill in a detail or make a change. In this way, you're combining questions and drawings to have a productive dialogue.

- It enhances listening and learning from your customer's contribution and feedback.

- In this age of increasing PowerPoint overload, it will make for a refreshing difference.

- It's useful for locking in agreements. For example, you may draw a timeline for the implementation of the solution, with action items for each side. It's one thing to say these things, and quite another to see the agreement in writing.

- Although it may be impractical for larger groups, it can get audience members actively involved if you put a pen in their hands and have them add to the picture.

What are some of the ideas that are best suited for interactive visuals?

Processes: Draw a flowchart depicting a "day in the life" of a user today, compared to what that user's day will look like after your solution is implemented.

Simple charts: By drawing the chart, you can make it more dynamic. For example, you could trace projected revenues under several different scenarios or choices.

Pros and cons: A simple T-chart listing pros and cons can be very powerful, particularly if you can influence through your questions what goes on each list.

Tradeoffs: For example, you could draw a graph with quality on one axis and performance on the other, to show how your solution compares to alternatives.

Timelines: These are very easy to visualize and to draw. If you want to create a shared sense of urgency, get the customer to specify a date by which the solution has to be in place, and then work backwards through the milestones.

Tasks and agreements: If you can agree on tasks and get people to volunteer their names by each you end up with a written contract. If you want to keep a record of what you drew, take a picture with your phone.

You don't have to completely cut the slide umbilical cord. There's no law that says you can't blend both approaches. You can show some slides, blank out the screen and draw a picture, go back to the slides, and so on. If you're game, go back through one of your slide decks and see which slides could work better as whiteboard drawings.

If you're like me, your lack of artistic talent or poor handwriting may deter you from trying it. The key point to remember is that it's not about being pretty, it's about being effective. Anyone can draw stick figures, arrows, boxes, and circles, and those are usually enough to get your point across.

Having said that, you definitely need to practice drawing the visuals you want to use during your presentation. Practice will help you ensure that you can draw a recognizable picture at the rate of normal conversation, while still maintaining focus on the audience. It will allow you to figure out and control the timing of the presentation as well, and to coordinate your questions with your visuals so you build a smoothly flowing story.

USING PEOPLE'S NAMES

This is a sure-fire way to make sure people are paying attention. If you haven't gotten to know all the attendees during the sales process leading up to the presentation, try to get there early enough to meet and greet participants as they come in, and *listen* to their names.

MOVING CLOSER

If you have any choice in the matter, it always helps to be as close as possible to the audience. If you've seen clips of Bill Clinton answering questions in a town hall setting, you can see how effective it can be to get close to people (without violating their personal space).

HANDOUTS

We've covered it in Chapter 10, but it might be useful to revisit the idea of using handouts. There are valid arguments on both sides of the question about whether to save handouts to the end or pass them out up front. On balance, I personally prefer to hand them out before the presentation; while it may increase the risk of disrupting my planned flow, it can be an excellent way to find out exactly what's important to your audience, because they will go immediately to what they care about.

The exception would be when you have to develop your story step by step to ensure buy-in, such as when your listeners are skeptical or hostile to your message.

DEMOS

Product demonstrations can be very useful in getting customers engaged, or they can be the easiest way to get them to tune out completely.

To get people engaged, set up the context for the demonstration first. In other words, set up the so-what of the demo. You'll have much more engagement if they have a clear idea of what they want to see, and you know what that is. What is the need that must be filled, and what does the demo have to show that will indicate the solution can perform as necessary to meet that need?

Don't get so wrapped up in running the demo that you lose track of how the audience is reacting. Whenever possible, let them run the demo themselves; put it in their hands, let them push the buttons and try it out, get them to play with it.

This last point should be obvious, except that the complaint came up often enough in my interviews that it bears repeating here: when possible, demonstrate the actual product or system they will be buying, not some standard demo product that you always carry.

DEALING WITH DISTRACTIONS

What about people who are obviously not participating? Ignore them, unless they're distracting the others. You may be speaking about an aspect of the issue that they don't care about by virtue of their position, or maybe they have already been convinced.

Above all, don't let your ego get away from you. If you're seen as calling someone out because they're not paying attention, you run a serious risk of creating an adversary. If a majority of the audience has tuned out, you obviously have to adjust. Maybe it's time to move on to your next point, or to ask questions to get them re-engaged.

PRODUCTIVE Q&A

Do you want to just deliver your presentation and get it over with, or do you enjoy the challenge of answering tough questions from the audience? If it's not the latter, it should be, and hopefully it will be after you read this section.

Q&A is not an ordeal that you try to survive in order to get the sale. Properly done, it can be an integral and productive part of your presentation.

Successful sales professionals view objections and questions as one of the most beneficial and important parts of the selling process. They understand that the absence of objections or questions is a greater cause for concern than their presence, and they take every opportunity to encourage listeners to raise objections and ask questions.

WHEN TO TAKE QUESTIONS

It's generally easier to maintain your flow and train of thought if audience members hold their questions until the end, but in most cases it's absolutely the wrong approach to take for a sales presentation, especially at executive levels.

First of all, senior-level people are not accustomed to waiting until they have permission to speak. Second, if they are asking questions they are actively involved. Third, their questions are usually an excellent gauge of where their thinking is.

What if the question concerns something that you plan to cover in a few more slides? My recommendation is still to give at least a brief answer, and then you can tell them you will go into more detail.

Probably the only exception to this advice is when you have a really large audience, or when someone in the audience is monopolizing the direction of the presentation in a way that is hurting your chances for making the sale. That's where you have to do a quick evaluation of the person's importance to the decision process and make a judgment call about shutting them down. Offer to take the discussion off-line, and you will satisfy the questioner and please everyone else.

USING THE Q&A SESSION TO YOUR ADVANTAGE

Think of the Q&A session as an extension of your presentation. It is an excellent opportunity to advance your message and elaborate on your key points. Because you are responding to the audience, you will be able to reinforce your message in precisely those areas that are of most interest to them.

It helps to identify what the audience is thinking. Even if you have gotten your point across, for example, they might be looking for something else. The type and tone of questions allows you to gauge your effectiveness in getting your message across.

It allows you to let more of yourself come out, because in responding to questions you're engaging in a dialogue where you can express yourself more informally.

Finally, Q&A is an excellent opportunity to reinforce your credibility by giving you the chance to be tested under pressure. Senior executives often like to ask tough questions just to scratch the surface to see how well you know your material and how deeply you believe in it.

THE HOW OF Q&A IS AS IMPORTANT AS THE WHAT

When you go to this level of preparation, you should be completely confident about your content, but it's still not enough.

Although I have harped constantly in this book about the primacy of content, Q&A is one aspect of sales presentations where process and style are just as important as content. *How* you handle objections is just as important as *what* you say.

That's because focusing too much on being "right" may win you the argument but lose you the sale. In fact, sometimes having an indisputable answer that slams the door on further discussion can easily turn into a liability.

HANDLING Q&A IS NOT THE SAME AS MANAGING OBJECTIONS

The first point to stress is that the way you answer objections and questions in a group setting is not exactly the same as handling objections during a sales call. There are some subtle but important differences.

In Chapter 6 we discussed the USE approach,[21] which is an example of the typical approach to handling an objection during a sales call. You probably learned some variant of it early in your sales career. The basic premise of all these approaches is that you don't treat the objection as a debating point that is confronted head-on. Instead, you set the stage for your answer by probing and listening, and then by getting a small agreement that leads to your response.

The USE model works great in individual sales calls, but once the audience goes above five or six people the dynamics change and it can actually backfire on you.

There are two key differences. First, the target of your answer is not necessarily the person who asked it, as it would be in a small group meeting. When there are only one or two people sitting across the table, you must answer the question to the satisfaction of that person before you can move on. In a larger group, the entire audience is listening to your response, and they — not the questioner — are the ones you must satisfy with your answer.

The typical scenario is when someone pursues a line of questioning that only they care about. You try too hard to satisfy that person; meanwhile, you lose the rest of the audience. In a group setting, it's okay to stray slightly from answering the exact question. You have to be careful when you do this, but keeping the group in mind as you answer question can help you keep control of the main message and meet the needs of the audience as a whole.

Further, because there may be a lot of questions and too little time, you can dispense with most of the probing and all of the softening you would use with an individual, and get straight to your answer. Keep the probing to a minimum because it gives too much control to the questioner. Drop the softening step because it starts sounding mechanical after the first couple of times. If you say, "That's an excellent question!" after every question you'll sound fake, and if you only say it to one person and not to everyone else who asks a question you may ruffle some feathers.

---

[21] USE: Understand/soften; Small agreement: Explanation.

WHAT IS THE AUDIENCE LOOKING FOR?

As I pointed out earlier in this book, in most cases the people sitting in your audience are not there to try to trip you up. They are usually on your side, and want you to do well.

They are generally asking questions for two reasons. First, and most obviously, they need more information before they are ready to make a decision. Second, there is an element of testing involved. They want to scratch the surface and see how your content holds up, and they want to gauge you to see how confident and composed you are in defense of your position, and of course still expect you to be clear and concise in your answers. They are watching you as much as they are listening for your answer.

THE "USE+" MODEL

Because of these differences, the USE model is modified slightly when in the context of a strategic sales presentation. This first thing you'll notice is that the first two steps are abbreviated.

Understand and soften: Listen carefully to the question and paraphrase or probe a little to ensure that you know what they're asking. In general, however, you will spend less time on the probing than you would in an individual sales call. Drop the softening. So for example, don't say, "That's a good question." If you say it to one person, you have to say it to everyone to avoid having people feel slighted. That will make you sound too scripted or patronizing.

Small agreement: You may keep the small agreement step, but often it won't be necessary to go into too much detail because your very thorough presentation would most likely have already contained the reframing, analogy, or other technique you used to get them to see things your way.

Explain: Give your answer concisely and move on. Try not to be too wordy in your response. The best way is to give a short answer, which is your "headline," and then build your response from there as needed.

Our approach is faster. It's faster because that's all we do, and this means you will be able slash your time to market, and introduce more new models in the same amount of time.

It's sometimes advisable to skip the confirmation step, so you can skip asking, "Did that answer your question?" which risks sending the meeting off track or giving control to someone in the audience who might have his or her own ax to grind.

If the questioner asks a very technical question in a mixed audience, give a brief answer that can be understood by everyone and offer to provide more details off-line.

The "+" in USE+: Now comes the fun part. Because you still have the floor, you can take an opportunity after you've answered a question to springboard over to a statement that reinforces one of the main messages of your presentation.

This is your chance to provide context and add a little something extra to your answer that reinforces the theme of your presentation. It's also a wonderful opportunity to turn around a negative or hostile question into a positive recommendation.

That's why it's crucial to begin implementation immediately.

Presentation guru Jerry Weissman calls this "topspin," and it's a great way to use the Q&A session to go from defense only to a more assertive and proactive approach.

A lot of salespeople view the Q&A portion of their presentations through a defensive lens, as one last obstacle to surmount on the way to a sale. Yet if you listen to the questions, answer them directly and concisely, and then add your own point at the end, the give-and-take can become one of your most important persuasive assets.

SUMMARY AND KEY TAKEAWAYS

By engaging your listeners during your presentation, you give up a little bit of control and efficiency, but gain tremendously in effectiveness.

Because senior-level listeners are going to make it interactive anyway, you might as well plan for interactivity and use it to your advantage.

- Gain their agreement on your agenda.

- Ask questions to tell your story, gauge understanding, and gain agreement.

- Use whiteboards and flip charts to create visual stories in real time.

- Use the Q&A to your advantage, answering real concerns and then turning the focus back on your key theme.

16
EFFECTIVE TEAM PRESENTATIONS

Everything covered so far in this book assumes that a single salesperson is crafting and delivering the presentation but the reality of strategic B2B sales is that they usually involve teams. This is a fact that has clearly emerged from my interviews with top executives. Everyone I spoke with said that the majority of presentations they attend at their level are conducted by more than one person, and some said *all* of them are.

It makes perfect sense because strategic sales are generally complex system sales, and systems have many parts, which generally can't be comprehended or explained in sufficient detail by one person. Individual parts of these systems require specialized knowledge.

In addition, these are not transactional sales; you are either establishing or continuing a close working relationship with the customer, and that relationship can involve multiple individual connections across various functions and levels.

Often, the senior-level executive is in the room precisely because the decision will have a broad impact across various functions within the organization. As a result, there are various people in the room who have a stake in the decision to be made and who will be working with various members of your team if you are successful. They want to get to know your team and gauge their compatibility.

The age of the heroic individual salesperson is over. Even if one person has all the knowledge and expertise to handle the presentation alone, it's not a good idea. If you're a short-listed candidate making a closing presentation, you have most likely already passed two crucial tests in the buying cycle: the customer has determined that the need is sufficiently important to invest in a solution, and they have agreed that your offering meets their minimum standards. The key remaining question at this point is: Can you deliver?

A team presentation goes a long way toward answering this question by addressing two important issues:

First, they want to know: Are these people we can work with over the long term?

An effective team presentation lets the customer see how your team works together and lets them try the team on for size. Several executives told me they pay attention to how the team works together during the presentation as an indicator about how they will work with the purchasing company. Numbers also count in terms of reassuring them that you have the depth of capability and talent to handle their needs.

When a team presentation goes well, the impact can be impressive and immediate. An executive who sat in on a presentation by a PR firm told me their team presentation was so impressive that "the foot of the last guy was barely out the door, and the president looked at me and said, 'Hire them.'"

What did they like so much about that presentation that clinched the decision? They became comfortable that the firm could deliver on its promises because each person who was responsible for the different aspects of the relationship had a chance to present. They were also impressed by the obvious camaraderie that the team displayed, and had the feeling that spirit would make them easy to work with.

Second, they want to know: Are we trusting our critical project to just one person? Actually, it's a bit more nuanced than that. They want to be assured that they have "one throat to choke" — a single responsible point of contact and accountability — *plus* the depth of an entire team to support their needs. The structure and delivery of your team presentation must convey both of those characteristics.

From a delivery standpoint, team presentations also help to add variety and maintain attention. Even the most dynamic presenter can get a bit stale after about twenty minutes, so it helps to have different speakers.

Of course, anything with such strong benefits is bound to carry some risk. Team presentations are much more difficult to pull off properly.

Any time you add moving parts to a system there is much more chance of something going wrong. Plus, any team is at the mercy of its weakest player.

Let's take a look at some proven practices to enjoy the advantages of team presenting without the pitfalls.

PLAN IT

The first thing to remember is that you are planning a *team* presentation, not a *group* presentation. Any collection of individuals can form a group at a moment's notice, but it takes time and care to mold a team. There is a big difference between the two.

A group presentation is a series of individual presentations that might or might not have a strong connection with each other. Each one could probably stand on its own. A team presentation, by contrast, is a single presentation with several participants. This is a critical difference because it changes how you plan it, practice it, and deliver it.

Because a team presentation is a single presentation, there is one plan for the presentation, and one person is in charge. As the USA Olympic basketball team has demonstrated on occasion, even a Dream Team of superstars is going to lose if you just have a collection of individuals trying to do their own thing. People have to keep their egos under control and see their part as a contribution to the big picture.

It does not mean that one person writes the entire presentation. They can still craft their own individual parts, just as long as they do it within the agreed-upon architecture. Their specialized knowledge only makes sense within the big picture, and that is what the account manager brings to the table.

The good news is that most of the process we have covered throughout this book is exactly what you need for a team presentation. Because it's a single presentation, the same principles apply. The additional complexity comes from meshing the individual contributions into a seamless whole.

Who does the planning? That's up to the sales team. The account manager could decide on the overall structure and then ask participants to build their presentation to fit. However, best practice is to have the team come together for at least an initial planning meeting. This brings several benefits.

First, as the old saying goes, "none of us is as smart as all of us." The combined input should result in a better presentation, especially as some team members may have specific information not known to the whole group.

Second, when everyone knows what everyone else is going to say, it helps them build references and links to other parts of the presentation. It also avoids the potential trap of having someone contradict a team member.

Finally, it provides a greater sense of ownership. Team camaraderie of the sort alluded to earlier in this section can't be faked or just turned on for the presentation.

A TEAM PRESENTATION IS JUST AN INDIVIDUAL ONE ON STEROIDS

Everything you have to do for an individual presentation applies to team presentations, but the addition of others adds another level of preparation. Let's review the required steps for a successful strategic sales presentation, and see what adjustments must be made for a team presentation.

Analysis: One of the benefits of a team sale is the diversity of connections, perspectives, and information that each team member has. The challenge is to get all that information out on the table so that the team has the information needed for effective analysis. The important task here is to connect the dots between the various collections of information that each team member has.

During the planning phase, the presentation team should have a common document so that all members of the team can see it. Besides the obvious benefit of "being on the same page," this process can often spark new ideas as knowledge is brought into the open and combined.

Shaping the conditions: This is somewhat outside the scope of this book, but the entire sales team should be working from a single opportunity planning template or document that details the buyer's decision-making process, with the relationships and influences clearly mapped out and understood by the entire team.

Core message: One of the most important reasons to have one clear theme in an individual presentation is to keep your presentation from being rambling and unfocused. Imagine how much more important that is with several people being involved.

It's absolutely critical to have the discipline of one message that everyone supports and sticks to during their portion of the presentation. Buyers will get confused if they can't connect all the threads, and even more so if presenters appear to contradict each other.

The reliance on a single clear theme was probably the most common denominator among the top team presenters interviewed for this book. One company called it the "central question," another called it the "win message," but nearly all insisted that this is the critical first step in all their team presentations.

Military planners use the concept of *commander's intent* to ensure that subordinates can respond to the unexpected while still furthering the purposes of the operation. In team presentations, the one clear theme serves the same purpose.

One benefit of having an agreed-upon core message is that when the presentation doesn't go exactly as it's drawn up during the planning — which it never does — the person speaking at the time can easily adjust and adapt, within the boundaries of the original intent.

Structure of the presentation: The main points that support the theme remain the same; the only difference is that each main point may actually be the complete presentation for an individual team member. By having a clear structure, individual presenters see their piece as a part of the whole presentation, and when the pieces are put back together, everything works as a seamless whole. It's like the way Boeing built the 787, with different contractors, each assigned a major assembly such as the wings or the tail, working to exacting specifications so that when it was all bolted together the thing would actually fly.

It's also important that each individual piece include references to previous and upcoming speakers, such as: "As Chris mentioned, one of the root causes of the problem is the fluctuation in density from one batch to the next, and our solution addresses that by . . ."

Evidence: The supporting evidence portion is put together individually, and then brought back to the team. It's not up to the team to parse the evidence, because the person putting it together is the recognized subject matter expert. However, it's useful to have the team review what will be said to reduce redundancy and avoid contradiction.

Introduction and close: The team leader is probably going to be the person delivering the introduction. Besides the standard ingredients of an individual presentation, the team leader should also introduce the individual presenters and briefly explain their roles. The emphasis here is on brevity because he or she will want to say a little more about each person just before handing off to them for their part.

The team leader may also take over for the close, or leave it to the last speaker to tie everything together. Since team presentations may be longer than individual ones, a brief summary at the end is a good idea.

Visuals: The only difference on visuals is just to ensure that the entire deck, if one is being used, should have a common look and feel. It should look like one presentation, not a patchwork.

PRACTICE IT

Once Boeing put together the first 787, they didn't assume their computerized plans were perfect. They had to test-fly the aircraft before they could put passengers on it. You should treat an important team presentation with equal care.

The rehearsal process is even more critical to a team presentation's success than an individual one because all the parts have to work together. Here are some practical tips that can go a long way toward creating an exceptional presentation:

Plan transitions and handoffs. There are two ways to handle this. The team leader can act as a master of ceremonies and handle all of the transitions. The advantage is that only one person needs to practice the transitions. Or each individual speaker can introduce the following speaker. The advantage of this is that there are fewer moving parts and it looks a little less choppy.

Plan what-ifs. An old military dictum is that no plan survives first contact with the enemy, and the same applies to sales presentations. The customer will always have a vote in how the presentation flows. It's important for the team to have flexibility built in, and for the team leader to follow the conversation closely and make adjustments.

Plan to shorten or omit parts as necessary. Sometimes the portion that one person worked so hard on becomes irrelevant because the customer prefers to spend more time on something else.

Plan on something going wrong. What will you do if someone is detained in travel?

Present in conditions as close to realistic as possible. It will make presenters more comfortable by making the actual scene much more familiar. It will also help to identify peculiarities of the venue that might interfere with some of the choreography of the presentation, such as where people sit when not presenting.

Videotape and review. There's no substitute for everyone seeing themselves performing individually and for the team getting a sense of how the entire presentation flows.

Rehearsing builds in safeguards against Murphy's Law. When everyone knows who will be saying what they are in a better position to step in and assist in case someone can't make it to the meeting, or someone has a momentary brain freeze and forgets a part or can't answer a question.

DELIVER

There seems to be a tendency among sales teams to bring more people to team presentations than necessary. It's understandable, because it seems it would demonstrate your depth of resources, and because you might need a specialist to answer a question about some esoteric aspect of the offering. Yet my interviews with top executives indicate that it can backfire.

One of the most common "don'ts" that came out of the interviews was not to bring more people than necessary, and to make sure that the people you do bring have a clear reason for being there. There may very well be times when there is value in bringing people just in case a specialized topic comes up, but in that case it's a good idea to explain that up front.

Make it a true team presentation; don't have one person do 90% of the talking.

If you bring in one of your own senior-level people, you have the delicate task of convincing that person to hold his or her ego in check. What does that mean? Make sure they know their role in the presentation and don't freelance. Don't let them go on too long. Coach them to ensure that they deflect most questions to you; otherwise they will undercut your authority and accountability, and the client will be confused about whom to turn to when they have an issue.

There are sales teams that err on the other side, expecting the senior person to carry too much of the load. One senior executive complained to me that his account managers seem to think that he can work some sort of magic just because of his rank. If it's your account, it's up to you to manage the process, set expectations, and use your senior management properly, as you would any other asset.

Most importantly, make sure you and your leadership are on the same page. Peter Rubenacker, VP of IT at Qualcomm, related a story about a presentation involving a professional services outsourcing firm. During the sales process, he had asked the account manager if his company would agree to letting Qualcomm hire any of its employees that they were impressed with, something that most of these firms avoid. The account manager said that, absolutely, they could do that; in fact, that was a strategic direction they were considering. When the company's C-level executive flew in for a meeting, that was the second question Rubenacker asked. The response he got from the executive was, "Hell, no. Why would we do that?"

Get agreement on the agenda and who will handle each part, ensuring a proper balance of talk time.

Transitions are important to maintain a smooth flow and keep people engaged in the forward progress of the meeting. The person handing off should tee up the next presenter by giving a brief explanation of how their topic follows. For example, you could say,

> You have very ambitious goals for your business in the next couple of years. Effective execution of your key business processes is going to be critical, and our next topic will address how we are enabling some industry-leading applications . . .

After a speaker has finished, it's a nice practice to do a brief summary of what they said and tie it into the principal theme of the meeting.

During their turn, each speaker should include links and references to what other speakers have said or are about to say.

Stay on top of the time. It helps to have one person designated to keep a close eye on time and have subtle signals arranged if things are going off track, such as an unobtrusive tap on the watch or the wrist.

It's a good idea to ensure that presentations are not designed to fill every minute they have available on the agenda. Since it's your goal to have a dialogue, there has to be enough time built in to allow for questions and necessary digressions. Sometimes digressions from prepared material are welcome, especially when ideas come up that point to potential customer needs.

There are times, though, that conversations can get sidetracked into unproductive threads. This is tricky because your customer may think the topic is important, so you have to be tactful.

What are some tactful ways you can bring the meeting back on track?

- Ask a question that redirects the conversation back to where it should be.

- Let the person know it will be covered in an upcoming presentation.

- Offer to "park" the question to be covered later.

- Offer to cover it offline (for example when the answer is far too detailed and is not interesting or important to the other participants).

Adjusting to the unexpected: No plan ever goes off exactly as laid out on paper. You need to be prepared to adjust the agenda based on what the customer says and how they react to various topics. Presenters must be prepared to cut back on their presentation time, for example, or to step up and speak extemporaneously on an unexpected topic.

What to do when you're not presenting: One of the easiest traps to fall into in a team presentation is for people who are not speaking to fail to pay as close attention to the current speaker as if they are hearing it for the first time. Even though you've heard it many times before, if you tune out, others will. Other audience members will take cues from you, so act interested.

In his book, *Perfect Pitch*, Jon Steel tells how his firm won a large contract because, as the client told him, "Each of you seemed to enjoy what your colleagues were saying as much as I did." The competitor's presenters, on the other hand, were studying their notes for their next part and even rolling their eyes at some parts.

Of course, another practical reason to pay attention is that a question might come up during the presentation that the speaker will send your way to answer. If your mind is wandering, it can feel like you're on an awfully lonely island when you have to ask your customer to repeat the question.

BEST PRACTICES FOR TEAM PRESENTATIONS: A CASE STUDY

Infrastructure engineering consulting is one industry in which companies depend for their very survival on the effectiveness of their team presentations. These companies compete for jobs to provide engineering services for major road, rail, and construction projects. Total billings for each job can run up to 20% of their annual billings, and decisions are handed down by major clients after short-listed firms deliver their presentations.

Because of what's at stake, most of these companies have developed rigorous protocols to ensure that they are at their best when it comes time to present. It might be instructive to look at the anatomy of one such presentation as seen through the eyes of one of their senior executives. In true team presentation style, I'm going to turn over the next two pages to Dave Thomas, SVP and National Director for Transit and Rail at Gannett Fleming, a 100 year old consulting engineering company based in Harrisburg, PA. In what follows, I'm paraphrasing his words as he describes the process.

CASE STUDY: GANNETT FLEMING'S STRATEGIC SALES PRESENTATION PROCESS FOR TEAMS

"When we receive notification that we are short-listed, we usually have a very short time to prepare, sometimes as little as a week, sometimes up to several weeks. Either way, our philosophy is that it's never too early to begin preparing.

The proposed project manager runs the entire process. The first step is to set up a war room in which the entire team can meet to begin preparing. The team includes the proposed project manager, marketing and business development staff, and the key discipline leaders, such as traction power, track, signals, etc.

We begin by pooling all the information that team members have about the proposal, the project, and the key hot buttons of the end customer, particularly the personal point of view of their project manager. We put all of this information into a document that is shared by the team.

From this, we develop the key themes of our presentation. We also brainstorm as a team all of the potential questions and issues the customer might have, and agree on our answers.

After the individual portions are written, the rehearsals begin. Up to fifteen or twenty people are there to watch the individual presentations and offer coaching and critiques. Presenters are timed and videotaped, and we play back the videos immediately so they can see for themselves what the coaches are saying. For some of the most critical presentations, we will bring in a professional coach to help.

Usually the first two or three times are rough, but they gradually get better. The last few rehearsals are full dress rehearsals; no one shows up in business casual. Since we usually have received permission from the client to see the presentation room ahead of time, we know where everyone will be.

We will rehearse at least seven or eight times, and our goal is to absolutely nail it three times in a row before we're satisfied.

On presentation day, we always arrive early to get set up. We're very conscious of Murphy's Law; for example, we have our entire presentation on foam boards in case there's a problem with the projector. On some occasions someone might get held up in travel, and another team member will have to pick up their part of the presentation. Usually it's the project manager, and it works because everyone has seen each other's presentation so many times.

The project manager is king during the presentation, acting as emcee, introducing each speaker, and taking care to keep the pace going so we don't lose attention between presenters. It's important that the client get a sense of a single point of contact who is fully in charge of the entire process and project. We typically limit it to three or four different speakers so that it doesn't get too choppy, although we will have discipline leaders in attendance in case questions come up in their own specialties.

My role as the senior attendee usually comes at the end to stress corporate support and to express our commitment to keep the project manager in place for the duration of the project, which is very important to our clients.

During the Q&A, the project manager is the only one standing to receive the questions, which he distributes to the right person.

It's a lot of work, but in the end, it doesn't cost any more to do it right the first time."

SUMMARY AND KEY TAKEAWAYS

Big deals often require team presentations, which are still single presentations delivered by well-coordinated teams. Because there are more moving parts, it's important to prepare and practice, with plenty of lead time as a team.

- One person should be in charge of the entire presentation.

- The entire presentation should have a common theme.

- Well-rehearsed transitions and handoffs will ensure a smooth flow.

- Participants should be prepared to cover for each other in a pinch.

- All participants should be fully engaged at all times.

17
HOW TO GET BETTER

We are what we repeatedly do. Excellence, then, is not an act but a habit.

—Aristotle

It's appropriate to leave the last quote in this book to Aristotle, who was the first to write a book on persuading crowds through rhetoric.

You don't need to read this chapter. If you've read this far, and you've tried some or all the ideas in this book, you will be more than good enough — you will be a better presenter than the overwhelming majority of sales professionals your customers will encounter. If that's good enough, feel free to stop here.

But if you have read this far, you are probably someone who blows through "good enough" like a stop sign on a deserted road. You want to be excellent, and you want to get better all the time. You know you're good, but not as good as you could be.

The ability to deliver excellent persuasive presentations comprises a complex set of skills that are not mastered overnight, and that you could spend years mastering.

Some of the best speakers in history honed their skills across decades of almost daily practice before they reached the heights for which we remember them. Lincoln argued cases in Illinois; Churchill gave a less-than-stellar maiden speech in Parliament in 1900, and then had forty years of practice before he deployed his eloquence to save his nation; Martin Luther King preached and spoke to civil rights meetings for years. In 1963 alone, King delivered 350 speeches.

You will not be an excellent speaker or salesperson just because you read this book, any more than buying new running shoes will make you fit.

Don't get me wrong — training in both fundamental and advanced skills can quickly take you from average to pretty good. And sometimes pretty good is good enough, depending on your competition. But to reach excellence, which I define very loosely as having a rare level of skill that makes your presentations eagerly anticipated and long remembered (and profitable for you and your customers), takes much more than reading a book.

DELIBERATE PRACTICE

Researchers tell us that genius in any particular skill or knowledge domain comes from one primary factor: simple hard work. In any field, from chess to composing to surgery, the best only reach that level after approximately 10,000 hours of deliberate practice.

Let me break that down. 10,000 hours means that mastery requires twenty-hour weeks of practice for ten years. It even applies to speakers.

Excellence isn't genius, though, so you can achieve it with far less than 10,000 hours of work. But you do need the *deliberate practice* part of the equation. Practice doesn't make perfect; practice makes permanent. Deliberate practice means that you don't keep practicing only what you're good at or what you like to do. You carefully study your performance and then work hard on your weaknesses one by one. You take chances, you fail over and over until you get it right, and then you tackle the next one. It takes self awareness and guts. It's not much fun, but by the time the big moment comes, excellent performance has been hardwired into your brain.

If you are willing to embark on the journey to excellence, here are some ideas that will help:

Seek out opportunities. Excellent speakers put in the time by seeking out opportunities to speak. You might join a local Toastmasters club, or take on roles that make you present often. Do some internal training in your company. When you have many more hours under your belt, you'll find that things that required effort become natural, freeing up mental energy for even greater improvements. You even find that the habit of developing habits becomes easier for you. When you know how to work toward a goal, excellence in many areas comes within reach.

Become self-aware. Be honest with yourself about where you need to improve. Develop your strengths, sure, but also expose your weaknesses and get them at least into the neutral column. Seek out feedback from people you respect. Videotape yourself when possible, however painful it may be.

Do after-action reviews. Immediately after every presentation, take a few minutes to reflect on what went well and what you need to work on for the next time. Then work on it.

Be patient. It won't happen overnight. If it did, everybody could do it, and you wouldn't be special. Use *kaizen* — constant and continuous improvement. Small actions are easier to do, and don't engage the resistance of your emotional brain as much as large actions. And they add up over time.

IT GETS EASIER — AND MORE FUN

In some ways, it gets easier. The process of filling out a template to prepare your first sales presentation may have been painful, and may have taken a lot of time, but if you keep it up you will find your mind easily slipping into a comfortable pattern.

Also, since your solutions tend to do the same thing for most of your customers, a lot of the material you put together easily transfers over from one presentation to another. The fun then comes in from constantly looking for ways to better get a specific point across, or to demonstrate a capability, or to make it unique for that specific customer.

APPENDIX 1: TEMPLATES

AUDIENCE ANALYSIS

SAMPLE: HOW TO USE THIS AUDIENCE ANALYSIS TEMPLATE	
ATTENDEE NAME *(include title if applicable)*	
Goal or "win"	*What does this person expect to gain from the decision?*
Criteria	*List their principal criteria for the decision.*
Attitude	*What is their attitude toward your solution?*
Status	*Need*
	Commit

ATTENDEE NAME:	
Goal or "win"	
Criteria	
Attitude	
Status	Need:
	Commit:

ATTENDEE NAME:		
Goal or "win"		
Criteria		
Attitude		
Status	Need:	
	Commit:	
ATTENDEE NAME:		
Goal or "win"		
Criteria		
Attitude		
Status	Need:	
	Commit:	
ATTENDEE NAME:		
Goal or "win"		
Criteria		
Attitude		
Status	Need:	
	Commit:	

PRESENTATION PREPARATION

EXECUTIVE SALES PRESENTATIONS PREPARATION
Customer: Date:
Presentation Goal (Call Purpose)
Actions You Want the Audience to Take
Value Proposition: What's in it for them?
Presentation Theme
Additional Work (if needed)

BUILDING THE PRESENTATION

Introduction	

Key Points	Examples/Evidence/Detail
1	
2	
3	

Close	

SOURCES & NOTES

Introduction: Your Leadership Moment

Page

8   **cannot wait for added value:** Mack Hanan, *Consultative Selling* (New York: AMACOM, 2004), 6 (hereafter cited as Hanan, *Consultative Selling*).

8   **involve an average of eight people:** Richard Shell and Mario Moussa, *The Art of Woo* (New York: Penguin, 2007), 23.

9   **your performance can have a huge impact:** Howard Stevens and Ted Kinni, *Achieve Sales Excellence* (Avon: Platinum Press, 2007), 5 (hereafter cited as Stevens and Kinni, *Achieve*).

11   **there is a different dynamic:** Max Atkinson, *Lend Me Your Ears* (New York: Oxford University Press, 2004), 68 (hereafter cited as Atkinson, *Lend*).

Chapter 1: Four Recurring Themes

Page

20   **it is the customer:** Peter Drucker, quoted in Stevens and Kinni, *Achieve*, 24.

20   **Seek first to understand:** Steven Covey, *Seven Habits of Highly Effective People* (New York: Simon and Schuster, 1989), 235. Also Roger Fisher and William Ury *Getting to Yes: Negotiating Agreement Without Giving In* (New York: Penguin Books, 1981).

21   **to whom it may concern:** Nancy Duarte, *Resonate* (Hoboken: John Wiley and Sons, 2010), 56.

22   **I communicated great things:** Ronald Reagan, Farewell Address to the Nation, Oval Office, January 11, 1989.

22   **CIOs want suppliers:** Michael Minelli and Mike Barlow, *Partnering with the CIO* (Hoboken: John Wiley and Sons, 2007), 4 (hereafter cited as Minelli and Barlow, *Partnering*).

23   **you will be unbeatable:** Bill Lane, *Jacked Up*, (New York: Mc-Graw-Hill, 2008), 211 (hereafter cited as Lane, *Jacked Up*).

24   **Steve Jobs would spend two full days:** Michael Evangelist, "Behind the Magic Curtain," *The Guardian Online*, January 4, 2006.

http://www.guardian.co.uk/technology/2006/jan/05/newmedia.media1

26   *Comments about genuineness came from Robert Craven, Mike Beck, and Carl Rapp. Interviews conducted by the author, November and December 2011.*

Chapter 2: Capturing the Listener's Mind

Page

28   **how hungry they are:** Roy Baumeister, *Willpower*, (New York: Penguin, 2011), 97.

29   **System 1 and System 2:** Daniel Kahneman, *Thinking: Fast and Slow*, (New York: Farrar, Straus and Giroux, 2011) (hereafter cited as Kahneman, *Thinking*).

29   **can make reasonably accurate judgments:** Nalini Ambady, Mary Anne Krabbenhoft, Daniel Hogan, "The 30-Sec Sale: Using Thin-Slice Judgments to Evaluate Sales Effectiveness," *Journal of Consumer Psychology*, 16(1), 4-13 (hereafter cited as Ambady, et al., *30-Sec Sale*).

30   **you have to change the way people feel:** John P. Kotter, Dan S. Cohen, *The Heart of Change*, (Boston: Harvard Business School Publishing, 2002), 29-30.

31   **substituting an easy question:** Kahneman, *Thinking*, 97-99.

31   **Can I trust you?:** Minelli and Barlow, *Partnering*, 6.

31   **the rest is window dressing:** Olivia Fox Cabane, *The Charisma Myth*, (New York: Penguin, 2012), 116.

32   **six powerful cues:** Robert Cialdini, *Influence: the Psychology of Persuasion*, (New York: William Morrow, 1993).

33   **more afraid of making a mistake:** Mark Goulston, *Just Listen*, (New York: AMACOM, 2010), 50 (hereafter cited as Goulston, *Listen*).

34   **potential regret can be a powerful motivator:** Kahneman, *Thinking*, 384.

34   **people will stick with the status quo:** William Samuelson and Richard Zeckhauser, "Status Quo Bias in Decision Making," *Journal of Risk and Uncertainty*, 1: 7-59 (1988)

        http://www.hks.harvard.edu/fs/rzeckhau/SQBDM.pdf

35   **respond to danger and stress:** Robert Maurer, *One Small Step Can Change Your Life*, (New York: Workman Publishing, 2004), 24-25.

35   **10% a week later:** Florence I. Wolff and Nadine C. Marsnick, *Perceptive Listening*, (Orlando: Holt, Rinehart and Winston, 1992), 3.

36   **continuous partial attention:** Linda Stone, "Beyond Simple Multi-Tasking: Continuous Partial Attention," Lindastone.net, blog post from November 9, 2009.

        http://lindastone.net/2009/11/30/beyond-simple-multi-tasking-continuous-partial-attention/

37   **magical number seven:** George Miller, "The Magical Number Seven, Plus or Minus Two," *Psychological Review*, 63:81-97 (1956) (hereafter cited as Miller, *Magical*).

39   **six qualities of sticky messages:** Chip Heath and Dan Heath, *Made to Stick*, (New York: Random House, 2008) (hereafter cited as Heath and Heath, *Made to Stick*).

40   **Roy Baumeister and colleagues:** Roy Baumeister, Ellen Bratslavsky, Catrin Finkenauer, and Kathleen D. Vohs, "Bad Is Stronger than Good," *Review of General Psychology*, 5:4, 323-370 (2001)

http://www.csom.umn.edu/Assets/71516.pdf, accessed 8/30/11.

40   **better than positive material:** Winifred Gallagher, *Rapt: Attention and the Focused Life*, (New York: Penguin, 2009), 32.

42   **applied equally to doctors:** Kahneman, *Thinking*, 367.

43   **Social styles:** Larry Wilson, *The Social Styles Handbook*, (USA: Nova Vista Publishing, 2004).

44   **law of least effort:** Kahneman, *Thinking*, **32.**

Chapter 3: Decision Making in Organizations

Page

54   **social judgment theory:** Richard M. Perloff, *The Dynamics of Persuasion*, (Hillsdale: Lawrence Erlbaum Assoc., 1993), 198-219.

58   **experience wasted time more painfully:** Art Markman, "Don't Waste My Time...," blog post from Ulterior Motives, *Psychology Today Online*, October 11, 2011.

http://www.psychologytoday.com/blog/ulterior-motives/201110/don-t-waste-my-time

59   **even the presenters seem bored:** Luke Lively, Interview with the author, November 14, 2011, .

60   **these qualities in your presentaion:** Ray Anthony, *Talking to the Top*, (Englewood Cliffs: Prentice-Hall, 1995), 71-77.

61   Stevens and Kinney, *Achieve*, xvi. The complete list of seven items on executives' wish list for salespeople is:

   • You must be personally accountable for our results
   • You must understand our business
   • You must be on our side

- You must bring us applications
- You must be easily accessible
- You must solve our problems
- You must be innovative in responding to our needs

Chapter 4: Shape the Conditions for Success

Page

69   **"box two" operational and functional managers:** this term comes from Hanan, *Consultative Selling*.

72   **widespread support for the supplier:** Matthew Dixon and Brent Adamson, *The Challenger Sale*, (New York: Penguin, 2011), 9.

75   For more on how to read an annual report and learn about industries, see Jack Malcolm, *Bottom-Line Selling: The Sales Professional's Guide to Improving Customer Profits*, (Seattle: Booktrope, 2011).

Chapter 5: Choose Your Message

Page

94   **"Ultimately, all decisions are personal":** Al Monserrat, interview with the author, June 14, 2012.

Chapter 6: Structure Your Argument

Page

100   **what you know now:** Heath and Heath, *Made to Stick*, 20-21. They call it the "Curse of Knowledge."

101   **impression of completeness:** Atkinson, *Lend*, 196.

102   **Research on message order:** Robert H. Gass, John S. Seiter, *Persuasion, Social Influence and Compliance Gaining*, (Boston, Pearson, 2007), 192.

103   **state clearly what you want:** Lane, *Jacked Up*, 289.

105   **neither would Welch:** Ibid., 234.

107   **grooves of the human mind:** Henry M. Boettinger, *Moving Mountains*, (Toronto: MacMillan, 1969), 37.

108   **Provide examples or analogies:** Andrew Abela, *Advanced Presentations by Design*, (San Francisco: Pfeiffer, 2008), 78.

110   **to what extent:** Thomas Freese, *Question-Based Selling*, (Naperville: Sourcebooks, 2000), 137.

113   **SPIN Process:** Neil Rackham, *SPIN Selling*, (New York: McGraw-Hill, 1988).

Chapter 7: Support Your Main Points

Page

128   **they are reasoning by analogy:** Giovanni Gavetti and Jan W. Rivkin, "How Strategists Really Think: Tapping the Power of Analogy," *Harvard Business Review*, April 2005.

133   **"transport" your listeners:** Melanie C. Green and Timothy C. Brock, "The Role of Transportation in the Persuasiveness of Public Narratives," *Journal of Personality and Social Psychology*, 79: 5, 701-721. (2000)

134   **simulate the action in their brains:** Stephen Denning, *The Springboard: How Storytelling Ignites Action in Knowledge-Era Organizations*, (Boston: Elsevier, 2001), 59. See also: Annette Simmons, *The Story Factor*, (Cambridge: Basic Books, 2001).

135   **Anchor and twist:** Chip Heath and Dan Heath, *Selling Your Innovation: Anchor and Twist*.

http://www.fastcompany.com/magazine/127/made-to-stick-anchor-and-twist.html

137   **Guacamole story:** Scott Plous, *The Psychology of Judgment and Decision Making*, (New York: McGraw-Hill, 1993), 127.

Chapter 8: Polishing

Page

144   **perceive you as less intelligent:** Daniel Oppenheimer, "Consequences of Erudite Vernacular Utilized Irrespective of Necessity: Problems with Using Long Words Needlessly," *Applied Cognitive Psychology*, 20: 139-156 (2006), Published online 31 October, 2005, Wiley InterScience.

www.interscience.wiley.com

146   **Words have meaning beyond their dictionary:** Frank Luntz, *Words that Work.* (New York, Hyperion, 2007), 129-132.

152   **The Spartans applauded:** Herodotus, *The Landmark Herodotus: The Histories,* (New York: Anchor Books, 2007), Book Three, Section 46.

155   **Ebbinghaus Illusion (circles):** B. Roberts, M.G. Harris, T.A. Yates, "The roles of inducer size and distance in the Ebbinghaus illusion (Titchener circles)," *Perception*, 34 (7): 847–56. 2005.

Anchoring: Kahneman, *Thinking*, 82.

process numbers emotionally: Kathryn Kadous, Lisa Koonce, Kristy L. Towry, "Quantification and Persuasion in Managerial Judgment," *Contemporary Accounting Research*, 22:643-686. 2005.

156   **when they heard the number:** Jacob M. Rose, F. Douglas Roberts, Anne M. Rose, "Affective Responses to Financial Data and Multimedia: the Effects of Information Load and Cognitive Load," *International Journal of Accounting Information Systems*, 5:5-24. 2004.

158   **83% thought:** Heath and Heath, *Made to Stick*, 144.

159   **strike 10% of the population:** "Numerical Information Can Be Persuasive or Informative Depending on How It's Presented." *Science Daily*, April 22, 2008. Web. 22 May 2012.

http://www.sciencedaily.com/releases/2008/04/080422150652.htm

160 **to double-check it:** or pick up a copy of Malcolm, *Bottom-Line Selling* (Seattle: Booktrope, 2011)

160 **almost equal to that of tangible assets:** Bill Birchard, "Intangible Assets Plus Hard numbers Equals Soft Finance", *Fast Company*, September 30, 1999.

   http://www.fastcompany.com/magazine/28/softfin.html

   See also Jan Hoffman, "Value Intangibles!" *Deutsche Bank Research*, October 19, 2005.

161 **it may not matter at all:** William Poundstone, *Priceless: The Myth of Fair Value (and How to Take Advantage of It)*, (New York: Hill and Wang, 2010), 7.

162 **data enforces boundaries:** Heath and Heath, *Made to Stick*, 147.

Chapter 9: Add the Opening and the Close

Page

168 **why they should listen to your presentation:** Charles Hand, Interview with the author, November 7, 2011.

172 **very difficult to work with:** Interview with the author, name withheld by request.

176 **We've got the deal. Let's go:** Andrei Mikhalevski, Interview with the author, November 15, 2011.

Chapter 10: Visual Persuasion

Page

183 **scientists played a dirty trick:** John Medina, *Brain Rules*, (Seattle: Pear Press, 2008) Kindle Edition, "Vision" chapter (hereafter cited as Medina, *Brain Rules*).

183 **auditory, visual, kinesthetic misconception:** See for example Scott O. Lilienfeld, et.al., *50 Great Myths of Popular Psychology*, (Malden: Wiley-Blackwell, 2010), 92-96.

183   **The best single tool we have:** Medina, *Brain Rules*, "Vision" chapter.

184   **retention goes up to 65%:** Ibid, "Vision" chapter.

186   **increase in retention of 30%:** Richard Mayer, *Multimedia Learning*, (Oxford: Cambridge University Press, 2009), 142.

186   **transfer of information by 105%:** Ibid., 143.

186   **A famous study published in 1956:** as quoted in Miller, *Magical*.

186   **probably as few as three or four:** Nelson Cowan, "The magical Number 4 in Short-term memory: A Reconsideration of mental Storage Capacity," *Behavioral Brain Sciences*, (1):87-114. 2001.

188   **contemptuous of slides:** Walter Isaacson, *Steve Jobs*, (New York: Simon & Schuster, 2011), 337.

190   **Complex slides are often a clue:** Bruce R. Gabrielle, *Speaking Powerpoint*, (Sevierville: Insights Publishing, 2010), 226.

196   **it makes more sense:** Kahneman, *Thinking*, 60.

197   **use headlines:** Michael Alley, The Craft of Scientific Presentations, (New York: Springer, 2003), 125-129.

198   **recommends three words or less:** Rick Altman, *Why Most PowerPoint Presentations Suck*, (Pleasanton: Harvest Books, 2007), 38.

200   **show the data:** Edward Tufte, *The Visual Display of Quantitative Information*, (Cheshire: Graphics Press, 2001), 105.

       Another excellent book about presenting numbers: Stephen Few, *Show Me the Numbers*, (Oakland: Analytics Press, 2004).

203   **they learn more:** Ruth Clark, Frank Nguyen, Jon Sweller, *Efficiency in Learning: Evidence-Based Guidelines to Manage Cognitive Load*, (San Francisco: Pfeiffer, 2006), 180-186.

Chapter 11: Executive Presence

Page

213 **People are highly attuned:** Ann Demarais and Valerie White, *First Impressions: What You Don't Know About How Others See You,* (New York City: Bantam, 2005). Kindle Edition (hereafter cited as Demarais and White, *First*).

217 **researchers in the courtroom:** Marcus T. Boccaccini, "What do We Really Know about Witness Preparation?" *Behavioral Sciences and the Law,* 20: 161-189, 2002.

219 **medium-confidence witnesses:** Robert J. Cramer, Stanley L. Brodsky, Jamie DeCoster, "Expert Witness Confidence and Juror Personality: Their Impact on Credibility and Persuasion in the Courtroom," *Journal of the American Academy of Psychiatry and the Law,* 37:63-74, 2009.

221 **evaluated on their likeability:** Demarais and White, *First*.

221 **An ounce of energy:** Roger Ailes, *You Are the Message,* (New York: Doubleday, 1988), 122.

222 **authority you project:** Dale Leathers and Michael H. Eaves, *Successful Nonverbal Communication,*(Boston: Pearson Education, 2008), 157-158 (hereafter cited as Leathers and Eaves, *Communication*).

222 **attractive people are more likely to get their way:** Ibid., 139-141.

Chapter 12: Dealing with Nerves

Page

226 **nervousness is different from worry:** John Eliot, *Overachievement,* (New York: Penguin, 2004), 23.

227 **and we built the Monster!:** H.A. Dorfman and Karl Kuehl, *The Mental Game of Baseball,* (Lanham: Diamond Communications, 1995), 93.

229   **Picture yourself doing what it takes:** Heidi Grant Halvorson, *Succeed*, (New York: Hudson Street Press, 2011), 206.

230   **labeling:** Goulston, *Listen*, 31.

231   **cause you to feel more powerful:** Amy Cuddy, "Body Language," Your Business: Do It Yourself, MSNBC, December 5, 2010, accessed at:

http://www.openforum.com/idea-hub/topics/lifestyle/video/do-it-yourself-body-language

231   **relaxed demeanor to the listener:** Ibid.

Chapter 13: Performing

Page

236   **Halo Effect:** Phil Rosenzweig, *The Halo Effect: ...and Eight Other Business Delusions that Deceive Managers*, (New York: Free Press, 2007), p.? (herafter cited as Rosenzweig, *Halo*).

      Anchoring: Kahneman, *Thinking*, 82.

      Thin slices: Ambady, et al, *The 30-Sec Sale*.

237   **Percy Barnevik description:** Rosenzweig, *Halo*, 35-49.

Chapter 14: Platform Skills

Page

244   **One very narrowly focused study:** The original study was by Albert Mehrabian and M. Wiener, "Decoding of Inconsistent Communications," *Journal of Personality and Social Psychology*, 6(1), 109-114, 1967. Mehrabian himself has tried to correct the misuse of his article. Note his own comments on his website at http://www.kaaj.com/psych/smorder.html. See also Olivia Mitchell, "Albert Mehrabian's Studies in Nonverbal Communication," blog post on her website, Speaking About Presenting.

www.speakingaboutpresenting.com/albert-mehrabian-nonverbal-communication

244   **often substitutes an easier question:** Kahneman, *Thinking*, 98.

247   **43% of the time:** Leathers and Eaves, *Communication*, 57.

248   **perceived as more credible with juries:** Leathers and Eaves, *Communication*, 218.

250   **they remembered more information:** Susan Goldin-Meadow, *Hearing Gesture*, (Cambridge: Belknap Press, 2003), 166.

251   **when they can't see their hands:** Joe Navarro, *What Every Body is Saying*, (New York: HarperCollins, 2008), 136 (hereafter cited as Navarro, *Body*).

251   **it detracts from the perceived quality:** Ibid., 136.

251   **Tiger Woods apology**, posted on his website, and rebroadcast on most major news channels, on February 19, 2010.

http://www.youtube.com/watch?v=FA7ty2LQwc0

Chapter 15: Make It Interactive

Page

257   **Do you like it:** credit for this question goes to Thomas Freese, Secrets of *Question-Based Selling: how the Most Powerful Tool in Business Can Double Your Sales Results*, (Naperville: Sourcebooks, 2000) 233.

267   **topspin:** Jerry Weissman, *In the Line of Fire: How to Handle Tough Questions...When It Counts*, (Upper Saddle River: Prentice-Hall, 2005), 93-94.

Chapter 16: Effective Team Presentations

Page

269   **looked at me and said, hire them:** Interview with author, anonymous by request.

275   **it's up to you:** Interview with author, anonymous by request.

275   **Peter Rubenacker:** Interview with author, November 10, 2011.

277   **even rolling their eyes:** Jon Steel, *Perfect Pitch*, (Hoboken: Jon Wiley & Sons, 2007), 145.

278   **Dave Thomas:** Interview with author, November 3, 2011.

Chapter 17: How to Get Better

Page

283   **10,000 hour rule:** Malcolm Gladwell introduced the concept to the general public in his book *Outliers*, but credit for the research and discovery goes to K. Anders Ericsson, who has written numerous papers on the topic, most specifically: K. Anders Ericsson., R. Th. Krampe, and C. Tesch-Römer, "The role of deliberate practice in the acquisition of expert performance," *Psychological Review*, 100: 363-406. 1993.

INDEX